OUTRAGEOUS!

OUTRAGEOUS!

The Story of Section 28 and Britain's Battle for LGBT Education

Paul Baker

REAKTION BOOKS

Published by
REAKTION BOOKS LTD
Unit 32, Waterside
44–48 Wharf Road
London N1 7UX, UK

www.reaktionbooks.co.uk

First published 2022
Copyright © Paul Baker 2022

Printed and bound in Great Britain
by Bell & Bain, Glasgow

A catalogue record for this book is available from the British Library

ISBN 978 1 78914 561 8

Contents

I

Welcome to Smalltown

I turned sixteen on 23 May 1988. In the UK, sixteen is a magical cut-off age signifying entrance into adulthood. In 1988, at the age of sixteen you could leave school without parental permission, get married, join the armed forces and have sex, as long as it was with someone of the opposite sex.

This year represented the triumph of the Conservative government in terms of its project to standardize education. They'd just passed a new law called the 1988 Education Reform Act, which created something called the 'national curriculum'. This covered around 87 per cent of children in the UK, ensuring they were taught the same things and had the same targets. On top of that, a new type of exam for sixteen-year-olds had been introduced, the GCSE (General Certificate of Secondary Education). It replaced the more complicated system of O Levels and CSEs, which had sometimes disadvantaged pupils who were entered for the wrong kind of exam.

My age cohort was the first one to sit these GCSEs and I was deep in revision of quadratic equations when I was called downstairs to attend my birthday party, which consisted of my mother, my twelve-year-old sister Helen, my Nanna Cochrane, my Great-Aunt Ethel and her neurotic black poodle Mimsy (my father was at work). As is the case in many working-class households, the television was rarely turned off, so we sat watching the end of *Neighbours* on our lime-green three-piece suite (bought in 1973) while my mother sliced the birthday cake in the background. I was too old for candles and 'Happy Birthday to You' so we were simply handed generous slabs on plates. *Neighbours* ended and then the news came on. A clipped, confident male voice declared, '*The Six O'Clock News* from the BBC. With Sue Lawley and Nicholas Witchell.' Nick was shown on the telephone as the opening credits played. Then Sue spoke. 'Good evening, the headlines at six o'clock.'

But something was not quite right.

In the background a muffled woman's voice repeatedly shouted something that sounded like 'Stop Section 28!' As Sue read the headlines over various clips of news footage (the Lords' vote on the poll tax, changes to nursing, the collapse of a football hooliganism court case, a glimpse inside the Soviet Army, a Reagan–Gorbachev summit meeting, cones on the roads) there were sounds of a scuffle happening off-screen. The shouting woman's voice seemed to have been suppressed as if someone, equally unseen, had placed a hand over her mouth.

When Sue returned, a box inset showing a picture of the Palace of Westminster appeared to be incorrectly imposed on the screen, blocking part of her face.

'Someone's going to lose their job,' observed Great-Aunt Ethel, while feeding Mimsy bits of cake. She'd been a nurse in the war so nothing fazed her anymore.

Momentarily, Sue seemed uncharacteristically alarmed and her eyes flitted down and around as what was happening off-screen battled for her attention. 'And I do apologize if you're hearing quite a lot of noise in the studio at the moment. I'm afraid that, erm, we have rather been invaded by some people who we hope to be removing very shortly.'

It is the *rather* that I love the most about Sue's apology. Throughout the twentieth century, members of the Establishment peppered their speech with these kinds of adverbs: *fairly*, *somewhat*, *vaguely*, *quite*. It's a Rather British Thing, helping them to cultivate an air of indirectness and detachment; nothing can ever really bother you if you're one of the elite. Nowadays it's a linguistic tic that marks you as old-fashioned and perhaps a bit posh, and instead we tend to unconsciously follow the more direct speaking style of the Americans, who have little time for such nonchalance.[1]

The news continued as normal although I wasn't watching it. I was thinking about what I had just seen, its oddness and suddenness. I was wondering how the news people in the television studio could have let it happen, and why it happened.

I was also wondering what Section 28 was.

While I knew that it was now legal for me to get married or have sexual intercourse with someone of the opposite sex, I also knew that wasn't for me. In those days I only had eyes for Bruce Willis, a smirking, balding 33-year-old actor in a detective comedy show called *Moonlighting*. Clearly this was not a realistic proposition but at sixteen I was old enough to know the sort of person I was attracted to. Yet if I wanted to have sex with a man, I'd have to wait another five years. In the UK, we tend to think of homosexuality as being legalized in 1967. However, it was decriminalized rather than legalized and only in certain contexts: sex was allowed to take place between just two men, both over the age of 21, in private (ideally in a locked room in your house with no one else at home), and only in England or Wales. It did not apply to the merchant navy or the armed forces, or to Northern Ireland, Scotland, the Isle of Man, Jersey or Guernsey.

Marrying a man was an impossibility, like time travel. In fact, I'd have had to time travel over a quarter-century to 2014 (2020 for Northern Ireland) if I'd wanted to marry a man in the UK.

An outrageous law

I came of age at the exact moment of a Very British Crisis, during a time when there was an enormous amount of fuss over my future sex life. I was the embodiment of the hypothetical young person whom the government so desperately did not want to be gay. During this period of our history, people expressed a great deal of concern about children. On my birthday the number one slot in the pop charts was occupied by a double A side of two Beatles hits: 'With a Little Help from My Friends' (by Wet Wet Wet) and 'She's Leaving Home' (by Billy Bragg and Cara Tivey). Proceeds went to the charity Childline, a telephone-based counselling service that had been set up for children and young people. Children suffering from abuse could (and still can) phone 0800 1111 and get help from a counsellor. The success of high-profile campaigns like this indicated that the British public loved children. Many of the actions described in this book were carried out in the name of children, because the people involved claimed that they cared about children and their futures, and possibly even because some of them fervently thought that they were doing the right thing.

The day after the BBC News studios were invaded by women protesting against the thing called Section 28, the law changed. Here is the full wording of Section 28. It isn't the most enthralling read, I'm afraid. There are five uses of *shall* (a word that by this point most English speakers had largely abandoned), and the fussy little phrasings like 'such inferences as to' and 'as may reasonably be drawn' cry out that this is a document written in the driest of legalese, which gives an air of importance and inaccessibility, effectively stating: 'You there, you little person, this is not your concern, go back to watching *Neighbours*!' But if the language is dated, the attitude it espouses is even more so.

28 Prohibition on promoting homosexuality by teaching or by publishing material
(1) The following section shall be inserted after section 2 of the [1986 c. 10.] Local Government Act 1986 (prohibition of political publicity) –
'2A Prohibition on promoting homosexuality by teaching or by publishing material
   (1) A local authority shall not –
      (a) intentionally promote homosexuality or publish material with the intention of promoting homosexuality;
      (b) promote the teaching in any maintained school of the acceptability of homosexuality as a pretended family relationship.
   (2) Nothing in subsection (1) above shall be taken to prohibit the doing of anything for the purpose of treating or preventing the spread of disease.

(3) In any proceedings in connection with the application of this section a court shall draw such inferences as to the intention of the local authority as may reasonably be drawn from the evidence before it.

(4) In subsection (1)(b) above 'maintained school' means, –

    (a) in England and Wales, a county school, voluntary school, nursery school or special school, within the meaning of the Education Act 1944; and

    (b) in Scotland, a public school, nursery school or special school, within the meaning of the Education (Scotland) Act 1980.'

(2) This section shall come into force at the end of the period of two months beginning with the day on which this Act is passed.

The most relevant parts are the bits in 2A section 1, subsections a and b, which state that local authorities should not 'intentionally promote homosexuality or . . . the teaching . . . of the acceptability of homosexuality as a pretended family relationship'. There is an exception part after that which seems to imply that local authorities are still allowed to give education with regard to 'treating or preventing the spread of disease'. It's not really clear what that means in practice, though. Also, how can you promote homosexuality as a *relationship*, pretend or otherwise? Homosexuality is a type of sexuality, not a relationship. The subsection would have been better worded as something like 'b) promote the teaching in any maintained school of the acceptability of people in a homosexual relationship as constituting a family'.

Indeed, a lot of the debate around Section 28 focused on the interpretation of words and phrases like 'pretended family relationship' and 'promote'. The term 'pretended' was mentioned 55 times when the bill was debated in the House of Lords on 16 February 1988. Many of those who were against the proposed law thought it was an insulting term. Baroness Blackstone said it was 'offensive to many homosexuals' and 'families take many forms.' However, Baroness Cox, who was one of the main supporters of the legislation, said that 'pretended family relationship' was too narrow and limiting so she was worried it might allow some positive representations of homosexuality to get in through a loophole. Lord Monson was more explicit, calling it a 'curious phrase' and then claiming it would imply that 'promiscuous homosexual relationships – such as those which, until recently, were said to be found in the bathhouses of San Francisco and New York in which men were said to have sexual relations with 200 or 300 different men every year – are in some way preferable to stable, quasi-family homosexual relationships.' As my old friends Julian and Sandy would exclaim, 'Ooh, I wonder where he spends *his* evenings?' Despite the opposition, an attempt to remove the word 'pretended' from the clause was defeated in the House of Lords by 43 to 20 votes.

During the same debate, the word 'promote' was mentioned 63 times. Lord Birkett wanted to change it to 'commend'. Lord Ritchie of Dundee said that 'promote' was too vague and noted that in the dictionary it meant 'to put forth into notice or publish'. However, Lord Campbell of Alloway had also been consulting his dictionary and claimed it meant 'active support or encouragement'. Lord Kilbracken had gone one better, noting he'd found references to 'promote' in seven different sections of his thesaurus but that none of them was very helpful. Baroness Blatch had had enough of all this and said, 'We can talk about the precise issue of the word "promote" but I suspect it is not the real issue,' before resolving to 'settle for the word "promote"'. But just when it appeared that the issue had been put to bed, Lord Henderson of Brompton had to jump in, wanting to know whether the word 'promote' had 'ever been used before in a statute without a concrete object'. And not to be outdone, Lord Monson complicated the matter further by claiming you could promote bisexuality (for example, 'try it out') but not homosexuality, which he maintained you were either born with or acquired at an early age.

The debate on 16 February 1988 was not the most thrilling of the many parliamentary debates about homosexuality and education that took place and I suspect that the word 'promote' got to stay in the final version of the clause because its detractors eventually lost the will to argue the point any further. Towards the end, Lord McIntosh of Haringey said (and I detect a note of weary sarcasm in the transcript) that he defended the right of any of the noble Lords 'to deal with this difficult – nay impossible – wording not only line by line and word by word but syllable by syllable if they want to'.

Telling the story of Section 28

Section 28 stayed as law until 21 June 2000 in Scotland and 18 November 2003 in the rest of the UK. I don't have evidence that anyone was ever criminalized because of the law, but it had many consequences, some bad, some good, depending on your point of view. This book tells the story of Section 28, or rather it contains lots of related stories: some are representative of the experiences of many people, while others relate to specific occurrences and actions involving individuals who played a key role. It involves a cast of thousands: Members of Parliament and local councils, religious leaders, journalists, political activists, pop stars, actors, teachers, parents and schoolchildren. In the course of writing this book I interviewed some of the main players, such as the actor Ian McKellen, the politician Chris Smith and the activists Angela Mason and Susannah Bowyer, all of whom gave fascinating perspectives on events that happened thirty or so years ago, providing insight, clarification and new threads for me to follow. I have also relied on newspaper and magazine archives, transcripts of existing interviews as well as political and academic debates and a wide range of books and academic articles. Of course, in relying on people's memories we have to accept that they will not always be accurate, while news reports can sometimes get things wrong. And I'm sure that I too will have interpreted something incorrectly or left something out. It would make for an arduous read if I put the word 'allegedly' before every statement made in this book but readers should try to envisage that word hovering above the page anyway.

This is not a story that began on 23 May 1988, and it is difficult to give an exact date, but in Chapter Two I identify a nebulous start as being around 1967 when homosexuality was decriminalized and almost immediately we find a politician complaining about the possibility of its promotion. And the story does not really end with the repeal of the bill in 2003, since echoes of Section 28 still resonate today. However, much of the story takes place in that brash and, for many, disagreeable decade: the 1980s.

Do you remember the 1980s? Here are some words and phrases from my memory in order of how quickly they popped into my head: leg-warmers, the miners' strike, Maggie Maggie Maggie, Falklands, Greenham Common, acid house, loadsamoney, AIDS, shoulder pads, MTV, privatization, GCSEs, New Wave, the *Challenger* disaster, *E.T.*, Zola Budd, yuppies, *Spitting Image*. It was the decade in which I spent most of my childhood and teenage years and (apart from some of its music and films) it is the one that I have enjoyed the least. For most people, the teenage years can be quite turbulent, what with bodies changing and growing, mood-affecting hormones, exam pressures and conflicts with other family members as your identity fluctuates around not-child and almost-adult. And that's if you're a normally sanguine, popular sort of person from a relatively privileged background in a stable family. Add on health or ability issues or being a member of a minority ethnicity, sexuality or gender group and these problems quickly start to multiply. I was a shy, nerdy, gay kid from a council estate in an overlooked bit of northeast England and Section 28 was the culmination of a set of attitudes which made growing up more challenging than it should have been. Once I left home for university in 1990, I consciously bade farewell to the previous decade and resolved to only think of the present and the future, rather than reliving past events and letting them define me. So revisiting the era has been a bit of a mixed bag for me. However, in writing this book, I've learnt a lot about why my childhood was how it was.

Although it didn't start off this way, I realize that one person I'm writing this book for is a younger version of myself. I wish I could send it back in my non-existent time machine to 23 May 1988, as a birthday present. I wish I could pass it on to the children and adults of that time who were affected by Section 28 and the homophobic climate of the 1980s, so they could read it and take solace in the fact that this wouldn't last forever. I'm also writing this book for the young LGBT+ people of today, to let them know about the ways that their elders campaigned, the gratitude we owe them and that if they could get through those years, then whatever comes along in your life, so can you. And I'm writing this book especially for queer people in other countries where homophobic laws are still in place, or are being passed; where they do not have the freedom that I have to marry or hold my husband's hand in public (we don't, as we're too self-conscious, but it's nice to have the option). I want this book to give you hope and inspire you to never give up. One day, years from now, someone will write a book about your country and its horrible history of homophobia and how eventually it went away. So, if you can, keep records, take pictures, make videos – future social historians will be needing them. Finally, I write this book to the queer people who were around in the 1980s and '90s – you're the stars of this story, and it's one that's worth telling.

This hasn't always been an easy story to research because the events in it affected me so strongly. In deciding what to call this book, I was drawn to the word 'outrageous' for several reasons. Straightforwardly, it can refer to something that is shocking, bad or excessive. Not only was the word used repeatedly in parliamentary debates to express horror at those who apparently promoted homosexuality, but Section 28 itself *was* outrageous. The story of Section 28 is one that easily provokes anger, both then and now. Anger can be a useful emotion – *if* it can be kept under control and used to inspire people to make positive changes. However, anger can also be horribly corrosive and holding on to anger long after an event has passed can be self-defeating. Anger also has a disappointing tendency to be misdirected at people who didn't cause it, or overextended towards a type of person who shares characteristics with someone who did cause it. We are living in a very angry time and it is not my aim to demonize those who supported Section 28 or inspire anyone to have a go at them.

Anger certainly has a strong role to play in this story but so does humour – the people who protested against Section 28 sometimes used comedic, camp or dramatic acts of resistance to get their message across. Another meaning of 'outrageous' is bold and unusual – and in this sense, some of those protests can be seen as outrageous. Indeed, the word echoes the name of the group OutRage!, which was created as a response to the homophobic climate of the 1980s. However, the word also has significance as a camp epithet – a little-known Canadian film from 1977 about a gay hairstylist was called *Outrageous!* Try saying the word with an emphasis on the middle syllable, drawing out the *rage* part for as long as is decent, or by giving the word a fake-sinister hiss at the end. What I love about the response to Section 28 was that the protesters were both real-outraged and mock-outraged. And their actions caused outrage too. The word 'outrageous' punctuates that very real sense of anger with a camp sensibility. And I think that's healthy.

Clause 27, Clause 28, Clause 29, Section 28 and Section 2A

Section 28 appeared in the Local Government Act (1988). This act was a bit of a ragbag: there was a part which meant that people no longer had to pay for a dog licence, something else on providing financial assistance for privately let housing accommodation and quite a lot on tenders for contracts. These parts were fairly uncontroversial, however, and it was really Section 28 that afforded the act its notorious place in history.

Section 28 resulted in the addition of a new segment (called Section 2A) to an earlier act, the Local Government Act (1986), which covered England, Wales and Scotland. I'd like to back up a bit now though, and talk about the process through which acts pass into law. Despite being a bit pernickety it's useful to know about this, both for this book and because you never know when it might come in handy (such as if you go on a date with an MP).

In the UK (and quite a few other countries), a distinction is made between a bill and an act, although they are essentially the names of the same thing at different stages in its legal life. The bill is a bit like the caterpillar and the act is the lovely legal butterfly that emerges at the end. So the bill is the proposed law which gets 'tabled' in parliament. The UK's Parliament is 'bicameral', which simply means it's divided into two separate assemblies, chambers or Houses (the Commons, which has green benches, and the Lords, which has red ones). The primary chamber is the House of Commons, which currently consists of 650 elected Members of Parliament (MPs) who represent constituencies. The leader of the party with the majority of MPs is the prime minister, who gets to appoint a cabinet of other ministers, covering areas such as education, defence, justice and transport. Together these ministers make up the 'government', occupying the front benches in the chamber to the right side of the Speaker of the Commons. Other MPs in the party are referred to as 'back benchers' (due to their seating position) while MPs from other parties are referred to as 'the opposition' and sit on the left side of the Speaker. The Commons is the primary chamber because in cases of conflict the Lords is meant to yield to it. However, counter-intuitively, the Commons is also known as the lower House, and the Lords as the upper one. The Lords consists of bishops and life peers who are appointed by the monarch, as well as hereditary peers. Sometimes retired MPs are given peerages, crossing from one House to the other. Prior to 1958 there were no female peers, and before 1999 there were many more hereditary peers (there are currently 92 hereditary ones out of 792 in total). The Lords are meant to act as a check on the House of Commons, although the non-elected and permanent nature of peers, the social background from which many of them come and their age (the average was 69 in 2017) has attracted criticisms of them as being out of touch with the concerns of ordinary people.

You may have heard Section 28 referred to as Clause 28, and some of the campaigns (both for and against it) used alliterative slogans such as 'Keep the Clause' or 'Kill the Clause'. The difference between the two relates to the distinction between bills and acts. Essentially, bills consist of a series of individual statements, called clauses, which are intended to divide it up into smaller portions so that it can be made easier to follow. However, once the bill becomes an act, what used to be called clauses are now referred to as sections. The actual numbering of any single clause can change over time as MPs and Lords attempt to tinker about with the bill, putting forward amendments that involve adding in new clauses and taking out existing ones. So, actually, Clause 28 was originally known as Clause 27 of the Local Government Bill (1988). Due to an additional clause being added in, Clause 27 got bumped up to Clause 28 and at one point it was even Clause 29. To make things even more confusing, you may have also read about something called Section 2A, which is sometimes seen as the same thing as Section 28. This is because the point of Section 28 in the Local Government Act (1988) was to put in a change to an earlier act, called the Local Government Act (1986). What Clause 28 did, essentially, was insert a new section (called 2A) into this earlier 1986 act. And in Scotland, Section 28 tended to be referred to as Section 2A. I'm referring to Section 28 in the title of this book because Section 28 represented the actual act, the culmination of the moral panic around homosexuality that took place over the 1980s. But you can't tell the story of Section 28 without talking about Clause 28 too. So when I'm talking about the bill, I'll refer to it as a clause, but once it is passed into law, I'll refer to it as a section. And if I'm talking about Scotland, I'll refer to it as Section 2A.

Some bills are introduced by ministers and represent government policy, but any MP can introduce a 'Private Members' Bill' (Lords can also introduce a 'Private Peers' Bill'). The bill usually undergoes a lot of scrutiny by the Parliamentary Business and Legislation Committee, which then decides if it starts off in the Commons or Lords (this is usually done to provide a balanced programme). Then, the bill is ready for its first reading. This is when the person responsible for introducing the bill stands up in one of the two chambers and announces it. This is more of a formality than anything else and, at this point, the bill is given a number and a date is set for it to have its more exciting 'second reading'.

The second reading consists of a debate about the bill. A government minister sets out the case for why the bill is needed, the opposition parties can respond and then other politicians chime in with their contributions. There are no changes made to the bill as a result of this debate, although Members of Parliament can indicate what might get proposed as a change later on. At the end of the debate, the House that has debated the bill votes on it. If the majority of people vote against the bill, then that's the end of that, although defeats don't usually happen very often at this point. Normally, the government are pretty sure they have the numbers to get the bill passed.

Bills then go to a 'committee stage' where the wording of each clause is carefully considered line-by-line, either in a specially convened committee or back in the Lords or Commons. Here the committee considers whether any of the clauses of the bill should be removed, amendments made or new material added. After that comes a 'report stage' to discuss the amendments, which takes place in either the Lords or Commons. This is followed (usually immediately) by a 'third reading'.

Both the Commons and Lords have to agree on the bill, so any amendments that are tabled in one House need to also be considered in the other House, which may reject those amendments or suggest further changes. This can result in a bill ping-ponging back and forth between Houses. The Lords are only permitted to delay a bill for two sessions or one year, after which the 1949 Parliament Act can be invoked in the Commons, making the bill law. This is one of the ways in which the Commons asserts its primacy; ultimately the Lords only have the power to delay if the Commons holds onto its resolve to pass a bill. Finally, once the bill has been passed by both Houses, it is given 'royal assent' by the monarch and becomes law, turning into an act. The act doesn't take effect immediately but there is usually a set period of a few months to give the government and those affected the time to make any changes or carry out the actions that are required of them.

Don't worry if you weren't taking notes – there won't be a test. You'll just have to find some other way to impress any MPs you end up dating.

What's in the rest of this book?

When I wrote Chapter Two it felt a bit like I was setting up a stage for a play, painting the backdrop, moving plywood trees and ornamental thrones into the right places, deciding where the main actors should make their entrances and choosing appropriate musical refrains to introduce them. The chapter deals with the recent historical context that led up to the introduction of Section 28. It begins in the 1960s with an examination of early uses of the term 'promote homosexuality' in politics, then moves to the 1970s to consider the antagonistic relationship between the Gay Liberation Front and the Nationwide Festival of Light. We go on to cover trendy lefty teaching methods, the Winter of Discontent, Margaret Thatcher's rise to power, the start of the HIV-AIDS pandemic and responses to it by the media, the government and the gay community. The chapter then goes on to discuss theories around whether sexuality is something you are born with or something that can be influenced by external factors such as your education or the society into which you are born. This segues into a discussion of lesbian separatist feminists and their role in organizations including the Greater London Council and the Inner London Education Authority London Youth Committee. If Chapter Two was an A-Level History essay it would conclude that 'There was not one single factor which precipitated the introduction of Section 28, but a combination of numerous interacting factors' (an answer which covers pretty much every A-Level History essay question).

Chapter Three, on the other hand, deals with the more immediate events that led to Section 28, as well as the process of it turning into your actual bona fide law. It begins with the publication of a book that has been variously described as terrifying, ridiculous, boring and famous. *Jenny Lives with Eric and Martin* is a large, thin paperback with a garish yellow and blue cover. It became the central focus of arguments around sex education (and specifically the bits relating to homosexuality) in the media and Parliament. The chapter then focuses on a series of frankly quite shocking events that occurred around the local council of Haringey in London. From people getting eggs thrown at them during a council chamber meeting to a vicar going on hunger strike and pretending to need a wheelchair, this chapter sees a fair amount of drama, and that's even before we get to the debates in Parliament that resulted in Section 28. There you'll find plenty of references to sodomy, reservoirs of venereal disease, piles of filth and disgusting and unnatural practices. If you like your homophobia pompous and authoritative, this is where you'll find it.

Chapter Four is even more dramatic if anything, covering the various ways that folk protested against Clause 28. It details the formation of the camp-sounding OLGA, one of the first groups to organize marches against the clause, then describes Sir Ian McKellen's avuncular self-outing on national radio. We go on to look at an unusual abseiling expedition that took place in the House of Lords, rousing speeches by soap stars at demonstrations, appeals to the queen and that memorable invasion of the BBC News studios during a live broadcast of the *Six O'Clock News*. The protests were many and varied, serious and hilarious, and I had a lot of fun writing this chapter.

We then get to Chapter Five, which details what it was like to live under the shadow of Section 28 from the decade following its passage into law under the sober watch of John Major. We look at the effect it had in schools, for teachers and pupils, and the demoralizing message it sent to lesbian mothers. The law sent the poor old BBC into a flap, causing gay characters to magically turn straight, while Channel 4 characteristically trolled Section 28, commissioning a TV series that shouted at legislators, 'Go on then, we dare you to say we're promoting homosexuality.' Things did not go so well for theatre groups, which relied on council funding, and this was a decade of distress for queer theatre. The chapter ends with the formation of two gay rights groups with somewhat different mission statements – Stonewall and OutRage!

Chapter Six covers the long road to the repeal of the law. There are two intertwined threads to this chapter, covering events that took place in Scotland and the rest of the UK. With a new Labour government in power from 1997, one question I wanted to address was why it took until 2003 to consign Section 28 to history – were Labour dragging their heels on purpose or were other factors at work? Scotland managed to dump what they called Section 2A earlier, in the year 2000, although the campaign to keep it was fierce, culminating in an attempted prosecution over a booklet called *Gay Sex Now* and a businessman using £1 million of his own money to have almost 4 million ballot papers sent out across the country. The latter half of the chapter covers the final set of parliamentary debates and the ways that the defenders of Section 28 desperately tried to keep it on the statute books in the face of dwindling opposition.

And in Chapter Seven we look at the legacy of Section 28. In the years that passed, did homosexuality get promoted in classrooms after all? Did the proponents of the law apologize for the aggro that they caused? And does it matter if they did? We might also ask whether the debate around teaching children about homosexuality in schools has been laid to rest for good or whether events in cities like Birmingham almost twenty years later suggest otherwise.

It's a bumpy, barmy, British story, and for much of it people were adorned in the deliciously bad fashions of the 1980s and '90s: gigantic glasses, frizzy perms, side ponytails with scrunchies, stringy mullets, dodgy moustaches, 'designer' stubble, oversized blazers with well-appointed shoulder pads, shapeless dungarees, flammable shell suits and, best of all, double denim.

The cover of Bronski Beat's 'Smalltown Boy' single – although it looks like clip art, this was pretty sophisticated in 1984.

In photos taken of me in the late 1980s, I'm wearing a baggy black blouson that makes me look nothing like the hunk from the Littlewoods catalogue where I'd got my mother to order it from, and my hair has an orange tint from spraying it with something called Sun In. But while this may not have been a time of sartorial elegance, in my opinion, the soundtrack of the 1980s and '90s is difficult to beat. Bronski Beat's 'Smalltown Boy' was released in 1984 and I get goosebumps every time I hear its mournful introduction. The video depicts a young gay man, played by lead singer Jimmy Somerville, who has been failed so he runs away to find a better life. More than anything, this book is for the residents of Smalltown. You don't have to run away.

2

Fractures in Society

I'd known about homosexuality since the age of about five, from staying over at my grandparents' bungalow watching *It Ain't Half Hot Mum*, a sitcom that never gets shown in repeats due to its use of blackface and sympathy towards colonialism, among other things. The opening credits feature Sergeant Major Williams (Windsor Davies) disgustedly mouthing 'Puffs!' at a Royal Artillery concert party performing 'Meet the Gang' on a makeshift stage. Puffs (or poofs or even pooves if you were from the South) was a word of the 1970s. I knew it referred to people like Gunner Beaumont aka Gloria (Melvyn Hayes), a yapping poodle of a man who liked to dress as a woman and frequently went into hysterics. Other signifiers of what homosexuality meant were provided by John Inman, who played mincing Mr Humphries in another sitcom, *Are You Being Served?*, and Larry Grayson, who was the camp compere of the family quiz show *The Generation Game*. They were friendly, funny, gossipy men, utterly harmless. On the one hand they were popular and much-loved but on the other, they were puffs, and nobody wanted to be a puff. It was a contradiction I could never resolve. I knew I was supposed to be attracted to

'Puffs!' Sergeant Major Williams and Gunner 'Gloria' Beaumont (Windsor Davies and Melvyn Hayes) in sitcom *It Ain't Half Hot Mum* (1974–81).

women with big eyes, red lips, yellow hair and large breasts, like the ones who chased Benny Hill around in fast motion. As this paragraph probably indicates, during my childhood I did pretty much nothing but watch television, but despite the almost-constant indoctrination of straight = normal, gay = awful, heterosexuality just didn't *take*.

'When did you realize you were gay?' is a question that is sometimes cited in those slightly bossy lists of things you shouldn't say to gay people. 'We never ask heterosexual people when they first realized they were straight!' goes the logic. All the same, I think it's a fair, and often illuminating, question to ask. During the twentieth century, your heterosexuality was pretty much always assumed; you internalized the messages about whom you should desire from television, film, books, magazines, family, school, church and dozens of other routes. The moment you realized you were heterosexual is a bit like the point at which you noticed your eye colour – in many cases it's not especially exciting. However, the narrative life twist of realizing you are attracted to persons of the same sex can be something of an occasion, although in the past it has not always been one for celebration. For my generation and those older than me, most of us were clued in enough to society's messages for that realization to involve anxiety and shame. And unlike the discovery of one's heterosexuality, this information can sometimes come from external sources (in such cases usually not conveyed as good news – 'Baker's a puff!'), rather than being a private self-discovery.

Speaking to various gay men and women over the years, the revelatory moment is sometimes associated with a strong, often strange, feeling of attraction towards someone, as if a switch has been flipped on or a new sense (or super-power) has been discovered. Teachers are often cited, as are classmates or celebrities. Compared to later decades, the 1980s was a relatively buttoned-down period and, while women were routinely sexualized, it was much less common for men to be presented as objects of desire, although that was starting to change. In 1985, an advert for Levi's 501 jeans featured 23-year-old model Nick Kamen strutting into a 1950s American laundrette. There was no dialogue or voiceover, just Marvin Gaye's agonized 1968 hit 'I Heard It through the Grapevine' performed by a sound-a-like session singer. However, despite its retro look, this was something new. There is a close-up of Kamen's hand, then his crotch, strangely noticed by a young boy. Sulky and quiffed, Kamen removes his shades, pauses momentarily and then pulls off his shirt in a single non-awkward move to reveal a hairless and taut (although certainly not 'swole' or 'hench') chest. Again, the camera goes into close-up as Kamen unbuttons, then bends over to strip down to white Sunspel boxer shorts. I like to think that the peak in divorce rates that occurred in the mid-1980s was due to the sexual dissatisfaction occasioned by this one advert. In any case, it was revelatory and resulted in sales of Levi's going up by 800 per cent as well as lots of pairs of boxer shorts being sold (I obediently bought a pair, although found them uncomfortable to wear). From that point onwards, male bodies were routinely objectified to sell things in the same way that women's bodies had been used to get us to buy things for countless years. It's not a gender equality moment we tend to shout about.

Despite the overt sexualization of the Levi's campaign, any chance that my thirteen-year-old self would be turned on by Mr Kamen was doomed as I found the advert to be a source of enormous embarrassment that invariably only got aired when Nanna and Aunty Ethel were visiting. Kamen was far too cool for me anyway. I couldn't imagine him spending his evenings playing Dungeons and Dragons, trying to work out who the killer was in Agatha Christie's *And Then There Were None* or typing pages of BASIC code from a computer magazine into his Spectrum 48K. Instead he looked like the sort of person who ate at somewhere trendy like McDonald's with about thirty of his best friends before going on to a nightclub somewhere in London. He probably even smoked. But there were other hunks and hotties in the early to mid-1980s that I could have crushed on – film stars such as Patrick Swayze, Mel Gibson, Kurt Russell and Tom Cruise or pop stars such as Simon Le Bon, Morten Harket and George Michael. None of these men did much for me, though. There was no 'awakening' when Ben from Curiosity Killed the Cat looked into the camera and announced that he was going to bring me 'straight back down to earth'. It is rather unfortunate to admit it, but the first 1980s man who made me realize that I was incontrovertibly, ridiculously and joyfully gay was the unthreatening television magician Paul Daniels.

The realization came to me around the age of ten or so, upon waking up from a dream involving him. It's probably best not to go into any detail. I've said too much as it is. But there we are. The heart wants what it wants. It was mostly platonic and I had no interest in the physical ins and outs, finding all that to be mortifying. But he was my first and remained the only one until he was supplanted a few years later by Bruce Willis of *Moonlighting*. Sorry Paul.

I'm not just telling you this to make you laugh but to point out how difficult it would have been to warp my sexuality into something that it didn't want to be. Nobody told me to fancy Paul Daniels. If anything, he was the *last* person in the world I ought to have been attracted to (especially by picky gay male stereotype standards). Certainly, nobody that I knew was going to find my desire 'normal' or even sympathize with my funny crush.

And it makes me wonder why people were so afraid that, if children were told that homosexuality existed and it was OK, it would somehow take them on a different path to the one they were destined for. Was homosexuality much more powerful, more seductive than heterosexuality? Or was it closer to the truth that gay people were required to be ashamed of themselves and to repress their sexuality as much as they could? What an ungenerous philosophy that would be.

Promoting homosexuality – the early years

To get a sense of the roots of Section 28 I'm going to take us back to November 1970 and introduce you to a married couple – what could be more normal than that? They are called Peter and Janet Hill and they have just returned to the UK after a four-year spell in India where they have been engaged in missionary work as evangelical Baptists. Anyone coming back to Britain in 1970 probably needed a kindly aunt or uncle figure to sit them down and say, 'Well my dears, there have been some changes since you've been away, do you have a few hours to spare while I get you up to speed?' As *you* don't have a few hours – here are some highlights. Something called a 'sexual revolution' had just occurred. The Abortion Act (1967) had legalized abortion and in the same year the contraceptive pill was made available to all women (before that it could only be accessed by married women). And in 1969 the Divorce Reform Act made divorce much easier (prior to this, women could only petition for divorce on the grounds of adultery). Victorian values were finally starting to go out of fashion and media people were talking of 'the permissive society'. Suddenly, young people were using terms like 'free love', 'groovy' and 'freak out' quite seriously and the word 'happening' was a noun for a while. Men grew long hair, women wore short skirts and some people were even taking marijuana, psilocybin mushrooms and LSD while listening to something called psychedelic music. This was characterized by surreal, dreamy, often literary-inspired lyrics and unusual instruments (sitars, harpsicords, theremins, electric jugs) and sound effects. Like many of the musical trends that will crop up over the course of this book, psychedelia was American-influenced, although you can see its impact in the late 1960s music of British bands such as The Beatles, Pink Floyd and Cream.

Homosexuality was another area where the law had changed. The Sexual Offences Act (1967) had partially decriminalized homosexuality, although it had been met with opposition in some quarters. For example, on 23 June 1967, as the change to the law was being debated, Sir Cyril Osborne (Conservative, Louth) unsuccessfully attempted to put in a new clause called 'Promotion of Homosexual Acts'. It would have made it an offence for anyone to publish lists of names and addresses of known homosexuals as a way of promoting acts of homosexuality. Like a teenage influencer trying to introduce a cool slang phrase into the vernacular of their friends, Sir Cyril must have really wanted to make 'promoting homosexuality' happen. On 8 November in Parliament he asked the Secretary of State for Defence if he would make a statement on his recent inquiries 'into the corruption of young guardsmen by a well-to-do vice ring promoting homosexuality in the Household Cavalry and the Welsh Guards'.

The concept of promoting homosexuality was starting to gain traction because it popped up again during an obscenity trial around the same time. The author Hubert Selby Jr had written a book in 1964 called *Last Exit to Brooklyn*, which dealt with prostitution, rape, homosexuality and drug use. Outraged, Charles Taylor MP (Conservative, Wimbledon) got the Attorney General, Sir Elwyn Jones, to start proceedings to prosecute the publishers, Calder & Boyars, under the Obscene Publications Act. On 23 November 1966, the all-male jury returned a verdict of guilty. During an appeal in 1968, Lord Justice Salmon said to the new jury:

A book may tend to deprave and corrupt a significant but comparatively small number of its readers or a large number or, indeed, the majority of its readers. The tendency to corrupt may be strong or slight. The corruption may also take various forms. It may be to induce erotic desires of the heterosexual kind, or to promote homosexuality or other sexual perversions, or drugtaking or brutal violence. All these are matters for you to consider and weigh up.

Despite its recent decriminalization, Lord Justice Salmon implied that homosexuality was a sexual perversion as well as equating it with taking drugs and brutal violence. But I mention all this because the phrase *promote homosexuality* is going to show up twenty years later in what will become Section 28, and it's worth noting that it had been around from the very moment that homosexuality was decriminalized. However, let's not get ahead of ourselves. The jury overturned the ruling over *Last Exit to Brooklyn*, signalling a change to British censorship laws – yet another example of the 'anything goes' mindset of the time.

So what did Peter and Janet Hill make of all this liberalization? They were horrified, of course. But what could they do? Then it came to Peter in a vision – tens of thousands of young people gathering in London, making a stand for Christian moral principles.[1] And so, in July 1971, they, along with journalist and author Malcolm Muggeridge, former Labour cabinet minister Lord Longford and Clean-Up TV campaigner Mary Whitehouse, formed an organization called the Nationwide Festival of Light. The group had two main goals – to oppose what they saw as media exploitation of sex and violence, and to promote the teachings of Jesus in order to recover the nation's morals. Over the next few months there were dozens of regional rallies. Bristol Cathedral, for example, was packed out as the festival protested against the opening of a 'sex supermarket' in the city. Not all of the rallies went as planned. One in Methodist Central Hall Westminster on 7 September had attracted an audience of 3,000. Peter Hill addressed the crowd and told them of his vision. But not everyone was there to pray. The hall had been infiltrated by members of the Gay Liberation Front (GLF), who were about to engage in a bold undercover mission called Operation Rupert (named after a subversive Rupert the Bear cartoon in the magazine *Oz*).

The UK branch of the GLF was relatively short-lived, existing between 1970 and 1973. It was a youthful, exuberant movement whose manifesto, published in 1971, said it would 'stand firm and assert our basic rights. If this involves violence, it will not be we who initiate this but those who attempt to stand in our way to freedom.'[2] Its members included several people who are going to feature at various points in our story: Lisa Power, Peter Tatchell and Angela Mason.

Radical chic – the Gay Liberation Front.

The GLF had managed to print 1,000 fake tickets for the Methodist Central Hall rally and on the day its members turned up in small groups, dispersed around the auditorium. What followed was a symphony of disruption, building gradually towards a chaotic crescendo. Initially, the activists tried to fit in with the crowd, perhaps emulating them a little too well. So when the Bishop of Stepney began speaking, GLF members applauded every sentence and kept on clapping in a show of insane enthusiasm. But when a female speaker described how Jesus had saved her from a life of depravity someone unexpectedly cried out 'Fuck you, cunt!' Then there was an unpleasant smell – had someone let off a stink bomb? Someone started blowing bubbles from the balcony. Someone else dropped pages of pornographic magazines from the balcony! When it was Malcolm Muggeridge's turn to speak, someone asked him a question about homosexuals. He replied, 'I'm afraid I don't like homosexuals, I just don't like them.'[3]

And just as if a code-phrase had been spoken, suddenly, members of the GLF were everywhere. A row of *mostly* women dressed as nuns did a conga to the front of the stage (apparently, Graham Chapman of the television comedy show *Monty Python's Flying Circus* had stumped up the money for the nuns' habits),[4] then got up on it and started performing the can-can amid fifty white mice that someone had released. Peter Tatchell describes how 'a GLF bishop began preaching an impromptu sermon which urged people to "keep on sinning".'[5] If that wasn't enough to cause pandemonium, other members of the GLF sounded horns and then the lights went off.[6] This was down to one GLF member, Martin Corbett, who walked into the basement of the building, ordered the staff to leave with a wave of authority, and then disconnected the broadcasting and electrical cables.[7]

A rally in Trafalgar Square on 25 September 1971 was the high point of the Festival of Light, attracting 45,000 people, who made their way to Hyde Park for a concert where performers included folk singer Judy Mackenzie, Dana, an Irish pop star who had won the Eurovision Song Contest in 1970, and

'Pray with me!' Morals-mad Mary Whitehouse and pop star Cliff Richard in their Nationwide Festival of Light days.

handsome, boyish pop star Cliff Richard. Cliff was something of a notoriety in my family, as my mother claimed he was the only man that she would have been prepared to forsake her marriage vows for (my father needn't have worried, there was precisely zero per cent chance of *that* happening). The GLF were up to their tricks again, letting off more stink bombs and heckling the singers. When poor Judy Mackenzie tried to sing 'He's got the whole world in his hands', audience members supplied their own lyrics: 'He's got the whole world between his legs, he's got the whole world in his pants!' As for Cliff Richard, an audience member shouted, 'Admit you're a homosexual!' That is not the only time in this story that this happens to Cliff.

Mary Whitehouse never forgave the GLF and in 1976 she turned her horn-rimmed spectacles towards *Gay News*, the first LGBT+ newspaper in the UK, whose founders had included members of the GLF. She brought a blasphemy case against the editor, Denis Lemon, in relation to a poem that *Gay News* had published called 'The Love That Dares to Speak Its Name'. The poem (by James Kirkup) was from the viewpoint of a Roman centurion who has sex with Jesus after he is crucified. Lemon was found guilty and given a suspended sentence (later dropped) and fined. Ironically, the extensive media coverage helped publicize *Gay News* and made many people more aware of its existence, although it is still illegal to publish the poem in the UK. No matter; what's important to us is that it is here where a set of deep battle lines have been drawn. Although the names of the organizations and some of those involved are going to change, this is where it all started, with incompatible views and confrontation and men dressed as nuns.

The year after the *Gay News* trial, Mary Whitehouse published a book called *Whatever Happened to Sex?* In it, she writes about the *Last Exit to Brooklyn* obscenity trial from a decade ago, quoting those words of Lord Justice Salmon about books that 'promote homosexuality'. It's an indication of who was influencing her thinking and how in turn she influenced others. We'll have to wait until the following chapter to see how those words ended up in Section 28, though.

I'm not writing this book to have a go at religious people in general, incidentally. But like many things, religions can be used by people who have their own agendas. A book like the Bible is massive and you can leaf through it, find a specific bit, interpret it in a specific way and then turn that into a fully fledged moral campaign. Religion *was* used to justify Section 28 but it involved a set of religious people who claimed to be speaking on behalf of many others when they were mostly speaking for themselves.

The Nationwide Festival of Light dimmed a little after those September rallies but it continued in a less high-profile role, employing a director called Raymond Johnston in 1974. In the next chapter Johnston is going to set off a chain of events that will contribute markedly to the formation of Section 28. But for now, let us leave him and drop in at a school in Islington which is in the midst of an almighty scandal.

The great debate

The scandal in question is rather grandly referred to as the 'William Tyndale affair', despite the fact that William Tyndale had already been dead for four hundred years. Tyndale was an English scholar who had worked on a translation of the Bible into English. In 1530, he publicly opposed Henry VIII's planned annulment of his first marriage, and he was subsequently tried for heresy and executed, aged 42, in 1536. After such a controversial and turbulent life, it is auspicious that the school that was named after him – a junior school, located practically on top of Islington Town Hall, sandwiched between posh Canonbury Square and the surrounding council estates – would also attract attention for all the wrong reasons. At the start of January 1974, a young man with shoulder-length hair and enormous sideburns called Terry Ellis became head teacher (or 'convenor' in his words) of William Tyndale, implementing a new system that was a radical departure from traditional teaching methods. Head teachers in Local Education Authorities (LEAs) had considerably more freedom then than they do today.

Imagine: no league tables, no national curriculum, no Ofsted inspectors. This 'just let them get on with it' thinking on the matter had been expressed as far back as 1854 by Ronald Gould, general secretary of the National Union of Teachers, when he said that democracy was safeguarded by the existence of a 'quarter of a million teachers who are free to decide what should be taught and how it should be taught'.[8]

Terry Ellis therefore had the freedom to institute a version of what was called a child-centred system. Child-centred education, also called progressive education, was an approach developed by John Dowey, Helen Pankhurst, Maria Montessori and others which drew on ideas from philosophers such as John Locke and Jean-Jacques Rousseau. It was a form of education that emphasized learning by doing, critical thinking, social skills, cooperative learning and personalized learning,

Life before Ofsted. Head teacher Terry Ellis (left) and deputy Brian Haddow at William Tyndale School, north London, 1975.

as opposed to traditional 'talk-and-chalk' methods where a (usually rather stern) teacher stands at the front of a room and instructs pupils from a textbook.

Child-centred education had started to appear in some 1960s and '70s classrooms but it was not to everyone's taste. The somewhat extreme version instituted by Ellis gave pupils a great deal of freedom to access all parts of the school, including the staff common room, and pupils were apparently allowed to choose what they did during open periods (every other hour). Children were encouraged to develop their own skills and so steel-band practice occurred for up to eight hours a week.[9] There were reports of spitting, swearing, fire starting, stone throwing, gambling of lunch money and a boy throwing milk bottles at the infants' school next door from the roof of the toilets. Some teachers at the school protested, along with parents, and it was claimed that Ellis told a governor that he 'did not give a damn about parents'.[10] In 1974, the school had 230 pupils. This had fallen to 144 by 1975 and just 63 by the summer of that year as, one by one, incandescent parents withdrew their children. There was no Parent–Teacher Association because the teachers felt it would be dominated by the middle-class parents, so instead, school managers became involved. The Inner London Education Authority (ILEA) sent in a team of inspectors, who ended up trying to teach the children themselves (some of the original teachers having set up a rival 'strike school'). A subsequent parliamentary inquiry (the Auld Inquiry), carried out from October 1975 to February 1976, interviewed 107 witnesses and cost £55,000.[11] It resulted in the dismissal of seven staff, including Ellis and his deputy Brian Haddow, and government intervention was urged in order to define and enforce educational standards. In a book written from their perspective, Ellis and three of his teachers claimed that the press had engaged in a 'witch hunt' against them, representing the staff as 'extreme left-wing child indoctrinators'.[12] And although the Auld Inquiry concluded that what happened at William Tyndale was an unfortunate but exceptional case, the general feeling was that progressive education was going too far.

It was on the back of all this educational drama that Prime Minister James Callaghan (Labour, Cardiff South East) gave a speech on 18 October 1976 at Ruskin College in Oxford, launching what became known as the 'Great Debate'. Callaghan noted that employers in industry were complaining that new recruits did not have the basic tools to do the job required and that there was unease from parents about the 'new informal methods of teaching', which produced 'excellent results in well-qualified hands but were more dubious when they are not'.[13] He called for 'a core curriculum of basic knowledge'. A 63-page document written by the Education Secretary, Fred Mulley, called *The Yellow Book*, noted that school-leavers lacked basic English and maths skills and that less able children needed more formal teaching. The Great Debate raged on, with a new education secretary, Shirley Williams, resisting the idea of a core curriculum that was prescriptive, while trade unions worried about centralized control of education. However, gradually, over the course of the debate, changes started to occur incrementally, paving the way for a more uniform, traditional and accountable form of school education. This, of course, would mean new laws and government intervention. In 1979, a document called 'Local Education Authority Arrangements for the School Curriculum' required local authorities to publish their curriculum policies, starting the long process towards a new standardized form of education. But what would it look like, and how would it treat sensitive topics like sex education?

Thatcher's children

Actually, the UK was in a bit of a mess at this point. The winter of 1978–9 was the coldest it had been in sixteen years, reducing spending and affecting the economy. The Labour Party had been in power since 1974, initially under Harold Wilson, then James Callaghan. Labour had grown out of the trade union movement and its key policies advocated government intervention in the economy and redistribution of wealth, including higher taxes. The party still had strong links to trade unions, which during the 1970s had called for larger pay rises, resulting in lorry, train and ambulance drivers, hospital staff, gravediggers and waste collectors going on strike. Bodies went unburied and Leicester Square in central London became a rat-infested dumping ground for uncollected rubbish – no wonder the period attracted the Shakespearian moniker 'Winter of Discontent'. Callaghan gave a press conference at Heathrow Airport on 10 January 1979, coming across as somewhat blasé by telling journalists that they were taking a parochial view of things. The following day, *The Sun*'s headline sarcastically read 'Crisis? What Crisis?' A few weeks later, the Scottish National Party withdrew support for the government, resulting in a vote of no confidence being passed by just one vote on 28 March. Callaghan was forced to call an election. It did not look good – private polling information had already led him to announce in autumn 1978 that he would not call an election. But now his hand had been forced.

The 1979 election was the only time that my mother voted Conservative. 'Don't do it, Our Marianne,' said all the older members of my family. 'The Tories only care about the rich.' But their leader, Margaret Thatcher, seemed like a new sort of politician. For one thing she was a woman (and the first female leader of a major British political party), and her father had owned a tobacconist's and grocer's, so she didn't come from an out-of-touch elitist background. Like my mother's family, the Thatchers were Methodists, and for a brief time during the Second World War they had sheltered a Jewish girl who had escaped from Nazi Germany – Margaret had even saved her pocket money to help pay for the girl's journey. No matter that her nickname was 'the Iron Lady'; she had sensibly decided to own it in 1976, making a speech that contained the line, 'I stand before you tonight in my Red Star chiffon evening gown, my face softly made up and my fair hair gently waved, the Iron Lady of the Western World.' While Mrs Thatcher was a credible candidate, I suspect that almost any Conservative MP would have won that election, since so many people were fed up with the strikes and wanted change.

Predictably, then, Callaghan was defeated by the Conservative Party in the election of May 1979. He at least won his seat, showing good humour during his acceptance speech while being heckled by campaigner Pat Arrowsmith, who stood against him on a 'Troops out of Ireland' ticket. And so Mrs Thatcher swept in, with 339 seats to Labour's 269 (the Liberals only managed 11, still reeling from the allegations that their former leader Jeremy Thorpe had tried to have his secret gay lover murdered – that's a whole other story, though). It's not often that the following words are really meaningful when they are written but things would never be the same again.

Everything that can be said about Margaret Thatcher has already been said a thousand times. She was divisive (Maggie! Maggie! Maggie! Out! Out! Out!), she was strong (the Iron Lady), she sold off the family silver (her privatization of the rail, energy and water industries), she was lucky (the Falklands War came along just at the right moment to give her a second election victory and she walked out of that bombed hotel with barely a scratch), she was terrifyingly bonkers (the *Spitting Image* puppet). Author and Literary Salon host Damian Barr grew up under her (somewhat neglectful) eye, calling his childhood memoir *Maggie and Me*. To him she was the woman who snatched his milk, smashed the miners and made millions unemployed. But she also saved his life, making a hero of the individual and a cult of the striver. She hated where he was from and made it OK for him to run away.[14] Maggie took the UK in a different direction, making choices that could be viewed as realistic or uncaring, depending on your political perspective. She wasn't everyone's cup of tea (certainly not mine), but she won three elections so was ultimately viewed by many as better than the alternative at the time.

Mrs Thatcher's rise to power coincided with the end of the 1970s, a multicoloured, high-contrast decade of which I have vague but mostly joyous memories – hot summers, snowy winters, Mr Men books and disco. I was a Disco Baby and spent a lot of my early years in a hyped-up haze, singing along to my parents' *Disco Fever* and Bee Gees LPs. I knew all the lyrics (and had dance routines) to 'Yes Sir I Can Boogie', 'Dance and

Shake Your Tambourine' and 'Stayin' Alive'. Disco was a silly, fun, bouncy style of music that combined futuristic-sounding electronic instruments with traditional ones like strings and horns. Although I didn't realize it at the time, it provided the soundtrack to a hedonistic, sexualized culture where people showed up at nightclubs in fabulous fancy dress costumes, took lots of drugs and copped off with people who had too much glitter on their faces. Queer people embraced disco – it represented sexual freedom, acceptance and diversity, and the coloured chequerboard of the dance floor was a space to meet interesting new people, strut your stuff and forget your cares, if only for a few hours. However, the same year that Margaret Thatcher became prime minister, another staunch lady, Ethel Merman (aged 71), doyenne of musical theatre, released her own, delectably dreadful disco album. Now rightfully reappraised as a camp classic, at the time it was seen as disco's elegy, as Merman bellowed her way through a series of Broadway hits in one take and a disco backtrack was added on almost as an after-thought. The party was definitely over and the tone was about to get much more serious.

The year following Labour's defeat in 1979, the party appointed Michael Foot as its leader. Foot was 67 with a dishevelled appearance and a penchant for wearing donkey jackets that earned him the nickname 'Worzel Gummidge', the name of a scarecrow on a (fantastic, incidentally) children's television programme. Initially, Foot was popular, although perhaps this was more by accident than design. The UK had gone into recession after an oil crisis that occurred in 1979 along with the Conservative government's adoption of monetarist policy to reduce inflation, which had the unfortunate effect of increasing unemployment. Polls of the time showed a double-digit lead for Labour. Foot advocated abolishing the House of Lords, unilateral nuclear disarmament, leaving the European Economic Community, more government influence on banking, the creation of a national minimal wage and a ban on fox-hunting. He was nonetheless viewed by some centrist members of the party as being too far to the left, resulting in them splitting off to form the Social Democratic Party, and despite his initial popularity, in 1983 he would lead his party to one of its worst electoral defeats, Labour's manifesto being famously dubbed 'the longest suicide note in history'. Again, this was arguably owing to events beyond his control (just as Thatcher's popularity was boosted as a result of her leadership during the Falklands War of 1982).

Mrs Thatcher may have been prime minister, but her power didn't stretch uniformly across the entire country. There were the couple of hundred Labour MP seats as well as numerous councils that were run by Labour councillors. The GLC (Greater London Council) was an especially prickly thorn in the side of the Tory government. Established in 1965, the sixth GLC election took place in 1981, giving Labour 50 seats, the Conservatives 41 and the Liberals 1. Its leader, Ken Livingstone, held court at the GLC's headquarters in County Hall, perfectly positioned on the South Bank of the Thames, facing Maggie's domain, Westminster, on the other side of the river. Livingstone was at the more radical end of the Labour Party, a socialist and champion of disadvantaged and minority groups, particularly women, lesbians and gay men, and people from ethnic minorities. He was Mrs Thatcher's ideological opposite although equally confrontational, erecting a series of provocative billboards on the front of County Hall that displayed unemployment figures or declared London a Nuclear Free Zone. In 1981 he set up the Gay Rights Working Party, a committee to investigate gay issues in the London area. It was particularly concerned with employment rights and police attitudes. The conservative press dubbed Livingstone 'Red Ken' and started printing stories about the GLC spending public money on minority interest groups. Ken had addressed a meeting of Harrow Gay Unity in August 1981, and *The Times* quoted Richard Brew, deputy leader of the Tory group on the GLC, who said 'Goodness knows what the electorate makes of all this absolute nonsense of supporting groups like this with rate-payers' money.'[15] The early 1980s were thus a time of strongly opposing ideologies and uncompromising political characters, which became ingrained in the memories of many of those who lived through that period. Years later, during the 2018 Labour Party Conference, Tosh McDonald, president of the UK Train Drivers' Union, stated that he detested Margaret Thatcher so much that he set his alarm clock an hour early so he could 'hate her for an hour longer' each day.

Another group of people who disliked Mrs Thatcher were encamped about 55 miles west of London outside a former Royal Air Force station in Berkshire, Greenham Common. In June 1980, it had been announced that, as part of the UK's role in NATO, the site would be used to house American cruise missiles. By September 1981, a group of women had established a camp at Greenham to protest against the missiles, chaining themselves to the base fence. There were several attempts at eviction but the growing numbers of women who called the camp their home were undeterred. In December 1983, 50,000

Badge for Greenham Common –
a finishing school for
non-violent direct action.

women encircled the base, sections of the fence were cut and
there were hundreds of arrests. One of the women who lived
at Greenham Common was called Susannah Bowyer and she is
going to do something amazing in Chapter Four. But for now
she is living in a tent, protesting by running around cutting
fences, spray-painting things and getting arrested. She told me
that Greenham Common was 'a very eroticized space – women
living outside together, lots of women came out or experimented
with same-sex relationships there, some for a long time, some
just for that time . . . it was a very open framework for being
a dyke. I mean there were hippy women with long hair, young
dykes with shaved heads, it wasn't my stereotypical idea of
lesbianism that I would have had at the time.' The women at
Greenham used non-violent direct action as a way of making
protest or trying to make change. They were used to being
arrested and appearing on the news. And as a consequence, a

few years later some of these women were destined to take the more dramatic roles in our story of Section 28.

But back in 1981, there was still the matter of how the children of the UK were to be educated. The Conservatives may have not agreed with James Callaghan's position on many things, but they found common ground over the Great Debate. A document called the 'School Curriculum' was published by the Secretaries of State for Education and Science and for Wales on 25 March 1981. The document noted that 'sex education was not a simple matter', but required 'fullest consultation and cooperation with parents' and that LEAs would have to inform parents of the way that it was provided.[16] The document also seemed to assume that children would grow up to become parents themselves and live in families, noting that 'Preparation for parenthood and family life should help pupils to recognize the importance of those human relationships which sustain, and are sustained by, family life, and the demands and duties that fall on parents.'[17] The government went on to publish a document called a White Paper in 1985. White Papers are made publicly available and are used as a way of putting (sometimes controversial) ideas 'out there' in order to gauge the impact of policies before the government attempts to make them into laws. This White Paper was titled 'Better Schools' and it indicated that the government intended to have a lot of control over the curriculum. This included the creation of the new GCSE exam to replace O Levels and CSEs. Its proposals eventually found their way into the Education (No. 2) Act (1986), which reduced the power of the LEAs and allowed parents to litigate. The act also said that sex education didn't have to be a compulsory subject but that governors had to have a policy on it and, if it was taught at all, pupils had to be encouraged 'to have due regard to moral considerations and the value of family life'.

As we'll see in Chapter Three, there'll be quite a ruckus in the media, with concern expressed about children apparently accessing materials about homosexuality in schools and libraries, particularly in what was starting to be known in the conservative press as 'loony left' councils. And in the press, the profile of gay people had already been raised considerably since the early 1980s, for an awful, terrible reason.

Vicar with a rifle

It is 1992, I am twenty and a nurse is taking blood out of my arm. My boyfriend and I are getting HIV tests. It is my first time and I am terrified. 'Of course, if you've got it, it's a death sentence,' a doctor has just told me in a very matter-of-fact way. 'Would you like some counselling?'

In those days, you had to wait two weeks for your test results and you were given them face to face. The time in the clinic beforehand was like being in a nightmare, the waiting room full of similarly glum-looking individuals. The walk to the office when your name was called always made my legs tremble. This wasn't the sort of test I liked – you couldn't revise for it. But it still felt like an evaluation of sorts – if not an explicitly moral one, then a test of how sensible you had been. On top of that was a sense that no matter how careful you were, there was still the chance of a slip-up, an accident. That first time, when I received my negative result, I surprised myself by bursting into tears in front of the nice woman who read it out to me. And, after a few days of relief, I realized I had started thinking about when the next test was going to be. That was as good as it got for gay men in 1992.

The early signs of the pandemic to come had begun a decade earlier with an article in a gay newspaper, *New York Native*, on 18 May 1981. Gay men and a group of injecting drug-users were dying of a rare kind of pneumonia that occurred in people with compromised immune systems. Another symptom involved an (also rare) form of skin cancer called Kaposi's sarcoma. As more cases emerged, the U.S. Centers for Disease Control and Prevention (CDC) formed a task force to monitor the outbreak. The illness did not have a name as yet, although the CDC had referred to it as the 4H disease because it affected heroin users, homosexuals, haemophiliacs and Haitians. It was also referred to as GRID (Gay-Related Immune Deficiency), although by 1982 it had been established that the disease did not just affect gay people and in July the term AIDS (Acquired Immune Deficiency Syndrome) was introduced, and taken up by the CDC in September. AIDS was caused by a retrovirus that was given the name HIV (Human Immunodeficiency Virus). It was passed on through blood and semen although it quickly died on exposure to air. The main ways to pass it on involved unprotected sex, sharing needles during drug use and blood transfusions, or from mother to child via pregnancy, delivery or breastfeeding. HIV compromised people's immune systems, resulting in them developing opportunistic infections that would eventually lead to death. Because the virus could live in the body for years before a person developed AIDS, it could be unknowingly passed on. At the time of writing there is no cure or vaccination although since the mid-1990s, antiviral medications have often been able to decrease the risk of progression to AIDS. If taken by people who are not HIV+, they strongly decrease the likelihood that they will become HIV+ if exposed to the virus. The World Health Organization estimates that since the start of the epidemic 76 million people have become HIV+ and about 33 million people (around the same number as the entire population of Morocco) have died from AIDS-related complications.[18]

It is difficult to comprehend the amount of fear, pain, suffering and grief that the virus has caused in the last forty or so years. Reverend Richard Coles, who formed the band The Communards in 1985, states that 'half the people you knew died. They'd be dead in a week. It was just so traumatic. We were so young. I really still miss some of the people. Mark Ashton – what would have he become? So many men were in their 20s and 30s. God knows what they would have been. I just wish they hadn't died.'[19]

In the 1980s, the British tabloids did not cover the HIV-AIDS epidemic in a restrained, sensitive or kind way. A selection of headlines include 'Britain Threatened by Gay Virus Plague' (*Mail on Sunday*, 6 January 1985), 'It's Spreading Like Wildfire' (*The Sun*, 6 February 1985), 'AIDS Victims Face Forced Quarantine' (*Daily Mirror*, 11 February 1985), 'Gay Plague Seals Off Death Prison' (*The Sun*, 6 February 1985) and 'My Doomed Son's Gay Plague Agony' (*News of the World*, 30 December 1984). Vicars featured prominently in some headlines, with '"AIDS Is the Wrath of God" Says Vicar' appearing in *The Sun* (7 February 1985), as well as '"I'd Shoot My Son If He Had AIDS", Says Vicar' (*The Sun*, 11 October 1985). This last article (a pitch-perfect exercise in camp horror) was

Not mincing words: Norman Fowler's 1987 'AIDS – Don't Die of Ignorance' campaign.

accompanied by a staged picture of the vicar (Reverend Robert Simpson) pointing a rifle at his son while the opposite page had a large advert for funeral expenses. Chris, the eighteen-year-old son, was quoted as saying, 'Sometimes I think he would like to shoot me whether I had AIDS or not.' Due to the fact that there were no further news stories about this extraordinary family, we should probably conclude that Reverend Robert Simpson did not end up shooting anyone.

The government's response to HIV-AIDS was late in coming. An Expert Advisory Group on AIDS had been set up in 1985 but it wasn't until 1986 that the epidemic was defined as 'high priority', with the Secretary of Health, Norman Fowler, advocating that information was the only vaccine. Fowler ran a public health campaign in 1987 called 'AIDS – Don't Die of Ignorance'. A short television advert, featuring scary music, a volcano and a tombstone with the word AIDS chiselled onto it, was solemnly voiced by John Hurt, one of the finest actors in the country (he had played Quentin Crisp, Caligula, Winston Smith and that chap who has an alien burst out of his stomach in the film *Alien*). Now he warned the entire country that 'if you ignore AIDS, it could be the death of you.' An accompanying information leaflet was delivered to every household in the UK. Despite using fear to put its message across, as campaigns go, it was at least non-judgemental. Fowler noted that Margaret Thatcher hadn't been keen on a campaign because she'd thought that informing people about unprotected sex would encourage them to engage in it.[20]

However, long before the campaign, gay men and lesbians had come together to provide care and support for those affected by HIV-AIDS. The first person to die of HIV-AIDS in the UK was a man called Terrence Higgins and in 1982 the Terrence Higgins Trust (THT) was formed, initially to raise funds for research but then to carry out community-based care for

Sinister! Norman Fowler's 1987 'AIDS – Don't Die of Ignorance' campaign.

patients. By the end of 1983, the THT was running a helpline offering information about the virus and publishing leaflets detailing safer-sex practices, and in 1984, it had established a buddying scheme to provide social support for those who had been affected. Between 1985 and 1999, the rate of HIV infection in the UK remained fairly stable at under 3,000 new cases a year. Up until 1995 the number of people in the UK who died of HIV-AIDS gradually rose to almost 2,000 a year. These statistics were too high and mask the vast amount of human suffering that extended well beyond them. But it's likely that they would have been higher still without the THT and the later government campaign. Additionally, gay men took the advice seriously, changing the ways they had sex en masse. Still, though, fear of HIV-AIDS affected millions of people in the UK.

What was the effect of the fear-mongering press articles on gay individuals? In a study I carried out as a young researcher, I examined samples of personal adverts printed in the publication *Gay Times* (formerly *Gay News*) in the years 1973, 1982, 1991 and 2000.[21] Comparing what men focused on at different points in time is telling about how trends in attractiveness changed. No matter what year you look at, masculinity (trying to appear butch and wanting a butch man) is always the main focus. But it comes over in different ways. The year 1973 was very much about clothing and accessories. Advertisers frequently used words like *jeans*, *leather*, *boots* and *sportswear*, as well as referring to objects like *pipes* and *motorbikes*, which signified that you were a 'proper' man. The 1970s were the decade of the 'clone' and a butch look could be easily bought off the peg, so to speak. Fast forward to 1982 and these overt costumes have become a bit of a cliché and are starting to look slightly naff. Unemployment is peaking at 13 per cent, so markers of economic success and security have become popular ways of selling yourself as a successful man, especially as the country makes its painful way towards market capitalism – calling yourself *solvent*, claiming you're *professional* or that you have OHAC (own home and car) are now very much in vogue.

Perhaps the onset of HIV-AIDS would be expected to be having an effect too at this point, but we are still in the early days and it isn't until the next sampling point, nine years later in 1991, that we see how the virus, the homophobia of the media and the general public's declining attitudes have taken their toll, with advertisers making a big deal about how actually not very gay they are, honestly. There's a lot of disavowal now, with phrases like *no camp* or *no effeminates*, alongside terms like *straight-acting*, which is frequently acronymed as SA. Advertisers even describe themselves using terms like *ungay* and *real man* in this period. *Straight-acting* was very popular in the early 1990s (I used it myself in one of these kinds of adverts) – we didn't talk much about what a self-defeating term it was. Not only were we implying that masculinity and heterosexuality were pretty much the same thing, but we were lauding heterosexual men as the ideal, as well as admitting that we couldn't really pull it off – the best we could do was put on an act. During this time many gay men seemed eager to distance themselves from the very idea that they might be friends with other gay people or hang out with them, so terms like *non-scene* and *discreet* were also popular. To hammer home just how butch these men are, they were more likely than in any other period to mention manly hobbies and occupations like *biker*, *trucker*, *forces*, *fireman*, *sailor* or *security guard*, and there was more emphasis than ever on having a hairy chest or beard.

This is also an era when gay men were much less likely to refer to having sex. The adverts in *Gay Times* hadn't been particularly explicit up until this point in any case, but advertisers had developed a succession of (not very difficult to decipher) codes to indicate their preferences. Terms like *active*, *passive*, *dominant*, *sub*, *daddy*, *masterful* and *strong-minded* (that is, into s&m) were used with about equal frequency in all four time periods apart from 1991, when they dipped significantly in popularity. So 1991 comes across as a much more uptight and self-hating year for gay men than 1973 and 1982. How fun for me, then, that 1991 was when I tentatively launched myself onto the gay scene while in my second year of university. One of the things I remember most about the late 1980s and early 1990s was how baggy the clothes were. It was almost as if they were designed to disguise the shape of your body so that nobody would ever get accidentally aroused by looking at you. They remind me now of the blue overalls worn by the citizens in George Orwell's dystopian novel *1984*, a society denoted by words like *sex-crime* and young people joining Anti-Sex Leagues. Relatively speaking, men's clothes today appear provocatively tight-fitting. But now we are in a much more liberal time and the direction we were moving in was already starting to be prevalent in 2000, the last time period I examined. Here, the focus was moving towards mesomorphic bodies, with descriptors like *athletic*, *muscular*, *gym-trained*, *fit*, *trim* and *nice physique* coming into vogue. Gay advertisers at the end of the millennium were eager to approximate the beefy Tom of Finland body shape and they were prepared to put in the effort at the gym to get the most masculine look. A literal arms race was now well under way.

Four snapshots, each revealing a different picture, each with different standards of what gay men thought would make them stand out as authentically masculine, with more difficult to achieve standards across each decade. Of course, there were some predictable constants – *slim*, *young* and *good-looking* were always going to get your dance card filled (and probably always will), no matter what year you set your time machine to. But it's the differences that I find fascinating, especially in 1991. A decade of fear and hatred had filtered into the way that gay men look for connection. And the men who *lived* through that era were the lucky ones.

The way the wind blows

We now take an illustrative interlude to consider the shocking events of the by-election that took place in Bermondsey on 24 February 1983. The darling of the dockers, sitting MP Bob Mellish had been safe in the seat for over thirty years, although he had recently become unhappy with the direction that the Labour party was taking, disliking the presence of voices from what he saw as the militant hard left. On the verge of resigning, he wanted John O'Grady, who was leader of Southwark Borough Council, to replace him. However, in 1981 the Labour Party selected ex-GLF activist Peter Tatchell as the parliamentary candidate for Bermondsey. Originally from Australia, Tatchell was a proponent of direct action, arguing that 'either we are forced to accept Tory edicts as a fait accompli or we must look to new, more militant, forms of extra-parliamentary opposition which involve mass popular participation and challenge the government's right to rule.'[22] Although Michael Foot refused to endorse him as a candidate, Tatchell was supported by the local Bermondsey Labour Party, and when Bob Mellish resigned, a by-election was triggered. The campaign that followed was one of the most vicious and dirty in British history, revealing much about attitudes towards homosexuality in the UK.

It was an odd time to have a by-election – the next general election was only three and a half months away – but by-elections can act as good indicators of the way the country is leaning and as is often the case when an election is for an important seat there were a lot of candidates clamouring for attention: sixteen in total. I don't have the will to go through all of them and I expect you don't want me to either, so I'll tell you about five of them. Tatchell was the official Labour selection, but his rival John O'Grady stood against him anyway under the banner of 'Real Bermondsey Labour'. The Liberal entrant was a new face – a wholesome-looking young barrister called Simon Hughes – while the Conservative Party put up a member of the GLC, Robert Hughes (no relation). The by-election was also the first outing of the infamous Screaming Lord Sutch of the Official Monster Raving Loony Party (he got 97 votes).

The Labour Party had persuaded Peter Tatchell not to speak about his sexuality, despite the fact that he was openly gay. However, the tabloid newspapers found out that he had been a member of the GLF and decided to make his sexuality public. *The Sun* ran a story that claimed (falsely) that he had been to a 'Gay Olympics' event in San Francisco (a place strongly associated with the HIV-AIDS epidemic), while the *News of the World* published a photograph of Tatchell that

had been retouched to make it look as if was wearing eye-
liner and lipstick.[23] Some of the other candidates chimed in,
deploying homophobia for political advantage. John O'Grady
toured around the Bermondsey constituency on the back of a
horse and cart singing a song to the tune of 'My Old Man's a
Dustman', which went like this:

> Tatchell is a poppet, as pretty as can be
> But he must be slow if he don't know that he won't
> be your MP
> Tatchell is an Aussie, he lives in a council flat
> He wears his trousers back to front because he doesn't
> know this from that . . .

Smear tactics weren't employed by O'Grady alone. The
Liberal campaign used male canvassers wearing badges that
claimed, 'I've been kissed by Peter Tatchell.' And its campaign
leaflet described the election as 'a straight choice' between
Hughes and Tatchell.

There was worse to come. Graffiti was daubed over almost
every subway hoarding, railway arch and bridge in the area,
proclaiming 'Tatchell is queer' and 'Tatchell is a communist
puff.' Towards the end of the campaign, an anonymous leaflet
was posted through local letterboxes which showed pictures
of Tatchell (again retouched in lipstick) and the queen. 'Which
queen will you vote for?' the accompanying text demanded. The
leaflet referred to Tatchell (who was a republican) as a traitor
and encouraged people to 'let him know what you think of him,'
helpfully printing his address and telephone number. Tatchell
received hate mail – more than thirty death threats – and was

violently assaulted over one hundred times.[24] He had to have his flat boarded up and police officers told him he was lucky not to have been killed.

The election saw a win for Simon Hughes, who received 17,017 votes (57.7 per cent). Peter Tatchell came second with 7,698 votes (26.1 per cent) while John O'Grady was in third place (2,243 votes, 7.6 per cent). It was a 44 per cent swing to the Liberals, the biggest in any by-election in recent history. Although the by-election suggested bad tidings for Labour and looked like good news for the Liberals, it was actually the Conservatives who won the general election by a landslide a few months later. Michael Foot resigned as leader of Labour a few days after Mrs Thatcher made her victory speech, being replaced by the more centre-left Neil Kinnock in October 1983.

Part of the reason why I've included the story of the Bermondsey by-election in this book is because both Hughes and Tatchell will go on to play very different roles in the opposition against Section 28 that is to come. But I've also highlighted it to point out the fact that all of this happened, that all of this was *allowed* to happen, without the whole by-election being written off – that should act as an alarm bell to wake the soundest of sleepers. This is what was alright in Britain in 1983.

Then there are the codas to this story, which make it all the more ugly and sad. Remember Bob Mellish, the original Labour MP whose resignation triggered the by-election, the one who wanted John O'Grady to replace him? After he died, Peter Tatchell claimed that Mellish was (secretly) bisexual and had persistently propositioned Tatchell, warning him not to make it public as no one would believe him.[25] And how about we fast-forward to January 2006, when the resignation of the

A straight choice
(although it wasn't):
Liberal–SDP Alliance
leaflet used in
the Bermondsey
by-election.

Sorry we didn't find you in !

one of **SIMON , HUGHES'**

Southwark and Bermondsey team

called

Would you like to help Simon's campai
Or have you any questions or problems that
you'd like to raise? Contact us at the
Liberal Centre, 30 St. James' Road,
Bermondsey SE16, or ring 231 06

This Election is A STRAIGHT CHOICE
On the one hand there is the divided and
declining Labour Party. On the other there
is local Liberal/SDP Alliance
SIMON HUGHES, known throughout Southwark
and Bermondsey for local action
in touch through FOCUS – and he's backed by
two national parties with clear, realistic
policies to fight unemployment, bad housing
and crime.

HE'S THE ONLY ONE TO BEAT TATCHELL !

**SIMON HUGHES
Liberal- SDP Alliance**

*battling for Bermondsey –
sound sense for Southwark*

then Liberal Democrat leader, Charles Kennedy, has just triggered another election contest? Simon Hughes announced his candidature for leader and was interviewed by a number of newspapers including the *Daily Telegraph*, *The Independent* and *The Guardian*. Questions regarding his sexuality kept coming up and Hughes denied that he was gay in each interview. Then *The Sun* told him they had evidence that he'd used a gay chat service and Hughes admitted that he'd had relationships with women and men. He also apologized for the Bermondsey campaign: 'I hope that there will never be that sort of campaign again. I have never been comfortable about the whole of that

campaign, as Peter knows, and I said that to him in the past
. . . Where there were things that were inappropriate or wrong,
I apologize for that.'[26] Peter Tatchell appears to have forgiven
him, endorsing his candidature for Liberal Democrat leader
and saying, 'Since his election, Simon has redeemed himself by
voting for gay equality. That's all that matters now. He should
be judged on his policies, not his private life.'[27]

Sexuality can be hidden. Not everyone is able (or wants)
to conceal it, and equally not everyone is adept at spotting
it. But the 1983 Bermondsey by-election showed that those
who were able to hide it could do so to their advantage and
that, sometimes, the voices that cry out most loudly in outrage
against us are those who are most afraid of their own secret
being discovered.

Made this way

The perspective that we are born with pre-set sexualities is
one which has gained traction (Lady Gaga had a hit song with
it, called 'Born This Way', in 2011). But during the 1980s, a
different understanding of sexuality was developing alongside
it, one chiefly being put forward by women like Sheila Jeffreys
who were sometimes called lesbian feminists. This was a view
called heterosexism, and it stated that sexuality could be and
was being influenced by society. Proponents of heterosexism
viewed heterosexuality as a social institution, a kind of ideology
or belief system under which everyone was encouraged, cajoled,
even brainwashed into thinking that heterosexuality was the
only and normal way of expressing sexuality. This could be
done through a number of processes – either by not discussing

alternatives like homosexuality or bisexuality, or, if they must be discussed, dismissing them as disgusting, some form of curable disease or just a phase. Sheila Jeffreys describes how, in 1985, a leaflet was produced by the GLC, entitled 'Harassment of Lesbians and Gay Men . . . and how to challenge it at the GLC'.[28] The leaflet stated:

> Lesbians and Gay men exist in all cultures, races and classes and religions and have existed throughout history. People are not born with a particular sexuality they acquire it. Heterosexism is a set of ideas and practices which assume that heterosexuality is the superior and therefore only 'normal' and 'natural' form of sexual relationship.[29]

In a talk given by Lynne Harne, who had worked as an equal opportunities officer for the GLC, she describes how gay men at the GLC weren't happy with the above wording and tried to get it changed. This all happened decades ago and we might naively wonder why those involved couldn't just work together or agree to disagree. Why did a rift develop between some of the lesbians and gay men who were involved in political activism in the 1980s? The concept of lesbian invisibility plays a part. Sex between women had never actually been made illegal, which, on the one hand, could be viewed as 'well, at least lesbians never got sent to prison or fined' but, on the other, implies that they simply weren't viewed as important enough for anyone to bother discriminating against them with a law. There is a somewhat apocryphal (that is, probably not true at all) story that lesbians were to be included in the Criminal

Law Amendment Act (1885), which made 'gross indecency' between men a crime, but Queen Victoria declared such a thing to be impossible so the relevant part of the bill was removed. Decades later, during the HIV-AIDS crisis, the media and government tended to focus on gay men (lesbians were not seen as a high-risk group), who bore the brunt, both in terms of becoming ill, dying, losing partners and friends, and experiencing stigma as disease-spreaders. Gay men were under a great deal of scrutiny, mostly for the wrong reasons, but where did this leave lesbians?

Another GLC document, called *Tackling Heterosexism: A Handbook of Lesbian Rights*, which was published in 1986, noted that while gay men were likely to suffer violence from heterosexual men, lesbians were even more likely to be attacked and on top of that they experienced sexual harassment from heterosexual men. While gay men were despised for not being real men, lesbians aroused anger because they demonstrated that women can get by jolly well without having to rely on a man.[30] Lesbians can be seen as being doubly oppressed – not only because they are attracted to members of the same sex but because they are women. Broadly speaking, men experience privilege in all sorts of ways, small and large, compared to women. A few examples: male graduates earn more than female graduates, even among those doing the same subject at the same university, there are fewer women managers, professors and high court judges, and two women a week are killed by a current or former male partner.[31] I remember being shocked when my sister told me that the only time that men stopped shouting rude things at her from cars when she was walking to the shops was after she started pushing her first baby around in a pram.

This is the sort of thing that women routinely experience, and I hadn't even realized it until she told me.

Go back a few decades and the situation is even worse. Female genital mutilation wasn't made a crime until 1985, and statutory maternity pay wasn't introduced until 1986. Throughout the 1980s it was still legal to rape your wife (this didn't change until 1994) or engage in coercive control of a partner (not an offence until 2015). Some lesbian feminists were 'separatist', wanting only to invest their energies in other women while limiting their dealings with men as much as possible. Another term, used to describe some lesbian feminists, was 'radical', which meant that you aimed to dismantle the system, as opposed to 'liberals', who wanted to keep the system but reform it.

The lesbian feminist take on sexuality could therefore be characterized as radical, having much more far-reaching consequences for society than the 'born this way' view, which tends towards the liberal stance. If we accept that a relatively small number of people are born gay, lesbian or bisexual and there is nothing that they can do about it, we can argue that we oughtn't worry about children being 'converted' and that discrimination against gay people is cruel because it is not their fault. Instead, we should campaign for laws to protect gay people from harassment and to ensure they are treated the same as everyone else. However, if we take the view that society has coerced large numbers of people into thinking they are heterosexual and that, in particular, women are being forced into becoming dependent on men, then this would require a complete restructuring of society to put things right. Taking this argument forward, as the heterosexist brainwashing begins practically from birth, teaching children about the existence of homosexuality alongside heterosexuality, at the very least in a non-judgemental way, would be an essential step in a project to dismantle heterosexism. And in the 1980s, groups within the GLC and the ILEA's youth service were beginning to do just that. One group, called Feminist Lesbians in Education, was set up to challenge heterosexism in education in London.

A number of Girls' Projects were organized by feminist lesbians in areas like Tower Hamlets and Hackney. The organizers ran consciousness-raising discussions with girls, getting them to think about why they wanted to get married or to talk about incidents of abuse or bullying they had experienced. These sessions were female-only and included activities where they would learn skills like car maintenance, self-defence, horse-riding and carpentry. It didn't always go well – some of the girls were wary of being taught by lesbians and responded by dressing in high heels, short skirts and make-up – but the women were careful to discuss issues that arose. Various short films were shown at some of the groups and used to instigate debate afterwards. One is a 25-minute drama produced by the Family Planning Association Education Unit in 1986, called *Danny's Big Night*. In the film, cockney teenagers with big hair, dangly hoop earrings, high-waisted jeans and baggy pullovers with geometric patterns showcase the horrors of toxic masculinity (despite this being a term that wouldn't be invented for several decades). In other words, Danny ignores his girlfriend Lorraine during a night out with friends, answers questions directed at her and is outraged to find a packet of condoms in her possession: 'What you got them in your bag for? Durex, Lorraine! Durex!' Another video called *How to Become a Lesbian in 35 Minutes* featured young lesbians talking about their lives. The title was meant to be ironic. It's certainly attention-catching and, as we'll see later on, is going to play a starring role in the debate around 'promotion of homosexuality' in the coming months.

In some of the girls' groups, young women saw lesbianism not just as an alternative to heterosexuality, but one that encapsulated a positive, political choice:

> I began to realize that there was a political affiliation, in some places, with lesbianism . . . I had thought it was just purely sexual, and then I finally realized that it had a lot to do with politics . . . And how it can be a political decision not to sleep with men . . .[32]

In 1981, a group of revolutionary feminists had published a booklet called *Love Your Enemy? The Debate between Heterosexual Feminism and Political Lesbianism*. The booklet defined a political lesbian as a 'woman-identified woman who does not fuck men. It does not mean compulsory sexual activity with women.'[33] Despite that disclaimer, not all feminists agreed with the stance. Beatrix Campbell described the notion of political lesbianism as 'crazy . . . It erased desire. It was founded, therefore, not on love of women but fear of men,' while Lynne Segal characterized it as 'advanced by a tiny band of vanguardist women . . . Its stance was tragic, because no, all men were not the enemy.'[34] However, for other women, like Julie Bindel, 'political lesbianism continues to make intrinsic sense because it reinforces the idea that sexuality is a choice, and we are not destined to a particular fate because of our chromosomes.'[35]

In the years to come, political lesbianism did not gain a lot of ground, perhaps due to having detractors among both other feminists and anti-feminists, the latter helping to perpetuate a stereotype of all feminists as angry, uncompromising, man-hating lesbians. As early as 16 June 1978, the *Daily Mirror* had warned that 'radical feminism is gaining aggressive support among the young.' During the 1980s, the 'angry feminist' trope appeared in the media in various comedic guises. It was not as commonly encountered as the 'camp gay man' stereotype and sometimes it was referred to obliquely, but it was there. For example, the 1985–6 ITV sitcom *Girls on Top* featured Dawn French playing Amanda Ripley, a radical feminist who wears a boiler suit and comes across as patronizing, bolshy and overly earnest. Over on BBC Two, the sketch show *Victoria Wood: As Seen on TV* ran a series of monologues by Kitty (Patricia Routledge), a formidable woman from Cheadle who regularly referred to her producer:

> She's a nice girl but when someone chain-smokes Capstan Full Strength and wears a coal-man's jerkin you're hardly tempted to sample their dumplings. The first day I met [her] she said, 'I'm a radical feminist lesbian.' I thought what would the Queen Mum do? So I just smiled and said, 'We shall have fog by tea-time.' She said, 'Are you intimidated by my sexual preferences?' I said, 'No and I'm not too struck with your donkey jacket either.'

The stereotype was most fully brought to life by the comic *Viz*, which featured a regular character called Millie Tant, embodying a complete caricature of a left-wing militant feminist. Tant refers to other women as 'fellow lesbians' and claims that fireworks are 'big explosive penises' that 'skewer and rape the virgin female sky'. The mainstream view of radical feminism was that it was something ridiculous to be laughed at or, more often, simply ignored.

Even within the ostensibly safer spaces of the GLC and the ILEA London Youth Committee, some of these women felt that they were being sidelined by gay men. Increasingly dominant was the 'born this way' belief about sexuality, along with a position that saw lesbians, gay men and heterosexuals as all essentially normal and not really different from one another. Down the line, this led to what tends to be the most popular model of thinking about sexuality that we see now in the UK. It is one encapsulated in the inclusive acronym LGBTQ+ and it involves a focus on help, support and counselling for gay people, which would result in them accepting their sexuality. However, some lesbian feminists wanted to inspire a kind of collective form of anger against societal oppression, which would challenge the status quo.

I'm inclined to believe that the 'born this way' and the 'heterosexist society' viewpoints both contain elements that make sense. I see sexuality as the product of multiple factors, including genes, brain development, hormones in the womb and all the messages we get from society through friends, family and the media. I believe we are all born with a set of sexual potentials (not the same potentials, though) and that our interactions with society will determine which of those potentials get expressed and how our sexuality manifests itself. I think of it as a bit similar to the height you reach. I'm 6 ft

1 inch tall. Had I been born in a different time period I probably wouldn't have had such good nutrition, so I would have been unlikely to reach that height. But my sister would never have reached 6 foot 1, no matter what her diet had been like. We just have different height potentials. Where sexuality differs from height, though, is that there is further capacity for change, although even that's more the case for some people than others.

Equally, I can see that activism that aims for small, incremental changes on an individual level, along with diplomacy, compromise and working within existing social and legal frameworks, is likely to be effective, and nobody needs to get a guillotine out. But I can also appreciate that in some cases people feel the need for a more radical activism that calls for enormous structural change, even if that can mean civil disobedience. When speaking to activists in the present day, quite a few of them also acknowledged this multifaceted perspective. But during the 1980s, it feels like these ideological positions were more at odds with one another.

Perhaps oddly, the lesbian feminism perspective could be seen as having quite a bit in common with some of the concerns that were coming from the 'moral majority' about the possibility that homosexuality could be 'promoted'. Although I view myself as a 'sexual solid' as opposed to having a fluid sexuality, I'm more than onboard with the view that plenty of people have a sexuality that is liable to change over time, or that some people haven't been able to fully realize their sexual potential due to society's insistence on heterosexuality. (As I'll describe later, when I was a teenager I tried to be heterosexual for a few weeks. Spoiler – it didn't go well.) Some people simply repress their sexual desires, take up a distracting hobby and go with what society wants. Others may have been kept in such ignorance that they haven't even properly considered other possibilities, while others still are more switched on and are willing to try different forms of sexual expression throughout their lives. I can imagine that the proponents of Section 28 would have had to concede that some people, like me, were just incorrigible homosexuals and it was pointless pinning my eyes open and forcing me to watch endless episodes of *Little House on the Prairie* because I was a lost cause. But for many others, they believed that there *was* scope for change, if people were given the right conditions.

It's ironic, then, that in some ways, some of the people who were opposed to Section 28 had pretty similar understandings of how sexuality worked to the people who were proponents of it. For example, on 8 May 1987 Jill Knight MP (Conservative, Edgbaston) relayed an anecdote told to her by someone who had been a colonel in the Indian army. It was

his belief that homosexuals were made if enough influence was exerted upon them. He said that in the hill country and in parts of Poona, when he was in the Indian army, drummer boys used to be sent out from England – they were often orphans – and sent up to the forward areas to the regiments. He said – I have never forgotten this – that not one of those children had a chance. They all ended up as homosexuals because of the life they were forced to lead. I find it outrageous that little children should have been perverted in that way.

Outrageous indeed. And on 2 February 1988, Lord Campbell of Croy argued, 'Young people at an impressionable age though basically heterosexual can be led into homosexuality even if it is for a temporary period. This can cause great confusion to them, upsetting their lives, their careers and their prospects of marriage.'

The claims about being made homosexual bring to mind the old joke: 'My mother made me a homosexual.' 'Oh good, if I get her the wool, will she make me one too?' Nowadays, it's not such a popular idea, although a related, somewhat more sophisticated version of it was starting to be voiced in academic circles in the early 1990s: queer theory. Queer theory holds that sexuality is fluid and unstable, only ever appearing to have a solid configuration due to the sexual categories that have been constructed as acceptable or even possible in any given society at any given point in time. I don't think that radical lesbian feminism took its arguments around heterosexism as far as queer theory, since it was more concerned with seeing the potential in women to be lesbians and to live apart from men. But the larger point I want to make here is that there was a fracture within gay and lesbian organizations, marked by differences in how sexuality was understood and what kinds of action ought to be taken to improve people's lives. It wasn't necessarily a fracture that received much attention outside queer political circles – and in any case, opponents of LGBTQ+ people tended to view anyone who advocated even the smallest move towards LGBTQ+ equality as equally militant.

And that points to another, more dangerous fracture that was growing bigger every day – between gay people and the rest of society. On the one hand there were gay men, who were being monstered in the press as sex-mad disease spreaders. And, on the other, there were radical feminist lesbians who were advocating a view of sexuality that would have had completely restructured society if it gained mainstream support. It was hardly a surprise that this was going to turn out badly.

3

An Uncivil Debate

It is 31 December 1979, I am seven years old and I have been allowed to stay up to 'see in the New Year'. The living room is cosy, with its Christmas decorations still up, and I savour the rare experience of being able to watch late-night TV with my parents, taking interest in a programme which claims that by 1990 everyone will have a household robot.

'Do you want to be the first foot?' asks my mother. 'You have to hold this piece of coal and knock on the door after midnight to bring us luck.' I still don't know where she got the coal from – we had central heating.

Being first foot sounds like a lark but as Big Ben strikes twelve I feel rushed and subsequently muddle putting on my shoes and coat. It's too cold outside and I get upset because I wanted to do it at exactly midnight; now I've left things too late and I reason that we'll now have bad luck all year. So, my earliest memory of the 1980s is my parents being mildly bemused at why I'm crying outside our front door. Not the best start to the decade.

As the 1980s continued, I was starting to realize that I wasn't having as much fun in this decade as I'd had in the previous one. I felt different to everyone around me and I was alienated by the values and the music of the time. The only pop song I liked was 'Don't Leave Me This Way' by duo Jimmy Somerville and Richard Coles, who had previously been in Bronski Beat, having released 'Smalltown Boy' two years earlier. I'd first heard it while being spun round on one of those fairground rides that you have to be 'this high' to ride on. I was fourteen and staying out late for the first time with my friends. The song was a cover of a disco classic, charting first in 1975 for Harold Melvin and the Blue Notes, then in 1976 for Thelma Houston. Disco would always be my favourite music and it took me a long time to get over the fact that the 1970s had ended – I wanted that decade to go on forever. It wasn't until much later I could appreciate that the pop music that came afterwards was also pretty good, just in a different way. The New Romantics, electropop, synthpop – this music was strange and sometimes mournful, with lyrics that seemed like commentaries on the chilly events of the early to mid-1980s when gay men were dying of AIDS, unemployment was high, miners' families suffered through a strike that lasted over a year and heroin use was on the rise. My friends scoured *Smash Hits* magazine, trying to decipher the meaning of the lyrics it printed for songs by bands such as Tears for Fears, Duran Duran, Human League, Spandau Ballet, Soft Cell and Ultravox. Unlike the smiling, bouncing disco groovers who usually assumed saucy or camp poses for their posters, these groups often looked sulky or wistful. Compared to disco, they sounded intelligent and angst-ridden – a serious sound for a serious time.

Because I didn't fit in, I retreated into a world of books. I read anything I could get my hands on, graduating from Enid Blyton to Agatha Christie to Jane Austen. I would have loved to have read books that featured gay characters but they were few and far between. However, such books did exist if you knew where to look. And it's one such book that this chapter is concerned with. Its heroine was called Jenny and she lived in a faraway land (actually Denmark). Unlike Enid Blyton's characters, Jenny wouldn't encounter any flying chairs or trees with different lands at the top of them. But still, there was something magical about this book. It had the power to change people's minds and the lady who'd written it had hoped that it would make other people be nicer to one another but in fact it made a lot of people very nasty instead. The book had such magical powers that you didn't have to read or even see the book to fall under its spell. So a curse fell upon the land and people were horrible to one another for quite a long time.

That's essentially a summary of this chapter, told as a children's fairy tale. The reality is even more fantastical.

Scandinavians don't wear pyjamas

The 'magic book' in question was *Jenny Lives with Eric and Martin*, a children's book by the Danish author Susanne Bösche. She had written the book after becoming 'aware that there were a lot of children in Denmark living with a homosexual father or mother and that there was a need for a book for these children to identify with'.[1] It had been first published in Danish as *Mette bor hos Morten og Erik* in 1981, then translated into English in 1983 by Louis Mackay. The book was taken up by a small independent publisher, the Gay Men's Press, with a run of 3,000 copies for UK distribution.[2] The initial response was small and a bit lukewarm.

Jenny Lives with Eric and Martin, one of the most burnt books of 1986.

The book is illustrated with black-and-white photographs that feature Martin, his boyfriend Eric and their five-year-old daughter Jenny (played by Bösche's own daughter). The characters go on a trip to the laundrette, have a birthday party for Eric and encounter homophobia from a woman in the street. At one point in the book, the three characters have breakfast in bed, and Jenny is shown sitting up between Eric and Martin, who are both shirtless. Bösche would later express surprise that this image was so shocking in England, describing how it is usual to have breakfast in bed in Denmark, and that Danish people didn't sleep in pyjamas in summer. She noted that a photograph of Jenny and Martin showering together had been removed for the UK version. However, had she known how the book was going to be received, it would have been further adapted to take into account English family customs.³ To my eyes, the breakfast in bed scene is innocent and loving, an event that occurs in many households all over the world (not just Denmark) – would as many eyebrows have been raised if one of the men had been a woman? But it is the confronting reality of those documentary-style photographs that perhaps explains the extent of the reaction in some quarters. Since then, many of the later books that feature same-sex families have used colourful drawings rather than photos, sometimes depicting animal characters instead of people.

In December 1983, John Izbicki, writing in the *Daily Telegraph*, rhetorically asked why he found the book so objectionable, deciding it was because the 'subject is to be forced on young minds that are not ready to absorb such information'.⁴ The following year, in the *Daily Mail*, Roald Dahl produced a searing critique of *Jenny*. Dahl is best known for his novel *Charlie and the Chocolate Factory*, where children suffer terrible fates such as being turned into a giant blueberry or shrunk to the size of a bar of chocolate. However, Dahl seems to have thought that having two male parents was even worse. He claimed the book is 'obviously . . . meant to condition very young children' while noting that 'reality is shirked or fudged, like the awkward matter of homosexuals often proving at least as promiscuous as "straight" men, so that partnerships are not necessarily stable or enduring.'⁵

In 1986, the *Daily Mail* reported that the book 'has been put into school libraries by the Inner London Education Authority and other Left-Wing authorities'.⁶ A couple of days later *The Times* quoted an after-dinner speech by the Minister for Arts, Richard Luce, who had said that the majority of the public would find the book 'totally unacceptable for stocking on open library shelves, although that was what was happening in the Labour-controlled Borough of Haringey'.[7]

Haringey London Borough Council had been created in 1965, the result of three smaller boroughs being amalgamated. It covers around 11 square miles of a parallelogram-shaped blob of north London and includes well-off areas such as Highgate and Muswell Hill as well as wards that are among the most deprived 10 per cent of the country. It is the home of Tottenham Hotspur Football Club, Alexandra Palace and Highgate Cemetery. In 1981, there were 202,641 people living there, and it had always been a Labour borough, apart from a blip from 1968 to 1971. By the mid-1980s, Haringey had become emblematic of a 'loony left council', in tabloid parlance. For example, on Guy Fawkes Night in 1985 a story in *The Sun* entitled 'Barmy Bernie Is Going Coffee Potty' claimed that Bernie Grant MP had 'ordered its workers to show solidarity with Nicaragua by drinking the Marxist country's grotty coffee'. While Nicaraguan coffee *was* available in the council's canteens, Grant had not issued any edicts about drinking it. The *Mail on Sunday* then ran a story on 2 March 1986 that claimed that 'Black bin liners have been banned by Haringey council because they are racially offensive.' Again, this does not appear to have been the case. The *Daily Mail* followed up with a story about how the song 'Baa Baa Black Sheep' had been changed to 'Baa Baa Green Sheep' in nurseries, which also does not appear to have been true.[8]

Meanwhile, the GLC (Greater London Council) found itself under attack by the government. The GLC had created a Gay Working Party in 1984, which had produced a detailed

Ken and his crew. The GLC's launch of *Changing the World*, with the help of Jimmy Somerville, Richard Coles and Miriam Margolyes.

document called *Changing the World: A London Charter for Gay and Lesbian Rights*. The document referred to heterosexism and its impact on gay people as well as discussing abuse faced by them in relation to schools, religion, health, disability, parenting, social services and the law. A year later, the GLC donated £750,000 to fund the opening of the London Lesbian and Gay Centre, which was housed in a former meat warehouse near Smithfield Market in Farringdon.

The government had had enough of this kind of spending, along with Ken Livingstone's mocking banners displayed across County Hall. It employed the Local Government Act (1985) to devolve the powers of the GLC to London boroughs, effectively abolishing it altogether. Aged thirteen, during a family holiday to London, I leaned on some railings that adjoined the Thames and asked my father why there was a banner that read 'We'll meet again' on the big building on the other side of the river. The GLC ceased to exist on 31 March 1986. However, Livingstone's banner was prophetic. Tony Blair's Labour government created the Greater London Authority in 2000, which had an elected Mayor of London. Ken Livingstone gained 58 per cent of the vote, also winning my vote for the best opening line of a victory speech ever: 'As I was saying before I was so rudely interrupted fourteen years ago . . .'

The GLC might have gone but there were still those local councils and their 'loony' policies. Focus shifted from the GLC to Labour-run London councils such as Ealing, Camden, Islington, Hackney and Haringey, and for the last council, in particular, 1986 was going to be a year that many of its residents would remember for a long time. Not for nice reasons either.

Cool knitwear styles
on Westminster Bridge.
With my parents,
aged 13.

The Battle of Haringey

The controversy around sex education was starting to ramp
up. During a House of Lords debate on schools' investment in
education and science on 7 May 1986, Baroness Cox referred
to *Jenny Lives with Eric and Martin*. She claimed the book was
being distributed from an education centre in north London,
and that there was urgent need to investigate the teaching of
subjects like the occult, witchcraft and homosexuality. In these
debates homosexuality frequently formed part of disparate
lists of things that the speaker wanted to link together as
equally bad, scary and weird – a kind of 'guilt by association'
strategy. So in the same debate Viscount Buckmaster noted
that many of the booklets like *Jenny* ... condoned if not advocated 'things like incest and homosexuality'.[9] And in another
debate later that year on 18 December, Lord Longford would

refer to 'the mentally disturbed, the blacks, homosexuals and criminals'.

On 20 May, Viscount Buckmaster (who was a member of a group called the Conservative Family Campaign, created that year) put forward an amendment to the Education (No. 2) Bill (1986). The amendment required that sex education 'shall have due regard to moral considerations and the promotion of stable family life' and could be seen as a weaker forerunner to what was to become Section 28 almost two years later. Buckmaster claimed that in London particularly, homosexual relationships, underage sex and incest (the 'guilt by association' strategy again) were being taught as acceptable. He then cited *Jenny Lives with Eric and Martin* as featuring 'two homosexual men naked in bed with the daughter of one of them between them. Can there be anything more repulsive than that?'

It's not fantastic to suggest that part of the reason for this attack on *Jenny* and north London councils was due to the fact that Labour again won control of Haringey Council in May 1986, on the back of a manifesto that declared their 'commitment to fighting heterosexism'. The manifesto defined heterosexism as 'the belief and practice that heterosexuality is the only form of sexuality'. In addition, the council promised to 'prioritize the needs and interests of lesbians' and to 'establish funds for curriculum projects from nursery through to further education which are specifically designed to promote positive images of gay men and lesbians'.[10] Femi Otitoju was one of the seven members of the council's newly created Lesbian and Gay Unit. She described how, when they first saw *Jenny Lives with Eric and Martin*,

some of the images in it, we wouldn't expect to see, even
with a heterosexual couple. You don't put bare-chested
men in children's books and we certainly don't show
couples in bed with their children when they're bare-
chested . . . In the '80s, even I was shocked . . . It was
odd . . . We thought the pictures were ridiculous. We
laughed at the bell-bottoms but we were still excited
to see something, anything, that showed that lesbians
and gay men could raise children. We were willing to
forgive it just about everything else.[11]

But the *Daily Mail* thought otherwise. On 5 June 1986,
one of its headlines read 'Save the Children from Sad, Sordid
Sex Lessons'. A month later on 7 July, *The Sun* had an article entitled 'Bernie Kids Get Lessons in Gay Love' while two
days after that the *Mail* had another article which referred to
'courses on homosexuality and lesbianism for all pupils from
nursery schools to further education'.[12] On 22 September, the
Mail brought *Jenny Lives with Eric and Martin* back to the
fore, with quotes from Andreas Hansen, who took the photographs for the book. Apparently, the 'bizarre truth about happy
family in the gay schoolbook' was that neither of the men were
Jenny's father in real life but the pair did live together and one
day were seen kissing in their garden, which was overlooked
by a kindergarten.[13]

The *Sun* published an article entitled 'Vile Book in School:
Pupils See Pictures of Gay Lovers', while the *Daily Telegraph*
decried 'An official sex industry that is at work in the classroom
and is poisoning the minds of children'.[14] Bösche's little book,
which was intended to make things a bit easier for gay parents

and their children and had hardly been seen by anyone in the UK, had become the focus of a full-scale moral panic.

Meanwhile, Viscount Buckmaster's 'moral considerations' amendment had been approved in the House of Lords, being subsequently debated in the House of Commons on 10 June 1986, where Education Secretary Kenneth Baker noted that it was important 'to give a clear signal reinforcing the institution of marriage as the foundation of a healthy family life and the very bedrock of our civilization'. The clause became Section 46 of the Education Act. It stated:

> The local education authority by whom any county, voluntary or special school is maintained, and the governing body and head teacher of the school, shall take such steps as are reasonably practicable to secure that where sex education is given to any registered pupils at the school it is given in such a manner as to encourage those pupils to have due regard to moral considerations and the value of family life.

Section 46 made no explicit mention of homosexuality and the references to 'moral considerations' and 'family life' were vague and open to interpretation. In fact, the Lesbian and Gay Unit provided a challenge to Buckmaster's understanding of those terms when they launched a campaign called 'Positive Images' in September. An eighteen-page resources booklet was produced, listing gay-friendly books, films, music, organizations and suppliers. In the introduction it was noted that the materials should be previewed (presumably by teachers) before use and that each item had been annotated for its suitability regarding age range. David Mallen, the Director of Education (Schools), wrote in the foreword that 'it will be for each school to make its own decision as to the quality of the material and its suitability for a particular age-range.'[15]

Perhaps naively, the unit wrote to all the heads in the borough to ask them how they intended to implement Positive Images, offering to help and meet heads of schools.[16] This did not go down well in some quarters, with the local, then national, press picking up on it, resulting in the formation of a protest group first called the Campaign for Normal Family Life, then later renamed as the Parents' Rights Group. It called for a 'return to normal family values' and 'an end to ridiculous words such as sexist and racist and a return to normality'. Another protest group formed around the same time was called the New Patriotic Movement – it suggested that Haringey's gay rights policy was intended to subvert society.[17]

The atmosphere in Haringey was becoming polarized and tense. A demonstration, organized by supporters of Positive Images, took place on the Roundway in Tottenham, with about 3,000 people marching in support of Haringey's gay and lesbian community. The route of the demonstration rather provocatively went around White Hart Lane, an area represented by Conservative councillors such as Peter Murphy, who had won a seat from Labour in 1986 by opposing racial and sexual equality initiatives. One of Murphy's campaign leaflets had stated, 'We are protesting against plans to introduce HOMO-SEXUAL EDUCATION throughout Haringey.'[18] Then there were counter-protests in Wood Green and the Parents' Rights Group did a sweep of local libraries, finding a copy of *Jenny Lives with Eric and Martin* apparently shelved in a section that was

Some lovely stitchwork: Haringey Lesbians and Gays march in support of the Positive Images campaign, 1986.

marked as parental advisory. No matter though. The *Mail* had an article on 17 September called 'Hit Squad of Parents to Burn Gay Schoolbook'. There were various claims that a copy of the book was ceremonially burnt on the steps of Haringey Civic Centre during a meeting on 30 September or outside a local Catholic primary school.[19]

There was chaos during a debate at a council chamber meeting in Haringey Civic Centre on 20 October 1986 regarding the policy to introduce positive images of gay men and lesbians in education. Peter Murphy proposed the motion, 'This council resolves that it will not allow teaching of homosexual or lesbian education in Haringey Schools and will permit parents to remove children from sex education lessons.' The motion was defeated but the meeting quickly descended into pandemonium with protestors on both sides clashing and screaming abuse at one another. Eggs were thrown from the public gallery, one hitting a Conservative councillor who threw the remains of it and a cushion at the chairmen's bench, striking a council worker on the head. The scene wasn't much better outside the hall, where the hundreds of activists who had been unable to get in waved placards and watched the unfolding drama on television screens. At one point, one of the Parents' Rights demonstrators was arrested after he chased a gay rights activist while brandishing a 35-centimetre bayonet. A Labour councillor had one of his car windows smashed by someone with a crowbar as he was driving away from the meeting.[20] In a speech in Parliament on 5 December, Jeremy Corbyn (Labour, Islington North) referred to the 'Tottenham skinhead clique that is led by Peter Murphy' and went on to claim that Murphy had tried to disrupt a council meeting while Bernie Grant was speaking on 20 October, then, three days later, had apparently shouted abuse through the letterbox of another councillor.

Jenny Lives with Eric and Martin was not to be the only target. An extraordinary 45-minute documentary film called *Framed Youth: The Revenge of the Teenage Perverts* had been made in 1983 by a group called the London Lesbian and Gay Youth Video Project. It won the 1983 Grierson Award for Best Documentary and featured 25 young lesbian and gay people, some of whom had been forced to leave home and were living in squats. In the film they talked about their sexualities, covering topics like coming out, sex, homophobia and relationships with parents. The group had been given access to video and editing equipment and it's clear that they were learning how to use the technology as they were making the film. Some of the techniques now appear a little gimmicky, although there is a lot of evidence of creativity on display too. Footage from news, film and television drama had been inserted into interviews and there is use of effects like freeze frame and slow motion, drawing on an emerging 'scratch' or 'remix' culture that was becoming popular with young people. There are some hilarious moments when one of the young women interviews people at a market, asking them to define words like 'lesbian' and 'heterosexual' (some are completely ignorant while others are horrified – one poor woman runs away). Some of the stories of homophobic violence are very upsetting.[21]

The short film is also notable in that those involved included Jimmy Somerville (referred to as Jimi) and Richard Coles of The Communards, mentioned earlier. Another participant was Mark Ashton, a young man from Northern Ireland who, with his friend Mike Jackson, formed the group Lesbians and Gays Support the Miners, which was immortalized in the film *Pride* in 2014. Mark Ashton died in 1987 of an AIDS-related illness. He was only 26.

Framed Youth was distributed by Albany Video, which received funding from the Greater London Arts Association via the GLC, and had been extremely popular, being shown at 66 screenings in the London area and accounting for many of Albany's bookings. Femi Otitoju, who also appeared in the film, said, 'We understood that it was different in terms of content and ownership. I don't think we understood how far reaching it was. We knew about the big screenings and television. But I also know that teachers were taking it into schools and youth workers were taking it into youth clubs and young people were showing it to other young people and it had an amazing reach.'²² In 1986 *Framed Youth* was broadcast on television at 11 p.m. on Channel 4 as part of a youth season called 'Turn It Up'.

These kinds of activities were seen in some quarters as an utter waste of money and morally dangerous. Do you remember the Nationwide Festival of Light from Chapter Two? It had turned into an organization called CARE (Christian Action Research and Education) with Raymond Johnston as its director. CARE was becoming increasingly concerned about how local councils were allocating money and in 1985 Johnston got in touch with a woman called Rachel Tingle. Ms Tingle had been a journalist at *The Economist* but had lost her job and was now looking for work. Johnston had an unusual offer for her – he wanted someone to carry out a three-month research project looking at how local councils were providing funding to teach young people about homosexuality. At first Rachel Tingle didn't want to get involved. She sat in a field for a day and prayed on it before deciding that she would agree. But once committed, she threw herself into the role, becoming a bit of a secret agent, going to places she didn't normally go and wearing clothes she didn't normally wear, in order to uncover what she believed to be a coordinated campaign to actively promote homosexuality in London schools, from nursery education upwards.²³ Johnston never got to see the impact of his research project. He died on 17 October 1985, aged 58. But I think he would have been impressed. The task had been left in Rachel Tingle's capable hands, and in the following year she was going to make sure that her findings, which included an excoriating analysis of *Framed Youth*, were well publicized.

The results appeared in an innocent-looking lilac-toned booklet, published in 1986, called *Gay Lessons: How Public Funds Are Used to Promote Homosexuality among Children and Young People*. There's that phrase 'promote homosexuality' again. The booklet begins with a ten-point 'ideology of the gay movement' then goes on to list the various grants that had been given to gay rights groups and associated resources, including a description of apparent propaganda methods in the experimental film *Framed Youth*. Tingle was quoted in the *Daily Mail* as claiming that 'Throughout the video, heterosexuals are portrayed as old-fashioned and rather stupid.'[24] CARE sent the booklet to every Member of Parliament as well as some members of the House of Lords. As a result, Rachel Tingle was asked to address a backbench committee on the family. Her views persuaded the Earl of Halsbury to swing into action.

In the House of Lords, on 18 December 1986, the earl put forward a Private Peers Bill called a Local Government Act (Amendment) Bill. Born in 1908 and educated at Eton, the earl (also known as Tony Giffard) had been Director of Research at Decca Records, where he had helped to develop the LP gramophone record. He'd taken his seat in the Lords on VE Day (8 May 1945) when the House was full, as members gathered to listen to Winston Churchill's voice as it was relayed from the Commons. He was now the president of an organization called the National Council for Christian Standards in Society. After a long and distinguished career, what he did on this day would go down as perhaps his most memorable act.

The long title of Halsbury's bill was clearly influenced by Rachel Tingle's booklet: 'An act to refrain local authorities from promoting homosexuality'. Halsbury's speech introducing the bill was shockingly offensive. It was actually an update of a speech he'd made in 1977 when he'd argued against a bill to reduce the age of consent for gay men to eighteen from twenty-one. In a recap of this earlier speech he referred to homosexuals as having a choice of making the best or worst of their situation. He then described those who chose the latter as sick and suffering from a psychological syndrome which involved exhibitionism, promiscuity, proselytizing, boasting and 'acting as reservoirs of venereal diseases of all kinds. Ask any venerealogist: syphilis, gonorrhoea, genital herpes and now AIDS are characteristically infections of homosexuals.' Halsbury was slightly nicer about lesbians, saying that they do not molest little girls or engage in 'disgusting and unnatural practices like buggery'. However, he warned that the 'loony left is hardening up the lesbian camp and that they are becoming increasingly aggressive'. His speech set the tone for the debate, with other speakers referring to homosexuals as 'often sad and lonely' (Lord Campbell of Alloway, who had helped to draft the bill), as 'handicapped people' (the Nationwide Festival of Light's Lord Longford) and as 'disabled sexually' (Lord Swinfen).

Halsbury proposed a clause containing four subsections of which the key one 'prevents a local authority from giving financial or other assistance to any person for the purpose of publishing or promoting homosexuality as an acceptable family relationship or for the purpose of teaching such accept-ability in any maintained school'. The bill passed its vote in the Lords and was scheduled to go to committee stage in the Commons in 1987.

That coming year, the focus turned to events that were alleged to have taken place at the ultra-respectable-sounding

Blanche Nevile School in Tottenham. Blanche Nevile, born in 1861, was a remarkable woman. She had become a teacher for deaf people when she was 23, founding her own school in 1895. For decades, the school had thrived with a blameless reputation. But that was about to change.

While the school catered to disabled students during the day, in the evenings it was used by various local community groups. In the early months of 1987, one such group, set up to support young lesbians, screened the short film I mentioned in the previous chapter called *How to Become a Lesbian in 35 Minutes*. Members of the Parents' Rights Group found out about the screening and one of its members, Mrs Rosemarie Thomas-Johnson, tried to gain entrance to the building. What happened next is unclear, and involves conflicting accounts. If this were a film instead of a book, we would go into split screen for a few minutes to show each version side by side.

On the left side of my imaginary split-screen, 21-year-old gay youth worker Kyriacos Spyrou, who was on the premises, had learned that Mrs Thomas-Johnson was trying to access the screening and refused her entry on the grounds that she was neither a lesbian nor under the age of 25. He told her that if she wanted to see the film, another screening could be arranged for her at some point in the future. Mrs Thomas-Johnson seemed to agree to this and left quietly.[25]

On the right side of the screen, Mrs Thomas-Johnson, who was apparently pregnant, claimed that she had told the people at the meeting that she had not come with violence in her heart and did not want to interrupt their meeting, but if they objected to her being there, they ought to phone the police. The men and women at the meeting responded by swearing at her. Then, a tall, strongly built man punched her in the stomach. She fell to the ground but nobody offered her any sort of aid. Managing to get to her feet, she staggered into the street and was taken to North Middlesex Hospital. She later had a miscarriage.[26]

Kyriacos Spyrou claimed that Mrs Thomas-Johnson telephoned him a few days later to ask his full name, accusing him of punching and kicking her. She then took out a summons against him, claiming that the assault had caused her to lose her baby. The papers couldn't resist. Although the film *had* been shown to a lesbian youth group (ages 25 and younger), the fact that Blanche Nevile School taught deaf pupils during the day suddenly meant that the film had been shown to children, and not just any old children but disabled ones. 'Handicapped Girls "Saw Lesbian Film"', screamed the *Daily Mail*,[27] quoting Mrs Thomas-Johnson, who claimed that there were four disabled girls present and the older people tried to hide them from her, while *The Voice* ran an even less restrained headline: 'Mad Bouncer Killed My Baby'.[28]

There was a private court summons, with Mrs Thomas-Johnson accompanied by a local evangelical vicar called Reverend David Rushworth Smith (take note of his name, there'll be shenanigans from him in a moment). However, the case failed because she was unable to recognize the man she had named as her attacker when he appeared before the court and she was also unable to produce any evidence of her pregnancy, the miscarriage or the assault. Still, that particular kind of mud has a tendency to stick – the negative press coverage ensured that Mr Spyrou received death threats and hate mail.

A pile of filth

The year 1987 was a general election year, but a forerunner to this was another by-election, this time in Greenwich, which was caused by the death of Guy Barnett. Greenwich had been a Labour stronghold since 1945, although the party had only scraped a win in 1983. No matter; opinion polls put them in front and they selected Deirdre Wood, a former GLC councillor who was regarded as being on the left of the party. It was a shock to Labour, then, when, on 26 February 1987, Rosie Barnes (SDP) won the seat. This provoked concern among some members of the Labour Party, and the leader's chief press secretary, Patricia Hewitt, sent a letter to Frank Dobson, who was leader of a London group of MPs and also Deirdre Wood's aide or 'minder'. In the letter Hewitt warned that 'The "loony Labour left" is now taking its toll; the gays and lesbians issue is costing us dear among the pensioners, and fear of extremism and higher taxes/rates is particularly prominent in the Greater London Council area.' The letter was leaked to *The Sun*, who published it on 4 March with the headline 'Gays Put Kinnock in Panic – Secret Letter Lashes Loonies'. It demonstrates how, at least among senior members of Labour, there was a feeling that policies and practices at Haringey and elsewhere were damaging their chances. Meanwhile, the Conservatives kept up the attack. On 16 March, Minister for the Arts Richard Luce complained that public libraries were stocking material like *Jenny Lives with Eric and Martin* while banning old favourites like Enid Blyton books and Biggles on the grounds of racism.

After the book burning and the egg throwing, the fractious situation in Haringey was set to take an even more dramatic turn when Reverend David Rushworth Smith went on hunger strike for sixty days to protest against the council's policies on sexuality.[29] Rushworth Smith knew a thing or two about not eating. His book *Fasting: A Neglected Discipline* was first published in 1954. In it, Rushworth Smith is actually rather disparaging about people who go on hunger strikes, claiming, 'To use fasting as a means of attracting attention for either a personal or a social matter defeats the teaching of Jesus relating to the all-important secrecy of true fasting. A hunger strike is neither Stoicism or Christianity; in fact it is exhibitionism.'[30] He had no such qualms about making an exhibition of himself in 1987.

Apparently the first ten days were the worst, then his weight 'began to level off' (a claim which didn't appear to fully convince Jolyon Jenkins, who interviewed Rushworth Smith in 2009). With an instinctive understanding of the power of theatre, the old cove attended council meetings in a wheelchair. 'At no time did I ever need a wheelchair, but I felt that the correct procedure was to portray a man in a weak state of health . . . who was going without meals for a reason.'[31]

The events in Haringey were beginning to attract attention in Parliament, with the Parents' Rights Group finding more than a few supporters there. On 23 April 1987, during the Business of the House, Michael McNair-Wilson (Conservative, Newbury) made a speech asking for a debate on an early-day motion (a motion set down for an unspecific day). The motion was: 'That this House expresses its abhorrence at the showing of a video entitled "How to be a Lesbian in 35 Minutes" shown at a Haringey Council community centre recently to an audience, including young people, and calls upon the Government to require local authorities to submit sexually explicit videos and literature to the Department of Education before such material can be shown to the public.' Peter Bruinvels (Conservative, Leicester East) then called for a debate on literature, complaining that Leicester teachers had published a book called *Outlaws in the Classroom – Give School Gays a Better Deal*. He warned that 'our children are in desperate danger of being corrupted by teachers writing books that promote homosexuality as the norm.'

A couple of weeks later the mantle of moral rectitude was taken up by Jill Knight MP (Conservative, Edgbaston). Knight was chair of a group involving child protection and claimed that 'scores' of concerned parents had contacted her about what was going on in Haringey and elsewhere. They felt that childhood was being taken away from children. On 8 May 1987, during discussion of the Halsbury amendment, she claimed there was 'evidence in shocking abundance that children in our schools, some as young as five years, are frequently being encouraged into homosexuality and lesbianism'. The infamous *Jenny Lives with Eric and Martin* was described as picturing 'a little girl of about six in bed with her father and his lover, both of whom are naked' (perhaps an exaggeration; the photograph didn't show whether they were wearing pyjama bottoms or not). She also referred to several other books (calling them a 'pile of filth'), including one called *The Playbook for Kids about Sex*, describing it as 'the most frightening piece of propaganda against children'.

The Playbook was authored by two American women, Joani Blank, who wrote the text, and Marcia Quackenbush, who provided the illustrations. It had first been published in

Such a bona riah: Baroness Knight, one of the architects of Section 28.

1978 by Down There Press (which had been founded by Joani) and was reprinted by a UK publisher called Sheba Feminist Publishers in 1980. This notorious-sounding title had already come up during the Earl of Halsbury's tabled amendment back in December, where Lady Saltoun of Abernethy had described it as so appalling that she could not bring herself to quote from it. This was rather convenient because it left the shocking content to the imagination, rather than subjecting the book to any real sort of scrutiny. Years later, in 1999, after Jill Knight had become Baroness Knight, she told the House of Lords that *The Playbook for Kids about Sex* had 'brightly coloured pictures of little stick men [which] showed all about homosexuality and how it was done'.

Given its mythos rivalling, perhaps even surpassing, *Jenny Lives with Eric and Martin*, I was reticent about getting hold of a copy of this book, even for research purposes, wondering if it would make me the subject of a complicated police sting – one of those ones with exciting codenames like 'Operation Sunflower'. But when I looked online, I found a copy on Amazon, which took the drama level a few hundred notches down. As we stared at the cardboard package that arrived a few days later, my husband pulled a face. I was reminded that we had friends visiting the next day with their toddler. It wouldn't look good to have such a book lying around, so I promised to hide it in the bedroom when they came round, under the wooden box containing the ashes of our much-loved cat, Larry.

The front cover didn't look very appealing. There were drawings of two naked homunculus-looking creatures (one blue, one yellow), and another homunculus seemed to be

The Playbook for Kids about Sex: content warning – you will see what gay men and lesbians get up to!

holding its stomach in pain. Many of the characters in Marcia's illustrations didn't have necks, so they affected a somewhat hunched posture, while some of their faces resembled cats. Inside, the book covered a range of topics: feelings related to talking about sex, bodies, masturbation, orgasms, intercourse, partners. There was a series of exercises, such as asking children to draw pictures of themselves naked and colouring in all the bits where they like to be touched. On one page the question 'Who is Sexy?' was asked, with thirteen options to tick, including 'all grown-ups', 'movie stars', 'people on TV', 'everybody', 'babies' . . . Babies? Most of the time, there was little or no indication that there were any wrong or right answers, although occasionally it was noted that some attitudes, like the view that masturbation was bad for you, were incorrect.

Towards the end of the book, I found the page that Jill Knight had described, with Marcia's pictures of stick men showing 'all about homosexuality and how it was done'. It contained a line drawing of two men with facial hair (both wearing bell-bottom trousers), each carrying a pot plant, and holding hands. Next to it, in a different box, were two women, about to fly a kite. One woman had her arm around the other. The text of the book informed readers that some people like partners of the same sex while some like the other sex. Some people think it's wrong to be homosexual or bisexual, while others think people should be allowed to have sex with whoever they want if everyone consents and it's in private. And then there's a part where we're told that partners do a lot more than just have sex with one another. Hmmmm.

To me, the title of the book is unnecessarily provocative. The term *playbook* has been used to refer to a sport's team's strategies, as well as relating to other kinds of strategies, such as those associated with crafty politicians who persuade people of things that aren't true. While *playbook* in this sense simply means a book to enable children to play, that secondary meaning hangs over the book in an unpleasant way. Putting the terms *kids* and *sex* in the same sentence is a no-no at the best of times. Anyway, as well as sex, the book is also about feelings and relationships, so the title doesn't do it justice. While there are aspects of the book that I don't like, the parts about homosexuality were sensible, non-judgemental and not explicit in the slightest. It is ridiculous that the book was used as 'evidence' in parliamentary debates around homosexuality without being properly examined – why didn't anybody on the opposition side get hold of a copy of it? With that said, times were different then and you couldn't purchase a copy of almost anything with just a few clicks of a mouse.

While the *Playbook* was clearly aimed at children, another book, written with teenagers in mind, was also cited as part of Jill Knight's evidence. *The Milkman's on His Way* was written by David Rees in 1982 and, like *Jenny*, was also published by the Gay Men's Press. During the 8 May 1987 debate, Knight said she would not shock the House by quoting from it (the same rhetorical flourish used by Lady Saltoun of Abernethy) but noted that 'it describes intercourse between a sixteen-year-old boy and his adult male homosexual lover. The book glorifies homosexuality and encourages youngsters to believe that it is better than any other sexual way of life.' Baroness Cox referred to its 'explicit – some would say pornographic – detail with the sexual intercourse between a teenager and his male adult lover', while on 1 February 1988, she claimed that a fifteen-year-old

THE MILKMAN'S ON HIS WAY
David Rees

THE GAY MEN'S PRESS

The Milkman's on His Way. Although he seems to have made
a slight detour to have a swim first.

girl had borrowed the book from a public library, noting that she had 'evidence to support that'.

My copy of *The Milkman's on His Way* arrived the day after the *Playbook*. A photo of a hunk in trunks adorned the front cover. The book tells the story of fifteen-year-old Ewan, a gay surfer living with his parents in Bude, who is about to leave school. He has a massive crush on his best friend, who, more out of sexual frustration than anything else, initiates non-penetrative sex between them. When he's seventeen (not sixteen as Jill Knight claimed), he meets a 23-year-old Londoner called Paul, who's on holiday. The two embark on a romance which involves penetrative sex. Since the age of consent between men was 21 at this time, this act counts as statutory rape, although had Ewan been female it wouldn't have been a crime. Ewan is certainly more than willing ('I wanted him inside me. I wanted to be fucked') and dismissive of the law ('I didn't care a damn about what the law said. That wasn't going to stop me'). But he is devastated at the end of the week to learn that Paul has a long-term partner. Ewan's parents read his diary and, brushing off their invasion of his privacy, respond to its contents with shock and disgust. Unable to reconcile them, Ewan moves to London, where he sticks up for a co-worker who is bullied for being gay.

Rachel Tingle had also read *The Milkman's on His Way*, providing her own review of it in her *Gay Lessons* booklet. She says it ends when Ewan 'establishes himself as one of the most promiscuous members of the London gay scene'. Putting aside the slut-shaming, I didn't get that impression at all. By the end of the book Ewan is twenty and in a happy, long-term relationship with a PhD student called James. I found it to be a sweet book, written with an honesty and insight that chimes with some of my own experiences as a teenager. The book doesn't glorify homosexuality. If anything, it points out the problems of being gay in a homophobic world, and when Ewan finally gets to London and starts to go out on the gay scene, it is represented not as a nirvana but, more realistically, as a place where human behaviour is not that different from anywhere else. I wish I had read it when I was in the latter half of my teens. Instead, I was reading a lot of 'the classics' for my GCSEs and A Levels – Elizabeth and Mr Darcy in *Pride and Prejudice* not necessarily being the most appropriate models for negotiating gay relationships in late twentieth-century Britain.

The inalienable right to be gay

The Commons vote on 8 May 1987 resulted in 20 Ayes in support of the Halsbury amendment and 0 Noes. Since fewer than forty members had taken part, the question was declared as undecided and that might have been the end of it. The debate had taken place on a Friday afternoon (perhaps MPs had decided to go home early). However, Jill Knight was undeterred. A week later, during Prime Minister's Questions, she asked whether Margaret Thatcher would 'give an assurance to the House that, in the next Parliament, she will, in legislation, protect both children and the concept of the family?' Thatcher responded by congratulating her on the promotion of the bill, noting it was a 'great pity' that it did not complete its passage. She encouraged Knight to bring the bill back before the House. However, there was the slightly inconvenient business of a general election to get out of the way first.

Conservative poster,
1987, warning that if
the left wing get in,
we'll all have bad hair.

The Tory campaign focused on a strong economy, stressing low taxes and noting the improving records on low unemployment and inflation. It played on Labour's policy of unilateral nuclear disarmament, showing a picture of a British soldier's arms raised in surrender. With public fears around the nuclear threat from the USSR, Labour's policy was never going to be very popular. Another aspect of the Tory election campaign involved casting Labour as a militant party that was going to bring homosexuality into schools. One campaign poster featured a sketch of a straggly gang of weirdos under the heading 'LABOUR CAMP'. They held placards reading 'MILITANT

Conservative poster, 1987 (no expense was spared on whizz-bang graphics).

RULES', 'Gay Lib' and 'GAY SPORTS DAY' (send in your answers on a postcard regarding what that last one entails). Another featured three books in a row, all with red (ergo 'run children – Communists!') covers. The titles of the books were *Young, Gay & Proud, Police: Out of School!* and *The Playbook for Kids about Sex.* The poster screamed, 'IS THIS LABOUR'S IDEA OF A COMPREHENSIVE EDUCATION?' The byline was deliciously hypocritical: 'Take the politics out of education. Vote Conservative.'

Around this time, a group of gay rights protesters staged a stunt by going to the Norwegian embassy in London in order to claim asylum, as a way of drawing attention to the ongoing hate campaign in the press. *The Sun* responded on 6 May 1987 with the headline 'Fly Away Gays – and We Will Pay!', rejecting their claims but then offering to buy the protesters a £162 one-way ticket to Oslo from Heathrow.[32] It is not known if any of the protesters took them up on this. The *Daily Express* had a headline 'My Love for Gay Labour Boss' on 17 May while on 6 June the *Daily Mail* had a front-page headline 'The

Left's Plan for a Gay Charter', listing demands that included allowing male prostitutes to solicit without fear of arrest and abolishing all homosexual offences (including gross indecency) in public places. *Sun* headlines included 'Labour Picks Rent Boy as School Boss' and 'Lesbian Plots to Pervert Nursery Tots'.[33]

Another anti-Labour campaign was spearheaded by a woman with the wonderfully camp-sounding name of Betty Sheridan. Sheridan was the vice-chair of the aforementioned Parents' Rights Group and she appeared in an advert that featured a headshot of her looking nonplussed (her mouth is just a horizontal line) above the words 'I live in Haringey. I have two children. <u>And I'm scared</u>. If you vote LABOUR they'll go on teaching my kids about GAYS & LESBIANS instead of giving them proper lessons.' The advert appeared in the national press in the week before the election as well as being distributed as a handbill. It didn't mention that Sheridan's children went to a private Catholic school that was not in the control of Haringey Education Authority, so her children were unlikely ever to be taught about GAYS & LESBIANS.[34]

And so the country voted on 11 June 1987, with the result being another landslide for Maggie. Only a couple of dozen seats changed colour – the Tories lost 21, Labour gained 20 and the Liberals lost 1, but this still gave the Tories a majority (376 out of 650 seats) and Mrs Thatcher became the first prime minister in 167 years to win three elections in a row. Hated as she was by so many, she won the popular vote by 3.7 million. It is no stretch of the imagination to hypothesize that the tabloid newspapers helped her out.

Did homophobia also help to win the Tories the election? When the British Social Attitudes survey was carried out in

1987 it returned to a question it had put to the public several times before: 'What about sexual relations between two adults of the same sex?' In 1983, half the respondents had said that this was 'always wrong' and the numbers had been going up since then, with 54 per cent answering 'always wrong' in 1984 and 59 per cent in 1985.[35] However, 1987 was the peak year, with 64 per cent of respondents saying homosexuality was always wrong and a further 11 per cent saying it was some-times wrong. That three-quarters of the nation were against homosexuality is chilling, and all the more so considering that this survey occurred only a few decades ago. True, HIV-AIDS had cast fear across the planet, and gay men were an 'at risk' minority group that had been disproportionately affected. Maybe in a kinder world, everyone would have rallied round and attitudes would have softened. I don't think most people were actively brimming over with hate but the 1980s were a divisive time and people were ignorant about many aspects of sexuality. Many of them didn't know anyone who was openly gay, and a lot of gay people were afraid to come out, so the situation was perpetuated, with a hostile media controlling the message.

It's perhaps a coincidence that this was a period when many working-class communities were being neglected or eroded by the Conservative Party's vision for the country. The loony left and their militant gays and lesbians were convenient distractors, enabling people to experience a frisson of superiority as they united behind a perceived enemy while the Tories positioned themselves as guardians of common sense. To me, it is one of the most disappointing times in my country's history and serves as a warning – that our capacity for empathy and kindness is limited, that we are not always at our best when the chips are down, and that our leaders are not always right.

After the election, as a way of signalling that the government was prepared to back Jill Knight, on 25 September 1987, the Department of Education and Science issued a written statement called a circular, outlining a set of policies, principles and practices to be carried out by public officials. The circular was titled *Sex Education at School*. It mentioned homosexuality a few times, for example, defining homosexual acts as 'buggery' or 'gross indecency'. It also included this paragraph:

There is no place in any school in any circumstances for teaching which advocates homosexual behaviour, which presents it as the 'norm', or which encourages homosexual experimentation by pupils. Indeed, encouraging or procuring homosexual acts by pupils who are under the age of consent is a criminal offence. It must also be recognized that for many people, including members of various religious faiths, homosexual practice is not morally acceptable, and deep offence may be caused to them if the subject is not handled with sensitivity by teachers if discussed in the classroom.

And if there was any doubt, remember David Rushworth Smith and his hunger strike? He recalled that on Day 59 he received a telephone call from someone claiming to be from 10 Downing Street. The speaker said that Mrs Thatcher was in the room with the caller and wanted David to 'please start eating again because we will introduce a bill that would prevent Haringey council from doing its own thing.'[36] That was good enough for

Maximum power! Margaret Thatcher receives a standing ovation at the 1987 Conservative Party conference.

Rushworth Smith. He ended his hunger strike. It didn't seem to have caused any lasting damage, as he died in 2012, aged 84.

In Blackpool at the Conservative Party conference on 9 October 1987, children were on the agenda. Mrs Thatcher, in a sensible Tory-blue outfit, made one of her most famous speeches, expressing concern about 'hard left education authorities and extremist teachers'. She warned that children were 'learning anti-racist mathematics, whatever they may be' (indeed, that's a new one to me), and that instead of being able to express themselves in clear English, children were being 'taught political slogans'. But worst of all, 'Children who need to be taught to respect traditional moral values are being taught that they have the inalienable right to be gay.' Thatcher continued, saying that such 'children are being cheated of a sound start in life, yes, cheated!' In today's parlance, this last observation in particular could be described as not having aged well, although her audience loved it, giving the speech an eleven-minute standing ovation.

The smell of fascism

On 2 December 1987, during the committee stage of the Local Government Act (1986), backbencher and new MP David Wilshire (Conservative, Spelthorne) took up Jill Knight's cause and proposed putting in an amendment which was pretty much the same as the Earl of Halsbury's shelved bill. The new text was initially referred to as Clause 14 (later 27, then 28, then 29, then 28 again). This time the government made it clear that they were fully in support. The Minister for Local Government, Michael Howard, said, 'The Government have always supported [these] objectives. The promotion of homosexuality, particularly in schools, by local authorities is an unacceptable development.' Howard proposed some changes to Wilshire's amendment, chiefly to add a section to ensure that local authorities would not be stopped in work relating to HIV-AIDS prevention.[37]

Initially, the clause appeared to be supported by the Labour Party too. Dr Jack Cunningham (Labour, Copeland) said that Labour did not believe councils or schools should promote homosexuality. One of the few MPs who argued against the clause was Bernie Grant (Labour, Tottenham) who said, 'If the new clause is accepted it will be a signal to every fascist and everyone opposed to homosexuality that the Government is really on their side.'[38]

At the time, there was only one openly gay Member of Parliament: Chris Smith (Labour, Islington South and Finsbury). No one was openly gay in the House of Lords. In November 1984, Smith had come out in public during a speech made at a rally in Rugby about the town council possibly allowing a ban on gay employees. It had been a last-minute decision and it earned him a five-minute standing ovation from the audience. However, other sections of the populace were less supportive, and *The Sun* ran a story in 1986 which read 'Chris Smith . . . is a self-confessed homosexual . . . He wants to ban Page Three while at the same time allowing homosexuals the right to buy magazines containing sado-masochistic porn.'[39]

I asked Chris Smith why Labour had initially been in favour of Clause 28 and he explained that 'there were some members of the parliamentary party who were frankly homophobic. They regarded all of these issues about lesbian and gay equality as being a diversion from demanding better conditions and rights for working-class people. There was also a nervousness on the part of the party leadership, Neil Kinnock a bit less so. Initially, Jack Cunningham was very nervous, he wasn't homophobic or antagonistic.'

The clause went through the Standing Committee on 8 December, where Simon Hughes, the Liberal MP who had defeated Peter Tatchell in the 1983 Bermondsey by-election, tabled several amendments that would weaken the effect of the clause. One (amendment 32) would allow children to be taught that different sexual orientations existed in sex education classes. Another (amendment 37) allowed teachers to provide counselling or advice to pupils relating to their sexuality, and a third (amendment 38) said that nothing in the section shall 'permit or encourage discrimination on the grounds of sexual orientation'.

A week later, on 15 December, the clause was debated in the House of Commons at the 'report stage', where Hughes gave a long speech arguing for his amendments. At one point he described a council advertisement for a job in Ealing which involved lesbian and gay rights. He was briefly interrupted by Eric Forth (Conservative, Mid Worcestershire), who exclaimed, 'They are all bonkers in Ealing.' Michael Howard advised the House to reject the amendments, quoting an approved reading list from Haringey (most likely the *Positive Images* document), which contained a book that called for a ban on teachers wearing wedding rings. He also mentioned that the reading list referred to *Young, Gay & Proud!* (recommended for children aged thirteen and older) as 'very helpful to everyone'. Howard said that it described 'homosexual acts in considerable detail'. He was right. *Young, Gay & Proud!* was published in 1977, first in Australia, then in 1980 in the United States with some changes. The 95-page book gives advice in a series of short essays on a range of aspects of homosexuality for young people, including coming out, sexual health and dealing with homophobia. There are sections that outline how gay men and lesbians have sex, as well as 'problem page' letters from various sixteen- and seventeen-year-olds. The book doesn't advocate that thirteen-year-olds have sex, although the descriptions are written as a direct address to the reader, for example, 'If you are doing the sucking, hold the other person's penis with one hand and put it in your mouth.' When I read this part, I wondered if I'd be comfortable with my nieces and nephews reading the book at age thirteen. But then I recalled that my mother had bought me an educational book when I was around twelve which outlined how heterosexual people had sex. Michael Howard wasn't complaining about those books, though.

One of the most shocking contributions to this debate was made by Elaine Kellett-Bowman (Conservative, Lancaster). It was in relation to an arson attack that had taken place just three days before on the morning of 12 December. A piece of lighted paper was pushed under the door of the office of *Capital Gay*, London's free weekly newspaper. The ensuing fire caused £20,000 worth of damage. Nobody was ever charged with the attack, although the newspaper's editor Graham McKerrow called it 'straightforward queerbashing'.[40] It reveals a lot about what life was like for LGBTQ+ people in the late 1980s, and in this debate Chris Smith referred to the arson attack as an example of how gay men and lesbians were treated as second-class citizens. Hansard (the official report of debates in Parliament) records an interruption at that point so it is not clear who spoke, although another MP, Tony Banks (Labour, Newham, North-West), accused Elaine Kellett-Bowman of saying 'Quite right too.' She replied, 'I am quite prepared to affirm that it is quite right that there should be an intolerance of evil.' Her remark implies that *Capital Gay* was evil and therefore deserved to be anonymously attacked by members of the public. The Speaker gently reprimanded her, saying, 'Let us keep the temperature down,' but Kellett-Bowman was not required to apologize or retract her remark.

MPs voted separately on Hughes's three amendments described above. Each one was resoundingly rejected, with just over two hundred MPs voting yes and over three hundred voting no in each case. The government then tabled their own amendments to the clause, which were designed to precisely define the application of the provision. The bill received its first reading in the Lords on 17 December (Hansard simply records 'Brought from the Commons; read a first time, and to be printed').

Christmas came and went. On 31 December 1987, the New Year Honours for 1988 were published. The Honours are appointments made by the monarch to reward and highlight good works by citizens. As a further mark of the state of the nation, Elaine Kellett-Bowman was made a DBE (Dame Commander of the Order of the British Empire). Happy New Year everyone!

The Lords had their second reading of the Local Government Bill on 11 January 1988. The debate not only covered the introduction of Clause 28 but referred to the abolition of dog licences, so it comes across as a somewhat odd sequence of non sequitur statements, with peers discussing extremist local councils promoting the 'nonsense' that homosexuality is a 'natural relationship compared with marriage' in one breath, and then moving on to complain about dogs fouling pavements in the next. Baroness Stedman took issue with the word 'promote', arguing that it could mean to push forward and encourage or to increase understanding. She was concerned that the clause would make countering prejudice illegal and would put advice centres at risk of closure. Baroness Blackstone called the phrase 'pretended family relationship' offensive to many homosexuals. Lord Peston called the clause nonsensical, illiberal, nasty and vindictive, saying, 'Are we asked to believe that homosexuals are less useful to society than the rest of us?' He accused those who supported the clause of not having 'the faintest idea of what they are talking about'. However, the clause had plenty of supporters. Baroness Cox quoted a playleader at a children's centre who had said, 'We have been on training courses where members have access to take this kind of literature into the playgroups but nearly everyone refused. Some of the books on display were terrible. I have children in here as young as two years old and I don't think they should be seeing pictures of grown men in the nude in different sexual practices.'

Unsurprisingly, the Conservative press was largely in favour of the clause. An article on 29 January in the *Daily Telegraph* said, 'Clause 28 or no Clause 28, there is no witch hunt on against homosexuals or against anyone else.'[41] A couple of days later the *Daily Express* also tried to play down the protests: 'What is lacking in the piercing protests of the Clause 28 agitators is any evidence that homosexuals are being persecuted . . . The British public find homosexuality oddly amusing. This may be irritating but it is not the stuff of pogrom.'

On 1 February 1988, the clause was debated in the House of Lords with an amendment proposed by Lord Falkland (Lucius Cary). The amendment had been drafted by the Arts Council, which had engaged a barrister to interpret the impact of the clause on the arts.[42] Lord Falkland's amendment removed the total ban on promoting homosexuality and replaced it with wording that said that local authorities would not publish representations of homosexual representations or acts as being more acceptable than heterosexual ones. There was also an exemption for anything that would serve a literary, artistic, scientific or educational purpose. Lord Falkland stated that the thinking and philosophy behind the clause was confused and that the homosexual community were at risk of a backlash of ignorance. He warned that the government was 'encouraging discrimination and violence' and that the clause 'uses a large hammer – a pile-driver – to smash a pane of glass. The splinters will go wide and far with the possibility of damaging and wounding a number of people.' Lord Soper also opposed the clause, reminding the other members that 'Jesus said nothing about homosexuality.' Lord Willis associated the clause with 'the smell of fascism', warning that it would embitter, isolate and frighten the homosexual community.

One strategy used by those in favour of the clause was to try to separate off the 'militant activists' from ordinary 'homosexuals'. Lord Annan said that the militants in the gay liberation movement wanted 'a first-class row' and 'do not represent homosexuals any more than student union activists used to represent students. Homosexual men and women ask to be left to live their own lives.' In a similar way, the Earl of Halsbury claimed he'd had a deluge of letters, many from homosexuals. He read out his 'favourite letter', which said, 'I want to say how fed up I am with my fellow homosexuals. They have brought it upon themselves, their unpopularity. They are too promiscuous, too aggressive and exhibitionist. I cannot stand the sight of them. I wish they would keep themselves to themselves.'

Lord Falkland's amendment failed with 111 voting for it and 166 against.

The debate continued in the Lords on the following day, with Lord Willis proposing that the clause simply be deleted altogether. It was during this debate that a group of women descended down ropes from the Peers' Guest Gallery into the main Chamber of the House. As thrilling as that sounds, we'll leave the detail for the next chapter, which describes the protests around the clause, and instead I'll concentrate on the other highlights of the debate.

The Earl of Caithness, who had been one of the architects of the clause, admitted that there were 'two areas in which the drafting may be worth further consideration' and that he had 'undertaken to come back to the House at a later stage on the wording' of specific paragraphs. Although many of the proponents of the clause were backed by religious convictions, belief in God did not always indicate support of it. A chief opponent of the clause was the Archbishop of York, who called it 'dangerous and unnecessary' despite claiming that 'homosexual lobbies' had 'behaved with quite extraordinary foolishness'. However, the majority of peers supported it. Lord Mason of Barnsley evoked the by-now familiar tabloid moniker 'loony left councils' in support of the clause, and played down the effect the clause would have: 'Homosexuals will still be able to live their form of orthodox or normal life.' Lord Boyd-Carpenter intriguingly claimed that 'young males . . . in many cases have a homosexual element or tendency in them which the vast majority of them succeed in restraining, to their credit.' He did not explain how he knew this but went on to say that 'if attempts were made to emphasize that side of their nature . . . it is fairly certain that some of these young people will be led to adopt a homosexual orientation.' Several peers argued that the clause was in line with popular opinion. Lady Saltoun of Abernethy referred to an Ipsos MORI poll that showed '85 per cent of people in this country are looking to us in this Committee today to pass this Clause' while Lord Bellwin referred to local authorities that were using 'public funds to promote controversial doctrines which are offensive to the majority of people'. When the vote came as to whether Clause 28, as amended, should stand as part of the bill, 202 voted in favour and 122 were against.

The Lords debated the amendments to the clause again on 16 February. By now some of the reworkings were getting rather fussy. For example, amendment 77 wanted to replace the words 'intended to promote' with 'with the intention of promoting' while amendment 79 would replace the word 'acceptability' with 'acceptance'. With this level of scrutiny it's amazing that any bills ever become acts. The number of proposed amendments was getting pretty unmanageable, and Lord Caithness had to intervene in the debate at one point in order to suggest which amendments should be discussed and in what order: 'I hope that if your Lordships are agreeable we should take the amendments of the noble Earl, Amendments Nos 72, 86 and 88. Then we should take Amendments Nos 73 to 75, 78, 80, 81 and possibly 104.' Amendment 72, which aimed to remove a couple of lines of text, was particularly controversial, with the Earl of Longford moving to reject it on the grounds that it would restrict the remit of the operation of Clause 28 to just schools. He said, 'I think that all homosexual activity, as distinct from homosexual feelings, is morally wrong.' Amendment 72 was rejected by 90 to 48 votes.

Lord Rea argued in support of amendment 76, which was to change the phrasing around 'pretended family relationships', which he found 'particularly offensive', especially as he was brought up by two women and had 'as rich and happy a childhood as most children'. He described *Jenny Lives with Eric and Martin* as 'a boring little book' that is 'enjoying considerable and probably undeserved fame' although argued that 'it was not produced to promote homosexuality, either intentionally or otherwise.' Amendment 82 was to get rid of the word 'pretended' and despite the fact that almost everyone appeared to hate this word for various reasons, only 20 peers voted to remove it and 43 to keep it, so 'pretended' stayed in.

There were a few surreal moments in this debate. Lord Boyd-Carpenter and Lord McIntosh of Haringey had an exchange about whether children were compelled to go to (and get corrupted) at discos. Baroness Strange (known as Cherry to her friends) complained about the 'mis-use of the splendid word "gay"', claiming that 'Some of my best friends are homosexuals but all my best friends are jolly and gay.' And Lord Monson seemed as concerned about syntax as he was about homosexuality: 'I do not think one can teach *The Milkman's on His Way*. Even if it were not for that grammatical fault the amendment would leave the door open to teaching that makes no use of material, such as off-the-cuff praise of homosexual behaviour.'

On 29 February, at the bill's third reading, the Lords were still tinkering with amendments. Due to the addition of yet another clause, Clause 28 was renamed as Clause 29 – although only briefly, eventually going back to being Clause 28. There was much less discussion now and at this point it was at the level of things like taking out the words 'it sees fit' and replacing with 'may reasonably be drawn from the evidence before it'. The Earl of Caithness noted (wearily, I imagine) that 25 hours had been spent on the bill at committee stage and more than 14 at report stage, and that 'very few stones have been left unturned'. He argued that the claims that Clause 29 would lead to discrimination and censorship and stop teachers dealing with homosexuality objectively or local authorities providing legitimate counselling and care could not be substantiated. After he had finished speaking, the bill was passed and returned to the Commons with a smaller number of amendments in tow, including a couple from opposition peers that were intended to reduce the impact of the clause.

Insolence and strong hand should prevail

The clause was implicitly referred to in the Commons on 8 March, with Michael Colvin (Conservative, Romsey and Waterside) asking the Secretary of State for the Environment whether he would discuss the expenditure on gay and lesbian groups by local authorities in London with the Association of London Authorities. Christopher Chope (Parliamentary Under Secretary of State for the Environment) gave the answer: 'No. Clause 28 of the Local Government Bill will ensure that expenditure by local authorities for the purpose of promoting homosexuality will no longer be permitted.' Later that day in the Commons, Jill Knight addressed Margaret Thatcher: 'Has my Right Hon. Friend seen that, following the reports last week that Haringey council was funding a bookshop selling anarchist literature to five-year-olds?' She then went on to refer to a 'recent report that infant teachers in Haringey are somehow using Home Office funds to produce videos promoting homosexuality, and terrorism in South Africa? Does my Right Hon. Friend feel that that is a right and proper use of taxpayers' and ratepayers' money?'

However, the clause was discussed in much more detail the following day, 9 March, in the House of Commons. A Lords amendment to add the word 'intentionally' to the phrase 'promote homosexuality' was to be debated, along with additional amendments by Labour. Although Labour had initially been supportive of the policy of not promoting homosexuality, the tide had changed by now, and numerous Labour MPS spoke against the clause (which was now being called Clause 27). The Labour position was led by Dr Jack Cunningham, who had changed his mind and argued that 'the clause represents a new and inherently dangerous direction for the law to take.' He stated that key words like 'promote', 'homosexuality' and 'acceptability' had not been defined and accused the government of seeking 'political gain from aiding and abetting bigotry and discrimination against gay and lesbian people'. Cunningham tried to add an amendment to the clause that exempted 'action undertaken for the purpose of discouraging discrimination against or protecting the civil rights of any person'. David Wilshire described this as a 'wrecking amendment', comparing it to the earlier Arts Council amendment that had failed.

Chris Smith told me that one of the key figures who persuaded Jack Cunningham to change his mind was Allan Roberts (Labour, Bootle). 'Allan was gay and he was part of Jack Cunningham's team on the front bench as a spokesperson on local government.' However, according to Smith, there was another reason why Labour shifted their position: the newly named Liberal Democrats, which had been founded six days earlier on 3 March 1988 as a result of a merger of the Liberal Party and the Social Democratic Party. It had been Simon

Hughes of the Liberal Party who had put forward amendments to weaken the clause and Chris Smith believes that 'the Lib Dems tried to corner the market in being against Section 28 and the Labour front bench didn't want to be outsmarted by the Lib Dems in opposing what the Tories were getting up to.'

It was the last chance saloon to get changes made to the clause before it went to 'royal assent', and the debate got pretty personal at times. Tony Banks and John Fraser accused Dame Jill Knight of lying and observed that during Radio 4's *Today* programme Knight had not provided any evidence to support her claims about schools promoting homosexuality. Knight replied that she *had* named the schools and referred to Mrs Thomas-Johnson ('a pregnant woman was kicked in the stomach and jolly nearly lost her child'), perhaps not the most reliable of witnesses. Banks replied that 'The Hon. Lady has not mentioned one school. She is clearly guilty but insane. I rest my case.' The shade of it!

Joan Lestor (Labour, Eccles) made an impassioned speech about how she had grown up with stereotypes of gay men as mincing and effeminate, to be laughed at and degraded, and noted that when such stereotypes were challenged and homosexuals were presented in a positive way, 'we are told, "My God, you are promoting homosexuality."' She presented sobering statistics that said that 20 per cent of young gay people had attempted suicide and 10 per cent had been thrown out of their homes. And a cerebral interlude was provided by Chris Smith, who quoted a speech from the Elizabethan play *Sir Thomas More*. In the speech, More tries to convince a mob who want to drive strangers out of the city that what they are doing is wrong.

What had you got? I'll tell you: you had taught
How insolence and strong hand should prevail,
How order should be quelled; and by this pattern
Not one of you should live an aged man,
For other ruffians, as their fancies wrought,
With self same hand, self reasons, and self right,
Would shark on you, and men like ravenous fishes
Would feed on one another . . .

Smith told me he had heard the actor Ian McKellen make the speech and had found it powerful. He'd thought it would be a good way of taking the high ground. I asked him how he'd felt during these debates and he said, 'It was really grim sitting through them. Some ridiculous things were said. It made you ashamed, it made you angry, it made you upset. But you had to sit there and debate it as politely as you could.'

And on the other side, the usual arguments were trotted out. Nicholas Bennett (Conservative, Pembrokeshire) referred to the Christian Church's view that for 2,000 years, 'homosexual genital acts and behaviour are intrinsically immoral.' Nicholas Fairbairn (Conservative, Perth and Kinross) made an extraordinarily horrible speech. Fairbairn was something of a flashy figure in Westminster, turning up in tartan with a silver miniature working revolver on a chain attached to his belt. He had decided to impress the audience by beginning with a little lesson in the Classics: 'In male homosexuality – homos in Greek meaning "the same" and homo in Latin meaning "man" – there is a perversion of a human function. It is using the excretory anus and rectum with a reproductive organ.' He noted that

as a lawyer, he had met plenty of psychopaths and bank robbers, 'people with all sorts of perversion, who decide either to
indulge in them or to refrain from them'. Then he hypothetically
described a child who tells his teacher he has an urge to shoplift
and the teacher says, 'You must not feel isolated, dear boy. It is
just another manifestation of the glorious diversity of human
behaviour. So be at home and worry not. There is no morality.'
As if equating homosexuality with psychopathy, bank robbing
and shoplifting wasn't bad enough, he then referred to it as 'a
morbid squint' (despite the offensiveness of the remark, I give
him credit for its unexpected assonance). He then resorted to
what had long been offensive historical terminology coupled
with some psychobabble thrown in: 'Sodomy and buggery are
not natural alternative sexual acts. They are perversions. They
result from deep-seated psychopathological perversion.'

However, one Conservative MP, Robin Squire (Hornchurch),
spoke against the clause, describing a cartoon by the artist
Franklin that had appeared that day in the UK's most read
newspaper, *The Sun*. It depicted 'a middle-aged man retiring
through the front door of his house, leaving his son, who is
drawn effeminately, hanging by a rope from a lamp post, having
clearly been hanged or attempted to be hanged'. The cartoon
featured the caption, 'I said your dad wouldn't take the news
so well Rodney.' He argued that if the cartoon had shown
someone from another group being strung up, people would
be horrified. However, Neil Hamilton (Conservative, Tatton)
queried whether the reason that the cartoon appeared was
due to 'the aggressive proselytizing by some local authorities
on behalf of homosexuals? That has tended to disgust the vast
majority of British people.'

I asked Chris Smith if any of the people who voted for the clause made any effort to speak to him around this time. He answered, 'None of them ever. During the course of the passage of Section 28, none of them ever came up and wanted to chat.' He also believed that there were some Conservative MPs 'who should have known better but they were very quiet at the time'. For example, Smith told me that Edwina Currie (Conservative, South Derbyshire) had come up to him previously in the Members' Tea Room and said, 'I hear you've come out. Well done!' before turning on her heel and marching away. In 1994, Currie campaigned for the age of consent for male homosexual acts to be reduced from twenty-one to sixteen and Smith believes that 'if left to her own devices, she would have not wanted to vote Section 28 through. But she and many like her did what they were told.' Robin Squire and Michael Brown were the only Conservative MPs who voted with Labour and the Liberal Democrats for Cunningham's amendment, although this made little difference and it was defeated by 254 to 201 votes. The amendment to get the word 'intentionally' added did pass though.

During the debate Smith told the House he'd hoped that in the last three months 'a degree of common sense and decency might have crept into the Government's thinking and that we might now be applauding their decision to withdraw the clause in its entirety from the bill and to reject everything that it stands for'. I asked him whether he believed there was ever a chance of this happening and he replied: 'Once they decided that this was what they were going to do, they went for it. I sort of knew it was a hopeless cause.'

Indeed, there was no doubt that the bill would pass, considering the Conservative majority. It received royal assent on 24 March 1988. Actor Ian McKellen, who has a starring role in the following chapter, has described how, 'The night it all ended, a few of us from the Arts Lobby got drunk with a bunch of sympathetic MPs, turning the Commons Bar into the gayest in town.'[43]

Clause 28 turned into Section 28, becoming law at the stroke of midnight on 24 May 1988.

*

So where did that leave Jenny and her parents? In the year 2000, Susanne Bösche wrote that 'it was absolutely shocking to see the book vilified as homosexual propaganda in the British press . . . I feel angry that my intentions in writing this book – namely to give children a little more knowledge about the world – have been twisted by grown-up people who chose to use it as a weapon in a political battle.'[44]

Were children ever taught from books like *Jenny Lives with Eric and Martin*? Could they read them in schools? Even now, there are conflicting accounts. Some sources claim that *Jenny* was kept in a teacher's resource centre and access to it was controlled.[45] *The Sun* said that a school run by the Labour-controlled Inner London Education Authority (ILEA) had a copy of the book in its library. Femi Otitoju said that it was in the parental advisory section of a library. On a Radio 4 debate, Neil Fletcher, the Labour leader of the ILEA, said, 'I certainly don't come across any evidence at all . . . I'm not aware of any child in any school anywhere in the country who was actually presented with that book in a classroom situation.' Baroness Knight said there was lots of evidence from 'scores of parents' but didn't produce any concrete examples. I haven't come across anyone who was a child during the 1980s who said they'd been taught with it. But even if they had, what harm would have been done? And consequently, what harm was done by removing such books from libraries? Instead of children being taught the inalienable right to be gay, Section 28 implicitly taught everyone to be homophobic.

Around this period, I had a brief, one-off sexual encounter with a boy my own age, which had left me feeling ashamed and embarrassed.

I was sure I was gay but was terrified of my parents finding out.

I was scared of becoming HIV+.

I was terrified of growing up in a world where I would have to try, probably unsuccessfully, to hide my sexuality.

I had no one to talk to.

4

The Path of Most Resistance

I'm meant to be going on a date with a girl from school but I can't face it. Despite fancying men, I'd grown up in a society where heterosexuality was aggressively promoted so I've decided to give it a go. I'd recently heard some girls in conference in a corner of the classroom. Apparently one of them liked me so I agreed to go out with her. I didn't find the physical side of things to be terrible and my body seemed to be enjoying it, but mentally, it didn't feel right. It was making me confused.

The problem pages in my parents' daily newspaper would sometimes have letters from people my age who thought they might be gay but the agony aunts would usually tell them not to worry and that many young people go through a homosexual phase. 'That must be it!' I reasoned. 'I'm in a phase.' I'd monitored myself anxiously for months, checking my response to various pictures of male and female models in the 1988 Littlewoods catalogue, in the hope that I would soon 'grow out of it'.

But I wasn't growing out of it. If anything, I was growing *into* it.

Too cowardly to face the girl, I write her a letter, ending things. I actually use the cliché 'it's not you, it's me,' which is at least truthful. I put the letter in an envelope with the girl's name on it, then Sellotape it to my front door. When she arrives, she reads it and then rips it up. After she's gone, I sneak outside, pick up all the bits and put them in the bin.

She doesn't know it, but she had a lucky escape. Thankfully, that is my last attempt at heterosexuality.

*

I don't know about you, but I thought the last chapter was a bit of a downer. The inevitability of the passage of Section 28 along with the insulting and untrue things about gay men and lesbians in the press and Parliament makes for depressing reading. For many young people, the summer of 1988 is remembered as an exciting and joyous time. This was the year that DJs at nightclubs such as the Hacienda in Manchester and Shoom in London inaugurated the rave scene in the UK. A form of electronic music called acid house was suddenly everywhere (I won't lie, it wasn't my kind of thing, though I now find it quaintly nostalgic). Acid house was heavy on rhythm while light on melody and lyrics. It was associated with the illegal drug ecstasy, which produced feelings of euphoria and love, and its emblem was a yellow smiley face symbol, emblazoned across the front of a baggy white T-shirt. So it is ironic that 1988 is fondly referred to as 'the Second Summer of Love' (the first one being in 1967, the same year that homosexuality was partially decriminalized). For those of us who were affected by Section 28, 'the Summer of Hate' felt more appropriate.

However, if you were feeling glum rather than ecstatic in 1988, then you were not alone. This chapter runs parallel to the last six months of the previous one in that it details the various actions that took place to protest against Clause 28 before it passed into law. Make no mistake, the amount of resistance against the clause was both substantial and diverse. There were glorious guerrilla-style stunts, impassioned media debates, rousing marches through city centres and bold acts of disobedience by local councils. Researching this chapter taught me that, despite the gloomy conclusion of the previous one, I was most certainly not alone. Plenty of people did care. And they were willing to devote large amounts of time and energy, not to say often putting themselves at risk, to stand up and shout 'Stop the Clause!'

A movement is born

The Organisation for Lesbian and Gay Action (OLGA) was a short-lived campaigning group formed in October 1987 as a result of a not very successful meeting of the Legislation for Lesbian and Gay Rights Campaign at Camden Town Hall, which had involved groups from a range of political perspectives and subsequently very little agreement. OLGA brings to mind a daffily eccentric upper-class lady ('Oh look it's Olga, she's lost her monocle again'), although its members were from a range of backgrounds with strong political commitments. Its co-founders were Jennie Wilson, who had been chair of the London Lesbian and Gay Centre, and Eric Presland (now called Peter Scott-Presland), writer, cabaret artist and founder of the Homo Promos theatre company. Other members included Kris Black, who had designed posters for the Lesbians and Policing Project, ex-GLF (Gay Liberation Front) activist and biographer Lisa Power, who had also been one of the early members of London Lesbian and Gay Switchboard, Ian Berridge, David Smith and Maureen Oliver. Its creation was timely – David Wilshire was to propose the amendment to the Local Government Act (1986) just a few weeks later in December 1987 and monocle or no monocle, OLGA was quick to act.

On 14 December, the day before the clause was debated in the House of Commons, OLGA organized a mass action with around eight hundred lesbians and gay men gathering at Westminster to lobby their MPs. In freezing weather, the lobbyists filed into the Grand Committee Room of the House of Commons to hear pledges of support from MPs, including Bernie Grant, Ken Livingstone, Diane Abbott, Robin Cook and Simon Hughes.

Jennie describes how OLGA organized the first national Stop the Clause rally, which took place in London on 9 January 1988. Jennie and Kris had to get the route approved by the police and they managed to convince them to let people gather together in the Temple area, saying that they'd be lucky to get 4,000 people on the march. It was all very short notice, and being the Christmas break, many people were away. And of course, back then there was no social media to spread the word. OLGA activists tried leafleting the gay bars although they met with little success, since at the start most people didn't understand how threatening the clause was going to be. As a result, not many people were expected to show up.[1]

Despite this, the turnout was impressive: different estimates put the number of attendees at between 10,000 and 40,000. The march had been advertised in the gay press just in time and news of it had quickly spread via word of mouth. Unlike smaller marches, which were often attended by the faithful few – experienced activists, who could be relied on to turn up whatever the weather – by now people had cottoned on to the fact that the clause was dangerous. It inspired those who had never thought of themselves as particularly political to get involved – an early sign that the backlash against the clause wasn't going to be limited to a few existing activists, but was acting as a form of recruitment for the gay and lesbian equality movement that was about to come into fruition. Songs produced for the march had a Christmas carol theme, poking fun at Jill Knight: 'Silent Knight' (sung to the tune of 'Oh Little Town of Bethlehem') and 'Margaret Thatcher: Once in Royal Maggie's City'.[2] When the marchers got to Downing Street, there was a moment of camp drama when someone shouted, 'She's home!' (meaning Margaret Thatcher). This caused what Jennie calls 'a good little riot for about twenty minutes' with protesters breaking through a cordon. The police threatened to bring horses in and had to get Jennie to disperse the crowd. In all, 32 arrests were made, with one person detained for carrying an 'offensive weapon' (a banner pole).[3]

OLGA was by no means the only organization that protested against Clause 28 in 1988. Groups sprang up all over the country – there were local ones in many cities and towns across the UK. For example, on 30 January 1988, local groups organized marches in Cardiff and Edinburgh. The Cardiff organizers asked demonstrators to bring placards with the names of the towns and villages in Wales where they had lived in order to demonstrate that gay men and lesbians weren't just located in cities but live throughout the country. The Edinburgh march was actually a day of action, incorporating a rally, public meeting and fundraising disco.[4] In Lancaster, where I work, a Stop the Clause group was also formed. The activists wanted to hold their meetings at a local pub, the Ring O'Bells, which was unofficially the city's gay pub. They asked permission of the proprietor to use a room at the back of the pub and she was apparently horrified, claiming she had no idea that many of the patrons were gay (that's North Lancashire for you). This caused a mass walkout as punters transferred their custom to another pub, the Yorkshire House, never to return.

There were also anti-clause groups formed to represent specific types of people, like the Trade Unionists against Section 28 (TUAS) group, which was set up in January 1988. And existing groups also campaigned against the clause. For example, the Pink Singers is a LGBTQ+ community choir that was formed in 1983. In 1989, the Singers and a women's choir called the Pre Madonnas hosted the European Lesbian and Gay Festival of Song, which was held in London in solidarity as a result of Section 28. The festival was called 'Singing the Blues Away' (blue being the Tory party colour).[5]

Robert debates with Ian and Peregrine

On 27 January 1988, the Radio 3 programme *Third Ear* discussed the potential effects of Clause 28 on the arts and education, with Robert Hewison leading the debate. One of the discussants was the editor of the *Sunday Telegraph*, Peregrine Worsthorne, who a few weeks earlier had referred in the paper's leader column to the 'bold and brazen, proselytising cult' of homosexuals of which many members had 'positively flaunted their aberrant sexual tastes'.[6] In the debate Worsthorne argued in support of the clause but conceded that it should be amended to exclude the arts. He viewed homosexuality as 'a great misfortune . . . the less frequent it is in a society the better'. He claimed that *Jenny Lives with Eric and Martin* 'had been introduced into schools by a particular local council with a view to teaching the . . . impressionable young that homosexuality was a perfectly normal and desirable condition'. Perhaps Worsthorne was protesting too much when he referred to homosexuality as 'disgusting'. He was married with children but had already talked about having been seduced on a sofa by the jazz musician George Melly while at public school and later had mentioned having 'homosexual adventures' in the army.[7]

The other participant in the debate was the charismatic actor Ian McKellen, who is now well known for his popular film roles such as the wizard Gandalf in the *Lord of the Rings* trilogy and Magneto in the *X-Men* series. My favourite McKellen role is that of Mel Hutchwright, a pompous and sponging author who appeared in ten episodes of *Coronation Street* in 2005, giving a memorable denouement speech to Emily Bishop and Ken Barlow among others. But in 1988 he had spent far more time on stage, having played roles such as Richard II, Dr Faustus, Romeo and Macbeth. McKellen was 48 and back from New York, where he had been acting in an adaption of a Chekhov play. Deeply affected by the HIV-AIDS epidemic, he had donated money from one-man performances and raised hundreds of thousands of pounds for charities such as London Lighthouse, standing at the front exit of whichever theatre he performed in, holding a bucket to collect additional donations as patrons left. It was during one of these collections, on 4 January 1988, that theatre critic Carole Woddis informed him about Clause 27, as it was then called. She handed him some literature on it, urging him to read it when he got home. He was horrified, realizing the effect it could have on the arts.[8] And although his sexuality was not a secret to fellow actors, he had grown up in a society where it had been completely illegal to be gay until 1967 when he was 28. Like many people in the public eye at the time, he was not officially 'out'.

In the *Third Ear* debate McKellen argued against the clause, saying that the book 'in question never appeared on a school library shelf, it was not used for teaching'. He also claimed that the clause 'will restrict the thought of people deciding what plays to do' and that the wording 'local authorities' was vague, not just applying to schools. He noted that there were no homosexual role models in society, and if children feared they were gay and received a 'dusty answer' from their parents, their next port of call would probably be their teacher. Then, employing a phrasing that sounds appropriately Shakespearian, he said that the law would 'restrict dangerously that perfectly proper activity of the schools' to reassure children that their sexuality was not against the law and not wrong. Worsthorne conceded that 'it would be very sad, if teachers, as a result of any new legislation, were frightened of seeming to be sympathetic to a homosexual boy or girl.' There was a wonderfully droll moment of sass from McKellen: when Worsthorne claimed that he knew the addresses of a number of gay clubs in London, McKellen interrupted with 'You mean like the Garrick Club?', referring to the posh gentlemen's club that is popular with actors, artists and writers.

A notable aspect of this debate is just how well-mannered everyone is, despite the clear divergence of opinion and the potential for it to descend into a screaming match. However, what's most interesting about the debate is that it marked a turning point, both in Ian McKellen's own life and in terms of the battle over Clause 28 and gay rights in the UK more generally. Four minutes in, McKellen casually says that the Clause is 'offensive to anyone who's, like myself, homosexual, apart from the whole business of what can and cannot be taught to children'. Although he had described himself as gay on a World Service programme on 19 January, it had largely gone unnoticed, while the *Third Ear* programme on Radio 3 had a much larger audience. At this time people still did not voluntarily come out in the media. They were either humiliatingly outed by the tabloids or they just stayed in the closet, thank you. What Ian McKellen had just done was simply *not* done. In the imaginary underground lair of Homophobia Central a klaxon was now going off and a huge bank of TV screens were all showing a close-up of McKellen's face.

I asked Ian McKellen about his memories of the interview, his coming out and what he made of Peregrine Worsthorne. He described him as

a rather dandy gentleman, overdressed. I think he was of the old school that of course it was alright to be gay but you just didn't talk about it and bring it into the open – he thought it was almost a matter of *taste*. Whether I went into that broadcast intending to come out, I don't know, although I was certainly ready to do it. But having heard it back it makes me squirm a bit. I think I mispronounce homosexuality. Indeed, I call myself a homosexual rather than a gay man. I

think I had an awful lot to learn about the language
and the attitudes.

But despite this, he told me that 'It was the best day of my life,
in a sense.' He had informed his family before the programme
was broadcast and other than the fact that it went out across
the whole country, it was a low-key coming out, sounding
almost like a throwaway remark with neither Worsthorne nor
Hewison evidencing any surprise or interest in pursuing the
topic. But make no mistake, Ian McKellen's self-outing was
a big deal. It was also a warning to those who favoured the
status quo. McKellen had referred to the dearth of famous gay
role models in the debate. Now, courtesy of him, the country
had one. And he was going to make it matter.

Indeed, who better than one of the country's most talented
theatrical actors, well-versed in captivating audiences, to be the
voice of the opposition against Clause 28? McKellen's coming
out gave him a purpose that he pursued with vigour, promoting and attending marches, putting homophobic journalists
in their place and lobbying, always lobbying. On 3 June he
appeared on the BBC early evening chat show *Wogan*, presenting an articulate seven-minute argument against Section 28.
The show was regularly watched by 13 million viewers and
it was appearances like this which helped to convince large
numbers of ordinary British people that the government had
made a mistake. Sincere and unflappable, McKellen brought
star quality to the fight against the clause. Obviously, he was not
always able to convince people to change their mind – a visit to
the Conservative Environment Minister Michael Howard was
undoubtedly never going to be successful. McKellen remembers,

'He had me round one Sunday to announce he'd given way and there was going to be protection and there was going to be none of the fears that I was representing about the arts for example, but it was very much a lawyer's niggling point that he'd presented.' At the end of the interview, Howard had the audacity to ask McKellen to sign autographs for his children. In one version of this story, he apparently wrote 'Fuck off, I'm gay.' However, McKellen told me, 'I did sign his kids' autograph books but I think I just put "best wishes". I think the [other] story's gone around because I said "I wish I'd put . . ."'

On other occasions, McKellen didn't hold back. In a speech made in July 1988, he characterized Section 28 as a pantomime: 'Enter stage right the ugly sisters, played by Dame Jill Knight, MP for Edgbaston and David Wilshire, MP for Spelthorne. They opened their act and their dirty minds by offering their dirtier little clause to Michael Howard, the local government minister. Mr Howard is the gentleman villain of this pantomime.'[9]

A full-page advert, with the title 'A Sense of Alarm', had been placed in *The Independent* on 1 February 1988, asking the Lords to look carefully at the clause and warning about the development of a climate of persecution. It was signed by a host of dignitaries from the arts, academia, science and politics. McKellen co-wrote the script with Matthew Parris, who had been Conservative MP for West Derbyshire between 1979 and 1986. McKellen thus acted as an important focal point for the emerging opposition to Section 28, bringing disparate sets of people together and hosting meetings at his home in Limehouse. It was at one such meeting on 16 February 1988 that Douglas Slater, a gay civil servant who worked as a clerk in the House of Lords, gave advice on how the activists should

operate within the context of Parliament. McKellen acknowledged to me that 'because I'd had fame elsewhere, I became
a representative of people who I had no right to represent . . .
But I never wanted to be a leader in that sense. I didn't think
I was qualified for that.'

Still, in the years to come, he was thrust into the spotlight,
becoming almost synonymous with the fight for gay rights.
And despite fears that coming out would harm his career or
make him a pariah, it had the opposite effect. He even became
Sir Ian McKellen in 1991. However, he wasn't the only person
to be knighted that year: 'When I went to collect my knighthood, standing next to me to get *his* knighthood was Peregrine
Worsthorne. It was bittersweet.' It was also very telling about
who the Establishment were prepared to reward.

[Interruption]

Ian McKellen's fame helped give him a platform to lobby against
Section 28 – he could summon up politicians and talk to them
face to face. However, lobbying was not the only strategy used
by activists, and less than a week after McKellen's self-outing, as
politicians debated Clause 28, they would be confronted with
an unexpected invasion – a form of direct action that would
become more newsworthy than the debate itself.

The Houses of Parliament were used to occasional vocal
'invasions' in the form of contributions from members of the
public galleries. For example, during the Commons debate on
the clause that took place on 15 December 1987, viewers in
the Visitors' Gallery (officially known as the Strangers' Gallery)
treated the proceedings like an all-in wrestling match, shouting

and clapping in a most unrestrained way. It got to be too much for poor Elaine Kellett-Bowman (Conservative, Lancaster), who complained about people in the gallery trying to 'inhibit debate', causing the Deputy Speaker to say obliquely, 'No one interrupts debates in this chamber, and I hope there will be no reference to any interruptions from elsewhere.' This did not deter the spectators, and later in the debate the Speaker felt it necessary to take up the mantle, warning that 'if we have disturbances from the Gallery I have the authority to clear it.' A bit later he gave 'one more warning', noting 'It may not be generally known that clapping from the Strangers' Gallery or even from the Benches is not permitted.' And a few minutes later he tried a third time, 'Those in the gallery must conduct themselves in good order.' The press loved the commotion and a headline in *The Sun* the following day read 'Screaming Gays Bring Commons to a Halt!' while *The Independent* noted that 140 people had cheered and hissed at the speakers. I asked Chris Smith what he'd thought about the audience participation. He said, 'Strictly speaking, the people in the gallery are not supposed to exist. The House of Commons has to proceed as if there was no one there. But the fact they were real people up there, and they were reacting, was actually quite useful for our side of the discussion. In the chamber we were vastly outnumbered.'

Richard Sandells, an actor with the theatre group Gay Sweatshop, told me that during the first reading of the Clause in the Commons he shouted his opposition from the Strangers' Gallery. Security guards rushed to arrest him but they had to fight their way past a line of determined women who all stuck out their legs to obstruct their passage. He was kept overnight in a cell beneath the House of Lords before being released after Chris Smith intervened on his behalf with the Speaker. Yet, despite the ruckus from the balconies, visitors kept to their allocated places. Security was ever-present in Parliament and visitors were subject to inspection before they were allowed in. So the debate on 2 February 1988 was historic because the floor of the House of Lords was invaded by members of the public in a most dramatic way. Sifting through the many (and sometimes conflicting) reports of the event, it is difficult to be certain that a completely accurate version of the incident can ever be told. Even the names of the women involved are difficult to ascertain. Different sources claim that Stella Blair, Paula Peake, Susannah Bowyer, Myriam/Miriam Preston, Janet McLaughlin and Rachel Cox were directly involved in the invasion. It has also been claimed that others present were called Sally Francis (who was also known as Sally Forth and Charlotte Despard), Olivia Butler and Angela Nunn.[10] The women are sometimes referred to as Lesbians against the Clause.

I interviewed Susannah Bowyer, one of the women who actually did descend over the edge of the balcony and into the Lords' chamber. She told me that at the time she'd used the pseudonym Rachel and that she and some of the women had previously been involved in protests at Greenham Common, described earlier. Another activist, Sally Francis, a native of Boreham Wood who had come out aged sixteen, has recounted how she had met some of the women during a visit to Lesbos in Greece.[11] From their previous participation in feminist and peace movements Sally says that these women had experience of taking 'imaginative, non-violent direct action . . . There was no hierarchy, they didn't have a name and were simply bound together by a commitment to draw attention to Clause 28.'[12] The women had recently organized a 'kiss-in' at Piccadilly Circus and after that, while at Susannah's flat in Clapham, were thinking of what to do next. Some of them had been attending the debates around Clause 28, getting into the Visitors' Gallery whenever they could. They first considered stealing a boat in order to board Westminster, but then realized that nobody knew how to operate one. They then thought about swinging in from the chandeliers. Sally Francis has described how Susannah had noticed the microphones hanging from the ceiling and had a Tarzan (or Jane) moment.[13] A plan was hatched. The women went to Clapham market and bought several lengths of clothesline, which they cut in half and distributed between them.[14] The following day, the group of activists, some wearing clothesline around their waists, set off for the Lords. Susannah recounts that

there was a really big queue outside to get in and we were worried that we wouldn't get in in time. My rope came off while we were talking to some police officers, trying to blag our way in. The rope fell off on the ground but they didn't clock it. Anyway, we were moving among that queue and one of the women was shouting out to people 'Are you a Lord? Are you a Lord? Can you sign us in as a guest?' as the queue was going up one side of the corridor and people were going in and out. And at some point Lord Monkswell said, 'Yes OK, I will.' So maybe half a dozen of us came out of the Visitors' queue and he signed us in to the Peers guest gallery on the side. So that was good because it's quite a few feet lower than the Visitors' Gallery. And we were right in the front row which we wouldn't have been [otherwise].

Who is this Lord Monkswell and why did he sign the women in? There's no evidence that he had met any of them before. Lord Monkswell (Gerald Collier) was in his mid-thirties, had inherited his title and, despite identifying as a socialist and disapproving of hereditary peers, believed that it was 'better to work from the inside to change the system, rather than from the outside'.[15] It's likely that he had correctly surmised that the women were there to protest the clause and was supportive of their position, but had no idea what they were planning. Another of the protesters, Paula, has described how only four of the women were able to get in as Lord Monkswell's guests, and so she and another woman were signed in as guests of Diane Abbott (Labour, Hackney North and Stoke Newington).[16]

As the debate progressed (see the previous chapter for highlights), the activists in the gallery engaged in the usual cheers and boos, although neither the Speaker nor Deputy Speaker is recorded as issuing any warnings this time (given that warnings were repeatedly ignored, perhaps they had given up). Susannah says that they didn't hear much of the debate due to being stuck in the queue and by the time they got into the Gallery they were quite hyped up. At the end of the debate, the Lords voted. Later that night, in an interview broadcast on ITV's *News at Ten*, one of the activists explained, 'We waited until the vote came through so that in no way were we going to change anybody's minds. We did the respectable bit and sat in there and listened to it and then they legislated against us so we thought, "Well, we'll just shake them up a bit."' The interviewer challenged her, noting that they had gone in with the rope. The protester responded with, 'No, we weren't going to do it. If the vote was on our side, we were going to walk out.'

At this point in the transcript of the debate from Hansard there is a single word in square brackets: '[Interruption]'. It is a word which does no justice to the thrilling events that were about to occur.

After the result of the vote was announced Susannah told me that 'it was a matter of getting these ropes out and tying them to these little cast-iron balcony railings that they have. And just kind of going over the edge. I remember getting rope burns on my hands. Not really having any technique in these matters and we didn't call it abseiling, the press called it abseiling, we thought we were just throwing ourselves over the edge.'

According to one of the other activists who was in the gallery, 'They had them out, they were all tangled up so they had them on their lap for about 30 seconds before anything happened. And then when we realised that they were tying them on and they were throwing them down the balcony . . . [we] just started shouting . . . silly outrageous things to attract security and they came for us.'[17]

Reports differ regarding how many women actually climbed over the railings and swung down. Some say it was just one woman; others claim that there were two, three or four, or even eight.[18] As some of the women probably gave false names when they were interviewed at the time, it is difficult to know exactly how many were involved in the abseiling, but my money is on three or four. A woman called Stella Blair was quoted in

The Times the following day: 'I have never gone down a rope before – I was quite frightened but it was not very hard. We had ropes inside our jackets. There was no attempt to try to stop us getting into the gallery but we lost our bags in the place where they have to be left.'[19]

According to Sarah Green, who was watching events unfold from across the other side of the Visitors' Gallery, 'the ropes were a bit too short but they managed to get on to the floor anyway, and one of them even managed to get halfway to the Queen's throne (she later explained she wanted to denounce the clause from there).' Green reports that 'some of the gay men in the Visitors' Gallery were appalled, and one of them rushed into my visitors' box to complain that this kind of behaviour would ruin the reputation of the campaign against Clause 28.'[20] The abseiling women were reported as shouting 'Lesbians are out!' The *Mail* referred to them as 'screaming lesbian activists'.[21]

The reaction of the Lords and Ladies in the chamber was one of utter amazement. No one had *dared* to do anything like this before. Lord Graham of Edmonton said that the peers 'were absolutely stunned. Incredible! We just couldn't believe that this sort of thing was going on inside the House of Lords.'[22] Douglas Slater, who was working as a clerk on the floor at the time, said that while most of the Conservative Lords were aghast, others began to chuckle. 'It was a fabulous gesture of sorts and has become one of the legends of the Lords.'[23]

The task of removing the women fell on retired Air Chief Marshal Sir John Gingell, who was Gentleman Usher of the Black Rod (usually just referred to as Black Rod) in Parliament. The role of Black Rod is to control access to the House of

Lords and maintain order (similar to the role of a nightclub bouncer but with a snazzier uniform). Gingell was standing in the vicinity of the demonstrators as they came down the ropes. He and his staff seized them, there was a bit of a fracas (which was characterized by *The Telegraph* the following day as being quite violent, with an usher being kicked and several others punched[24]) and then they walked them out of the chamber. Susannah Bowyer relates what happened as follows: 'I got grabbed by the Black Rod, an ex-military man, he was very quick on getting me into a half-nelson, shunting us out of the room.' Elaine Kellett-Bowman was reported in the *Telegraph* as saying, 'It was a pure Tarzan act . . . They flung ropes over the gallery and started shinning down them. One chap almost lost his trousers in the melee.' In other words, this was British Comedy Gold.[25] Ian McKellen, who was one of the viewers in the gallery, enjoyed the show, telling me, 'Good for them. It was the spirit of theatricality which appealed to me. What a good sense of humour – for people watching the debate going on, they must have thought, "These gays! They've got some chutzpah and style."'

One of the abseilers, who later gave her name to the press as Stella Blair, said, 'I had expected to be bundled out very quickly. We got dragged out – and then the man let go of me. I just walked away and went straight out of the building.'[26] Due to the pandemonium, two of the women who had been involved got away but six others were arrested, two of whom had had little to do with the action. According to Sally Francis and Susannah Bowyer, they were all put in a cell next to Big Ben. Paula Peake describes how the arresting officer was a fan of the suffragettes and she took the women on a detour to show them the cell where Emily Pankhurst had been held. While under arrest the women were given tea and coffee and allowed to watch television. They were held for about six hours, then released in the evening without charge. Apparently, they would have been released earlier if they hadn't made fun of Black Rod's buckled shoes, silk stockings, knee-breeches and wig.[27] The women adjourned to a pub by Westminster Bridge that was popular with journalists. Sally Francis says that the journalists didn't understand why they hadn't been charged and she offered to tell them what had happened if they bought her a drink. Susannah Bowyer remembers that although they'd done actions before when they had been at Greenham Common, 'for me at least it was quite a big thing to be saying, "As lesbians we're doing this." That felt like stepping over a line into a different kind of press identity.' Susannah (credited as Rachel Cox) had her photo taken among a group of activists and was described as being the one who went over the balcony. She is reported as saying, 'We did it because we are very angry lesbians.'[28]

The women may have got off scot-free, but Lord Monkswell was not to be so lucky. It was obvious that someone had signed the women into the guest gallery, and it didn't take long for Lord Monkswell to be fingered. The House of Lords was packed out two days later on 4 February 1988, and a rare silence fell over the expectant and rather cross lords and ladies as Monkswell admitted that he must have signed the pass to allow the four women into the gallery. He said

I should like to make a short personal statement in connection with the demonstration which occurred after the vote on Clause 28 last Tuesday. On that day,

Released after being 'detained at their Lordships' pleasure': the ladies who abseiled, 2 February 1988.

Released after being 'detained at their Lordships' pleasure': the ladies who abseiled, 2 February 1988.

four young ladies were admitted to the visitors' gallery in my name. Until today I was under the impression that they were not involved in the demonstration. However, I have been advised that those young ladies were involved. On the basis of that advice, I tender my apologies to Black Rod and his staff for any difficulties that they had to contend with as a result of my actions. While neither condemning nor condoning the demonstration, I believe that it was understandable, given the results of the vote on Clause 28. I conclude by repeating the words spoken by a twelve-year-old girl yesterday as regards Clause 28: It is just what the Germans did to the Jews.[29]

Some apology – he basically just called the government a load of Nazis. Monkswell's speech was punctuated with cries of 'Shame!' and afterwards he was quoted as saying, 'I do not go out of my way to upset people but one of the things I feel very strongly about is that people should speak the truth and unfortunately that hurts some people sometimes.'[30] The apology was seen as inadequate and in *The Times* he was described as unrepentant and shunned by his fellow peers. In fact, his speech was seen as such a disgrace that Lord Belstead, the leader of the House, warned that an informal investigation would be held into the procedures for making personal statements.[31]

The women had made their mark. But as we'll see, at this point they were just getting started.

Never going underground

A number of (mostly Labour-majority) local councils decided to publicly defy Section 28 by either denouncing it or saying they would not acknowledge it. These included the councils of Hammersmith, Camden, Hackney, Islington, Kensington and Chelsea, Newcastle, Liverpool, Aberdeen and Hillingdon. Some councils made a stand even before Section 28 had passed into law. For example, the *Uxbridge and West Drayton Gazette* reported 'a blazing row over gay rights' that took place at a council meeting in Hillingdon in early March 1988. Councillor

Jane Rose-Williams (Labour) said, 'This is probably the biggest attack on minority civil liberties seen in Europe since Nazi Germany in the 1930s. Publicity, teaching, funding and all local authority work which has a bearing on homosexuality will be banned. Lesbians and gay men residing in Hillingdon pay rates and taxes, and their contribution to our society is no less because of their sexuality.' The council held a vote to denounce Clause 28 but local Conservative councillors tried to get an amendment to the denouncement attached, which disapproved of so-called 'deviant' relationships and called for sex education to be taught in the context of love, marriage and the family. This was defeated, to cheers from the public gallery, and instead a Liberal amendment was passed to oppose the clause and show commitment to non-discriminatory practices while not promoting homosexuality.[32]

Lotte Cash, Margaret Thatcher impersonator extraordinaire, during the Never Going Underground march in Manchester, 1988.

Birmingham City Council did not offer much help to the local gay community and it was up to around one hundred members of the Birmingham Stop the Clause group, led by Steve Bedser, to organize their own demonstration. On 13 February, leaflets were given out and signatures were collected for a petition. The rally ended with the burning of replicas of books by gay authors like Oscar Wilde and E. M. Forster outside the city library, in an effort to show the effects of censorship.[33]

Birmingham was the home of Jill Knight's office in the Edgbaston area, and campaigners regularly picketed her when she was in residence. Knight complained that her constituents were apparently terrified to come to see her because she was effectively barricaded in the building by militant homosexuals.[34] A decade later, on 6 December 1999, in a speech made in the House of Lords, she claimed, 'I did not only incur verbal abuse for my pains but physical abuse too. On one occasion, opponents of Section 28 attacked me outside my constituency office and tried to turn my car over with me inside it. I was saved by the swift arrival of several police cars with sirens blaring.'

A council that did decide to denounce Clause 28 was Manchester. Councillors worked with the Campaign for Lesbian and Gay Rights to organize a large rally in the city centre on 20 February 1988, which was followed by an evening music festival. The rally made use of the slogan 'Never Going Underground', which was also adopted as a logo. With a gay village that was concentrated around Canal Street, a Labour-run council and a history of gay rights activism, Manchester was becoming established as a haven for gay men and lesbians, despite the prejudiced presence of chief constable James

Anderton, who organized regular patrols around the village and complained that sodomy was against the word of God.[35] Remember how Ian McKellen had received his knighthood alongside his debating partner in 1991? If that were not galling enough, James Anderton was knighted that year too.

But Anderton did not put people off and they came to the march from far and wide. A 'Pink Express' was chartered to bring protesters from London and the rally attracted more than 20,000 people. It was reported that the procession stretched for nearly two miles around the city streets.[36] Tom Robinson performed his 1976 hit 'Glad to Be Gay' and the *Manchester Evening News* even printed alternative lyrics from Robinson that satirized James Anderton.[37] Meanwhile, speeches were made by a range of dignitaries, including the leader of Manchester council. Ian McKellen gave one, telling the assembled crowd,

> I'm here because I'm one of millions of normal homosexuals who are affected by this new law. Clause 28 is in parts designed to keep us in our place, but it didn't work with me. Because I, like you, am now out and about in the streets of Manchester. We must be out and about in the media, we must be out and about in pubs and clubs and in the classroom, talking about homosexuality, encouraging our friends and family to think about homosexuality and in fact, in that sense, promoting homosexuality.

I asked him why he'd emphasized coming out and jokingly he told me, that's what all people who have just come out want to do. It was a wonderful day. Manchester's my home turf really as a kid, it was the first gay march I'd ever been on, and it was absolutely about Section 28, which was extremely unpopular in a radical city like Manchester. And in between the march and the speeches we were entertained by the Lord Mayor in the City Hall. We were welcome, we were part of the Manchester establishment. I felt I'd really become a citizen of the country. I felt I belonged and I was not going to be rejected any more by society.

Another speaker was Michael Cashman, an actor who had become famous two years earlier as a result of his role as Colin Russell in the popular BBC One soap opera *EastEnders*. Colin was one of the first gay characters in a British soap and, unlike the gossipy camp gay characters who had flounced around television screens in the 1970s, he was quiet, minded his own business and wore sensible shirts in muted colours. Despite the initial mystery around him, Cashman described him as 'a bit of a damp squib. He was ordinary, in fact he could blend into a magnolia wall.'[38] Michael Cashman told me that he'd wished Colin had been more dynamic, but thankfully the writers never listened to the actors – they knew what they were doing (although he was able to get them to change a couple of lines so Colin could refer to the Lesbian and Gay Switchboard in one storyline).

Even before Colin had arrived in Albert Square, *The Sun* had its welcome wagon out in force with the front page headline 'It's EastBenders: Gay Men to Stir Up TV Soap', while later the *News of the World* had the misleading headline 'Secret Gay Love of AIDS Scare EastEnder', also printing Cashman's address and 'outing' his partner. After that article was published a brick was thrown through their window. It gets worse. Cashman has also described how one journalist informed him that he was almost certainly dying of AIDS while another sent two young children to knock on his door asking for money, no doubt with the telephoto lens set to kill.[39] I asked Michael Cashman what he'd made of this treatment and he said,

> It was terrible because they dirtied you, they used language that dirtied us all and that was how they wanted to represent us. Indeed, that was how they represented us: it was the gay plague, we abused children, we were paedophiles, we lurked in the shadows, we were people who were not worthy of being treated equally and we should be sacked, certainly if we were anywhere near nursing or education. So it was a nasty time in British social life.

Really, how could this kind of treatment *not* politicize you?

On 17 November 1987, Colin had briefly kissed his live-in partner Barry on the forehead, and in the months to follow the *Daily Express* went slightly insane, calling the program 'filth'.[40] In 1989, Piers Morgan wrote in *The Sun* of a 'homosexual love scene between yuppie poofs' when Colin kissed a character called Guido. I never missed an episode of *EastEnders* and had watched (studied) Colin covertly, half-acknowledging that he constituted a role model for me. Speaking to the crowd that day in February 1988, Cashman said, 'Gay men and lesbians are ordinary men and women made extraordinary by society's focus on what we do in bed. And as ordinary men and women we demand the same rights . . . as other ordinary civilized human beings.' Another part of his speech was quoted a couple of weeks later in the 9 March 1988 Commons debate by Allan Roberts: 'we could round up gay people, we could shoot them or gas them, but they will not go away. As long as men and women procreate, they will continue to create homosexuals, and there is nothing that we can do about it, even if Conservative Members want to.'

Actors from another soap opera, *Brookside*, which was broadcast on Channel 4, also made speeches. Sue Johnston, who played the iconic Sheila Grant, told the audience, 'When I first heard about Clause 28 I thought about Hitler's burning of the books. And we all know what happened there and it must not happen here.' Another *Brookie* actor who spoke was Stifyn Parri, who had joined the cast in 1985 to play Chris, the handsome and cheeky boyfriend of regular character Gordon Collins. Parri told me that playing Chris on *Brookside* had been an education for him, a kind of dress rehearsal for his own life, as the writers made his character deal with homophobic attacks and graffiti. And while Cashman and McKellen were 'out and proud' at this point, he was not, and wasn't especially politically minded. On photographs taken of the march, McKellen, Cashman and Parri are front and centre, along with Peter Tatchell, holding a huge banner that reads 'Lesbian & Gay Rights – Human Rights'. Parri described how being at the front of the march felt like being in a machine. 'It was quite a pressurized day for me because I was playing two parts.' His speech to the crowd was effectively his coming out. He said,

'. . . like being in a machine'. From left: Stifyn Parri, Michael Cashman, Ian McKellen and Peter Tatchell at the front of the Never Going Underground march, 20 February 1988.

'No government is going to force lesbians and gays back into the closet . . . It is you now who must fear us . . . who the hell's going to get a closet big enough for all of us?' Parri says that on the same day as the march, a kiss between Chris and Gordon had been scheduled to appear on *Brookside*. It was no more than a peck on the cheek but it made the 'And finally' segment on the *Nine O'Clock News* as the first gay kiss on UK television.[41]

Pat Karney, who was chair of the organizing committee, said that 'the march changed people's lives. It was quite courageous that 20,000 people went out on it and I think it was a pivotal moment in gay and lesbian history, because the confidence of people soared when they saw so many people out on the streets.'[42]

Some 45 miles away in Leeds, protesters had gathered to lobby local councillors before a council meeting. The Independent councillor for Pudsey South, Peter Kersting, argued that Clause 28 didn't go far enough and that 'all homosexuals and lesbians should be barred from public buildings.' He then added, 'They should be totally barred from leisure centres.' Leisure centres! A Conservative councillor, Ann O'Brien, complained that Leeds City Council was giving out grants to gay and lesbian groups and council leader George Mudie tried to play it down, saying that only a grant to an AIDS helpline had been given and he had personally vetoed a number of grants.[43] A group that had been formed in December 1987 called Leeds Women against the Clause organized a march that took place on 5 March, involving over 2,000 protesters, who met in Victoria Gardens and marched through Leeds city centre.

The 'Stop the Section' campaign had been set up at the start of the year. Rebecca Flemming, a student of Sanskrit and Urdu, had dropped out of her studies to become a full-time organizer. There was a small office to start with, with just a telephone and typewriter and an enormous number of volunteers, many of whom had never been involved in a political movement before. While some of the stories around the fight against Section 28 involve the more glamorous acts of resistance that drew media attention, we should not overlook the fact that behind the scenes there was an awful lot of organizational and administrative work going on. Phone calls had to be made, leaflets typed up, printed and distributed, and meetings organized and attended. Flemming recalls that she spent a *lot* of time in meetings – large ones that tried to coordinate the whole thing and small ones that involved sub-groups such as trade unions or local government groups. With so many meetings, she says it would have been easy to get ground down but that didn't happen, because even though they could be quite chaotic at times, things were happening, tasks got allocated, people did them and then came back and said what they'd done.[44]

With each march that took place, the numbers got bigger as the opposition to the clause grew. Saturday 30 April saw another, organized by the Stop the Section campaign, which took place in London, starting at Embankment with a rally and ending with a festival in Kennington Park. While police estimated that 15,000 people attended, the organizers put the number at 50,000.[45] Two protesters who made the journey were from Swindon: 73-year-old Rodney Oakley and his partner Graham. Rodney described the event as 'absolutely awe-inspiring. The young, the old, the disabled and the fit, we're all here. It is the proudest day of my entire life.'[46] Leaders of the Labour and Liberal parties, Neil Kinnock and David Steel, sent messages of support to the marchers and the *Pink Paper* reported that even the police seemed to be on the side of the protesters this time.[47]

At the march pop star Boy George performed his new song, 'No Clause 28', twice. George was the lead vocalist of the group Culture Club, which had achieved twelve Top 40 hit singles and two number ones. Despite his talent, the media had tended to focus on his androgynous dress style, labelling him a 'gender bender'.[48] The single version of the song was officially released in June, with the cover featuring artwork of George dressed as Enid Blyton's Noddy. The song begins with a Margaret Thatcher impersonator saying, 'The aim of this government is to make everyone as miserable as possible.' Drawing on acid house, the video version features people dancing in smiley-face T-shirts and a DJ scratching records on a turntable. Words like FIGHT BACK, PRIDE and GROOVE flash across the screen while George sings about not needing Clause 28. Another protest song out that year was 'Smash Clause 28! Fight the Alton Bill', by the group Chumbawamba. Proceeds went to the London Lesbian and Gay Switchboard and the Women's Reproductive Rights Campaign. The song refers to Clause 29 (which, you'll remember, was what Clause 28 was debated as at one point) so it stands as a testament to the fluctuating parliamentary processes around getting a bill passed into law. It is difficult to classify 'Smash Clause 28!' as belonging to a single genre of music since it combines punk and rock with sampling of poetry and choral music. Neither song was a chart-topper and listening to them today, I have to admit that they both feel dated by some of the less enduring musical signatures of the late 1980s.

Pleas to royalty

On 8 March 1988, a group of activists demonstrated outside Buckingham Palace and five women from the group chained themselves to the palace railings. The date of the demonstration was timed to coincide with the seventieth anniversary of the suffragettes, who, decades ago, had done the same (1914 seems to have been the year when this was popular). Sally Francis was one of the activists. She describes how the women 'dressed up as Suffragettes and got a lift in a friend of mine's van down to Buckingham Palace, and chained ourselves to the railings. We were there a long time because the police came and had to cut through the chains with bolt cutters. And we got taken to Cannon Row police station for that and we all gave Suffragette names to . . . make a connection with feminism and homophobia.'[49] Other activists demonstrated outside the gates of the palace. The banners read 'International Womyn's Day – 70th Anniversary of Suffragettes – Dykes against the Clause' and 'Lesbians against Clause 29'. One banner directly appealed to the queen, in her role as the Crown-in-Parliament who had to give royal assent to new acts. It read, 'Elizabeth you preached tolerance. Please practice [sic] it. Don't sign the Clause.' Despite what the queen may have thought, she was unlikely to interfere. Her role in Parliament is meant to be impartial and it would put everyone in an enormous tizzy if she ever openly disagreed with anything or refused to perform her expected duties. The last time a monarch refused to give royal assent to a bill was in 1707.

After the clause had come into law, there were other protests aimed at members of the royal family. On 5 July 1988, the queen and Prince Philip visited the Netherlands to mark three centuries of Anglo-Dutch friendship. Occurring only a few weeks after Section 28 had become law, it was perhaps not the wisest of decisions to have them walk around Amsterdam, one of the world's most liberal and gay-friendly cities. Only five months earlier, on 2 February, the windows of the British Airways Office in Amsterdam had been paint-bombed as part of a protest against Clause 28.

In central Dam Square the royal couple were greeted by activists who chanted, 'It's OK to be gay!' and 'Say no to Clause 28.' A large banner humorously proclaiming 'Lillibeth! Save Your Queens (from Clause 28)' was unfurled from a nearby building. Later that day, the royal couple were driven to the

Begijnhof Amsterdam, a medieval inner courtyard where women of the Catholic sisterhood had lived. While the queen toured the Begijnhof, activists threw a smoke bomb, which landed about 18 metres (60 ft) away from her waiting limousine. The bomb was extinguished and no one was hurt or arrested. One of the protesters was quoted as saying, 'We don't think there is a need to show Dutch–British friendship because of what is being done to lesbians and gays there.'[50]

And two years later, on 12 July 1990, the Queen of Hearts herself, Princess Diana, came face to face with Section 28 activists, after making an (also ill-advised) speech to the Sixteenth International Congress for the Family, which had been scheduled (somewhat incongruously) to occur in Brighton of all places. Brighton might be where the Conservatives held their annual conference but it was, and still is, one of the UK's most gay-friendly cities – it was the first place I thought of to carry out fieldwork when I started researching the gay language Polari. I suspect Diana would have been more comfortable getting to know the locals at Club Revenge or the Queen's Head but here she was, resplendent as always, in a white jacket over a black polka-dot outfit, claiming that the Congress for the Family was worthwhile and ambitious, given the problem of defining what the word 'family' actually means. The congress had conservative views on issues such as sexuality and family planning, and Diana's participation had already caused concern in some quarters. She at least tried to offer a more inclusive understanding of the family as having many different definitions.

After her speech, she had taken her seat on the panel when activists from the group Brighton Area Action against Section

From one queen to another – anti-Section 28 demonstration
during HRH's trip to Amsterdam.

28 climbed onto the stage. They stood in a line, each holding up a placard that spelt out the words 'Lesbian mothers are not pretending.'[51] Then they quietly left the stage, placing the placards on the desk that Diana sat at, walking behind her as audience members jeered and cried 'Shame!' The leader of the group, Danielle Ahrens, was quoted as saying, 'I don't know whether the princess was embarrassed, but it was not our intention to embarrass her. The delegates to this congress are trying to make people believe that lesbian mothers and gay men looking after children are not real families but are pretend family groups. We are not pretending and we have no lesser values than any other family.'[52]

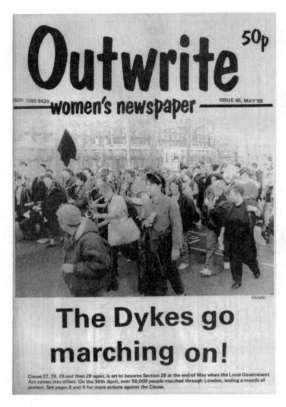

On trend with 1980s saxophones, the 30 April march in London.

Fucking hell! We've got nutters in the studio!

The House of Lords. Buckingham Palace. Where next? What location could represent the ultimate in normal, normal, normal? How about the 'Ideal Home' exhibition? An annual event that took place in London's Olympia, the exhibition was devised by the *Daily Mail* back in 1908 and was a showcase of all the latest delights of domestic gadgetry for Mrs Housewife, as well as the newest housing designs. On 13 March 1988, the exhibition was the target of a series of increasingly inventive Clause 28 protests. It was Mothering Sunday and 28 lesbians, some with their children, occupied one of the show homes to tell the world what they thought about the 'pretended family relationships' wording in Clause 28. A number of banners were unfurled from the windows of the home. One read, 'One of these days these dykes are gonna walk all over you' (a reworking of a line from the Nancy Sinatra song 'These Boots Are Made for Walkin''). Another stated, 'The ideal home is one without any men in it.' And of course, there was one which simply read, 'Stop Clause 28.' The women, who were from a group called Dykestrike, occupied the house for nearly half an hour, giving leaflets to people who had stopped to watch, until they were ejected by a police escort.[53] One of the women, Julie Bindel, said that the group chanted, 'An ideal home contains at least one lesbian.'

However, the most famous piece of direct action was the invasion of a BBC studio during the *Six O'Clock News* on

The talk of Olympia: non-violent direct action at the Ideal Home Exhibition, 13 March 1988.

23 May 1988, witnessed by 8 million viewers as it played out live on television.[54] Time was running out – at midnight Clause 28 would become law and this was the last chance to get people to take notice before that happened. Some of the women who took part had also been involved in the House of Lords abseiling protest. One of them was Booan Temple, a carpenter who worked for Haringey Council as part of an all-women team that had built a refuge for Asian women and a women's centre. She described how frustrating it was that the media were not reporting stories about Clause 28 and she and fellow activists formed a plan to raise its profile. 'We could not get the news to report on it so we thought, "Well, we'll just be the news . . ."'[55] Susannah Bowyer, who was present during the planning of the action but did not take part in it, told me how the women had heard about some hippies who had got out of the *Top of the Pops* studio and had invaded the filming of the news, which had given them the idea.

Sally Francis was one of the women who was involved. She described how a previous attempt to get on the news had descended into farce, with around 25 women breaking into the BBC Studio in Lime Grove, a residential street in Shepherd's Bush. This studio had been in use since 1950, originally as a temporary measure while Television Centre at nearby White City was being built; however, the women hadn't realized that this was not where the *Six O'Clock News* was filmed and having gained entrance, they ran around the building, through studios, hiding in broom cupboards, trying to find something that was being broadcast on-air. They even climbed through the window of Esther Rantzen's dressing room. Sally Francis says it was like an episode of the *Keystone Kops*.[56]

Susannah Bowyer recalls that 'a friend of one of the women worked as a runner or something in the BBC at the time and gave them a floor map of where the news was recorded.' Additionally, the *Daily Mail* quoted one of the women, who claimed that she had gone to 'case the joint a month ago. I couldn't believe how easy it was to get in. I just tagged on to the back of a group who were visiting.' She had wandered off from the others and found the news studio on the sixth floor.[57]

On 23 May, the women met outside Television Centre, armed with the map to get in via a side entrance. Bowyer recalls 'they had some argy-bargy at the gate door with the doorman but they managed to get through there, and did a good job of getting their way through that. And then this map didn't really correspond to where the news was broadcast from so there was a lot of running around.' Booan Temple describes how they had to 'leg it up what seemed like five million stairs. We got to the top, we knew where some loos were. We changed into our T-shirts with the big pink triangles on.'[58]

Meanwhile, in the news studio, completely unaware of what was about to happen, broadcasters Sue Lawley and Nicholas Witchell were taking their places behind the news desk. Both were popular presenters – Witchell was a BBC stalwart; he was the first presenter on the *Six O'Clock News* when it launched in 1984. And a few weeks earlier, Lawley had landed a job presenting the much-loved radio programme *Desert Island Discs*, a position she would hold for the next eighteen years.

Interviewed that night on ITN's *News at Ten*, one of the activists said, 'We walked around, we kept our eyes open, and we managed to get to the right place with seconds to spare.' As soon as the lights changed to signal that the studio was on-air, the women 'burst in'.[59] If this was a film, a simple split-screen wouldn't cover what happened next. You'd need at least four screens to do justice to the chaos that took place.

Two of the women got onto the news floor, one of them immediately handcuffing herself to the desk behind which Sue Lawley and Nicholas Witchell were sitting, the other handcuffing herself to a camera cable. The newsreaders and crew were shocked. But there was no going back. This was live television. They'd just have to do what the British are so good at doing in a crisis – pretend it isn't happening and muddle through somehow. After the opening credits were shown, viewers briefly saw Nicholas Witchell hang up a telephone and then Sue Lawley started announcing the headlines as usual. Except it was not as usual.

On recorded footage which purports to show the behind the scenes 'talkback' (the instructions that the director gives to the studio crew) a man's voice is heard saying the following:

> Run titles. On the air. Oh fucking hell! We've got nutters in the studio! Get 'em out! Get security quickly! Get security quickly! Cue Sue. Run A. Run B. Get her out now! Animate Charisma. Animate Charisma. Run C. Animate Charisma (unclear) Reagan. Animate Charisma. Run D. Coming up Sue. Animate Charisma. (unclear) Camera 2 invasion Camera 2 with inset. Cut. Cue Sue. Cut. Wide shot on 2![60]

This brief monologue is a delight to read, as the director switches between expressing his utter horror at what he is witnessing, to then having to shift into work mode and issue instructions regarding the animations that appear as Sue gives a rundown of the day's headlines. On top of that, he's trying to get the invasion under control, repeatedly calling for security. It's a hilarious multitasking headache of technical and informal lingo. And in case you're wondering, Charisma was the wonderfully old-fashioned animation software system that was used by the BBC in the 1980s and '90s. In my household the phrase 'Animate Charisma!' has become a catchphrase, to be uttered mechanically in moments of confusion or panic.

While Sue Lawley made her way through the news headlines, just off-camera Nicholas Witchell had unplugged the microphone from his desk and was attempting to subdue one of the women by sitting on her and placing his hand over her mouth. The protester is quoted as saying that he kept whispering to her to 'Shut up.'[61] Her muffled cries can be heard on the live broadcast. A member of the television crew sat on the bottom half of her body. The protester later said that she thought she was going to suffocate.[62] According to a report in the *Pink Paper*, one of the cameramen told Witchell, 'Give her one,' and he replied, 'I'm trying to give her one but she won't fucking sit still.' One of the protesters said, 'I couldn't believe his language, especially someone from the BBC. It seemed so out of character and, in my opinion, so unnecessary.'[63] Witchell has given a somewhat milder version of the event: 'I lowered myself gently astride the dear lady ... You could hear all these muffled cries and groans. I think it came as a shock to us both.'[64] Meanwhile, Booan Temple was rugby-tackled to the ground by some of the staff.[65] The activists had admiration for Sue Lawley – 'She was very cool ... [I'll be] listening to

Desert Island Discs on Sunday' – but they didn't approve of the way that Nicholas Witchell had responded: 'The man was not particularly professional.'[66]

There was a break from the live footage when the news cut to a filmed item and at that point 'all hell broke loose' as staff who had been off-camera were now able to intervene.[67] Eventually, someone produced a set of bolt cutters and the women were removed from their handcuffs. But the cameras continued running. Footage later that night over on ITN's *News at Ten* showed one of the women politely saying 'thank you very much' as she was cut free (only in Britain). The women were then led away and Booan Temple was filmed telling the camera, 'We're protesting about rights for lesbian and gay people.'[68] The police had been called and the women were taken out of the building, put in cars and driven to Shepherd's Bush police station.[69] When asked who they were, the women gave the names of famous lesbians. This included Charlotte Despard (a suffragist), as well as Eleanor Butler and Sarah Ponsonby, who were known as 'the Ladies of Llangollen', two upper-class Irish women who had lived together in a mansion in north Wales from 1780 until Butler's death in 1829.[70] Booan Temple noted they were treated with kindness by the custody sergeant, who told them, 'Well done ladies, I think you've done a good thing.'[71] In the meantime, staff at the BBC held an impromptu meeting and decided not to charge the women. They were released later that evening and Booan Temple says that they then went to the Houses of Parliament to join activists there, where they were cheered for taking a stand.[72]

The media coverage was extensive and not especially uplifting. The following day the *Daily Mirror*'s front page sneered,

Here is The Six O'Clock News . .

BEEB MAN SITS ON LESBIAN

By JOHN PEACOCK and GRAHAM BARNES

FOUR lesbian demonstrators burst into a TV studio last night as Sue Lawley started to present the BBC Six O'Clock News.

In the chaos, co-presenter Nicholas Witchell swiftly SAT on one who had handcuffed herself to a desk beside Sue.

He put his hand over her mouth to silence her shouted slogans.

Another lesbian locked herself to a TV camera . . . but Sue kept her cool and pressed ahead.

As millions of viewers heard muffled shouting and the picture shook on their screens, Sue said calmly: "We have rather been invaded."

The commotion went on for four minutes during the bulletin before BBC staff managed to drag the women away.

The four lesbians came within feet of getting "on camera" to protest about the Government's law banning local authorities from promoting homosexuality, which came into effect at midnight.

Attack

Last night a major security investigation was underway at the BBC over the raid on the Shepherds Bush studios in London.

Security was tightened last year after a gang of robbers squirted ammonia into the face of Jan Leeming as she was preparing to read the Ten O'Clock News.

A BBC man said last night: "Clearly, something has gone very wrong."

Ron Neil, the BBC's deputy director of news and current affairs praised the actions of the Lawley-Witchell team.

He said: "Presenting

● Turn to Page 2

..while Sue reads on with woman chained to her desk

WITCHELL: Gagged shouting lesbian

LAWLEY: Stayed calm during drama

The *Daily Mirror*, characteristically restrained in its reporting of the BBC *Six O'Clock News* invasion.

'Here Is the Six O'Clock News: Beeb Man Sits on Lesbian'. The *Daily Star* was even less subtle: 'Loony Lezzies Attack TV Sue'. It referred to the women as 'a gaggle of screeching, lesbian harridans' as well as calling them 'dotty dykes' and 'hirsute harpies'. The *Daily Star* also patronizingly contrasted the protesters with 'the fair and feminine Sue Lawley', who came off-air to a standing ovation from the studio staff. My favourite headline though was from the *Pink Paper*, which subversively related the event as 'Dykes penetrate Auntie!'[73] Booan Temple has observed that 'Quite often activism by lesbians is treated as somehow amusing because of a deep-felt bigotry against lesbians' but she notes that despite the skewed coverage at the time, she heard from young gay people who were watching at home and felt empowered by the action.[74]

On 27 May, two of the women (credited with the pseudonyms Sarah Ponsonby and Eleanor Butler) appeared on the late-night television debate programme *Central Weekend Live*. The not-very-impressed presenter sternly asked the activists, 'Wasn't it a ridiculously irresponsible thing to have done?' and followed up with, 'If you asked everyone here what you did they'd all have remembered what you did but I doubt very many would know why you did it.' The activists brushed off her admonishments. One of them, credited as Eleanor Butler (actually Sally Francis), asked the audience, 'Did you hear Section 28 mentioned?' and several audience members shouted in the affirmative.

I can understand why people would find the invasions carried out by the women to be amusing. Suzanne Bowyer agrees with that. 'Part of it was the humour side of it – it appealed to people, the slightly *Carry On* vibe about it that people quite liked at the time. And that it's good-natured, nobody got hurt and both [the House of Lords and the BBC] pin-pointing a seat of power.' The invasions do feel a bit like scenes from a *Carry On* film. In fact, in *Carry On Girls* (1973), female activists sabotage a beauty contest by putting itching powder in the contestant's costumes, sprinkling sneezing powder everywhere, throwing oil on the floor and turning on the fire-system sprink-lers. Of course, *Carry On Girls* is a case of art imitating life, as in November 1970, while the Miss World beauty contest took place at the Royal Albert Hall, members of the Women's Liberation Movement threw flour and stink bombs and heckled the host Bob Hope.

I can also sympathize with Booan's frustration at the media coverage at the time. More was made of the protest itself than the reasons for it. And in some quarters of the media, the protesters were treated dismissively. We can at least console ourselves with the fact that it may have taken a few decades, but Booan and the other women have had the last laugh.

Chris Smith told me, 'One of the very useful things that Section 28 did was it succeeded in activating large numbers of LGBT people across the country in a way that nothing previ-ously had. Because it was so outrageous, everyone felt so upset about it, that they decided they needed to become politically active in fighting it. And that catalyst for political action was really valuable.'

The movement against Section 28 was actually a series of movements, some coordinated and connected to others, some involving small numbers of people working separately. While methods differed hugely, the ultimate goal was the same, and to me, all of these different approaches were important and necessary. Depending on your point of view, it's easy to tut-tut at the lobbyists for working within the system or to clutch your pearls at the women who invaded public spaces. But it is harder to quell a movement that is actually lots of movements, all using different tactics. As Jennie Wilson explains, 'The more sophisticated message about why it was bad out there [was] from particularly Artists Against the Clause, Stop the Clause, OLGA, the work that we were doing there, but then these stunts that caught the public's attention, who was never going to listen to those messages, but suddenly realized that there were people who were very agitated by it. It was a perfect package to be a perfect storm to make a lot of noise.'[75]

Naively, we might view the protests that took place in 1988 as a failure because they did not stop Section 28. Considering that public attitudes towards homosexuality were so negative in 1988, not to mention the hatred that a large segment of the press had sustained towards gay men and lesbians for years, it is unlikely that the campaigners would have been able to change large numbers of people's minds in a matter of months. However, where the campaigns were successful was in galvanizing large numbers of LGBTQ+ people to reject the status quo and demand equal rights.

Ironically, the Section 28 protests caused gay people to have fun, meeting each other, exchanging ideas, copping off and even falling in love. Chris Smith remembers one of the lobbying meetings that took place in the House of Commons:

> It packed out one of the large committee rooms in the Commons by activists from all around the country who had come, and there were three of us who were MPs who were there, to discuss with them what all the tactics should be. One of the people who came to do the lobbying was a very attractive young man who I noticed across the crowded room. We ended up living together for 24 years. So something good did come out of it!

The main impression I get from looking at all the photographs of the marches, rallies and meetings that took place up and down the country was that the faces of those involved conveyed emotions like happiness and pride. Stifyn Parri told me, 'On that day I remember joy and I remember power. Safety in numbers. And that made me come out. It wasn't about me being the only gay in the village, which I thought I was, but there were 18,000 people around me. And standing next to Ian McKellen I thought, "what am I hiding for?"'

Indeed, one of the key messages of the protests around Clause 28 was 'come out'. It is much easier to oppress a social group if they are in hiding and unknown to one another, sometimes even hiding from themselves. Fear of being found out is an effective method of social control. And it is much easier for people to hate an abstract concept as opposed to someone you know and like. But with social attitudes towards homosexuality hitting the worst ever levels measured, the late 1980s were not an easy time to tell friends, family and work colleagues that you were gay. It often involved an emotional or difficult conversation and there was always the risk of rejection – a risk I decided to take.

*

While studying for A Levels, I took the bus to the Big City (Newcastle-upon-Tyne) and bought a book written by Terry Sanderson called *How to Be a Happy Homosexual*. Sanderson had been writing a column called MediaWatch for *Gay Times* since 1982, charting press homophobia as it was spewed out, month by month. His book had a part on the effects of Section 28 and there was a chapter on coming out to your family, detailing how important it was and giving advice on how to go about it. Because of this book I decided to take the plunge, preparing my mother a few weeks beforehand, stating that I had a secret but wasn't ready to tell her just yet.

'Have you murdered someone?' she asked.

I had to reassure her that my secret didn't involve burying bodies and when I did tell them, my parents were supportive although concerned for me, realizing that life might not always be easy. My mother joined a parents' group called Acceptance and set about getting herself up to speed on gay rights, then embarking on a vigorous letter-writing campaign to a range of magazines and newspapers, asking for more representation of gay people on the television shows she watched, as well as contacting her GP and asking for information leaflets for gay helplines to be put on display in the waiting room. In 1993 we ended up being interviewed by Linda Grant for an article in *The Independent* where we both described the effect of my coming out on the family. I didn't think about it but my coming out was a small political act of defiance against Section 28 and what it stood for, inspired by a key message from activists of the time.

Yes, the fractures still existed, but for the most part the idea – Stop Section 28 – was able to override all that. And in the years following the passing of the act, one thing was clear: the issue was not going to go away.

5
Under the Shadow of Section 28

I am on a date. He must think something of me because he has bought a new coat from Burton (you get bags more buzz at Burton's, as the advert says) for the occasion and stumped up for train tickets to London for the two of us. We meet at the station and I see that he is carrying a copy of a magazine called *Private Eye*.

'What's that about?'

'It's a comedy magazine about politics and stuff.'

'Oh. Are you into politics?'

'Yes, a bit.'

'I don't know what I'll do if the Conservatives get in again. That'd be four times in a row!'

A pause.

'Actually, I voted Conservative last time.'

Another pause.

I say, 'I don't think I've met many people who've voted Conservative.' I think, 'How can he be gay?' Then, 'Don't spoil the day by making a thing of it.' I make a mental note to bring it up another time.

We have a nice day out in London, visiting Gay's the Word

bookshop, First Out café and Harrods, where we buy branded tea towels for our mothers so they can show them off to their friends and we can swish about for the rest of the day with Harrods plastic bags. Everyone will be impressed by that!

Towards the end of the trip we go for a walk along the Thames and then collapse exhausted on a park bench near the Palace of Westminster. A rather skimpily dressed young lady stands near us, hovering a bit too close to the kerb.

'Watch out, she's plying her wares,' says my date. I'm shocked. I'd never seen what we used to call a prostitute and now call a sex worker. I'm also impressed – he's so worldly to notice things like that.

Then a bus pulls up. The lady's elderly mother gets off and they hug and walk off together.

We exchange ashamed glances, then laugh. 'Well, that'll teach me to judge,' he says.

There is a long pause.

He says, 'I think I'm falling in love with you.'

I tell him I feel the same way. We check that nobody is looking, then surreptitiously hold hands.

I was nineteen and he was several years older. It felt natural, and at the time I didn't even notice that I was sitting in the shadow of a building where people I'd never met had decreed that my relationship would be illegal.

They *really* didn't want me to be gay. But here I was anyway, flaunting it (sort of), right in front of them. Perhaps it was because they'd left it too late to stop me. But now Section 28 was here, those kids who came after me would be different. They'd all grow up to lead happy, normal, moral, family lives. Wouldn't they?

Goodbye Maggie, hello John

In 1989, a memorable headline on the front page of the *Pink Paper* read 'Maggie's Unbelievable U-Turn Sees Section Scrapped'. A closer look revealed the publication date to be 1 April. Section 28 wasn't going anywhere. But instead, Mrs Thatcher's days as prime minister were numbered. Opposition to her brusquely regal style had been growing for years. The satirical puppet show *Spitting Image* had a sketch where Thatcher treats her cabinet to a meal at a restaurant. A waitress asks how she'd like her steak and she replies, 'Oh, raw please.' 'What about the vegetables?' asks the waitress. 'Oh, they'll have the same as me,' says Maggie. Perceivably excited by the birth of her first grandchild on 3 March 1989, she greeted the press with, 'We have become a grandmother.' This use of what looked like an appropriation of the royal 'we' was commented on as a sign of how imperious Mrs Thatcher had become.

Then there was the Poll Tax. A new system of community tax was introduced in 1989 in Scotland, then England and Wales in 1990. The previous system had been based upon the notional rental value of your house. However, the Poll Tax was based on charging each person for the services provided in their community. Students and the unemployed only paid 20 per cent but it was seen as unfair, particularly towards less well-off members of society. Mass protests occurred across the UK and a demonstration that started at Kennington Park and ended at Trafalgar Square on 31 March 1989 involved between 180,000 and 250,000 people, with some participants rioting. The tax was seen as an out-of-touch policy and an example of Tory disregard of working-class people. Afterwards, a couple of by-elections in 1990 resulted in Conservative losses, causing worries about how they would do at the next general election. Mrs Thatcher survived an initial leadership bid in December 1989 but then Michael Heseltine, a former Secretary of State for Defence, challenged her for leadership on 14 November 1990. She won but not by enough to stop a second round of voting. Her cabinet advised her that they doubted she would win and so she resigned. A second vote, held on 27 November, saw John Major, who had been recently appointed as Chancellor of the Exchequer, winning enough votes for the other candidates to withdraw.

After the oft-dramatic reign of Mrs Thatcher, Mr Major was not seen as especially exciting (like Maggie, his *Spitting Image* puppet talked about vegetables but in his case it involved excruciatingly boring conversations about peas with his wife Norma). Under him, and to the surprise of many, the Tories won the 1992 general election, with 14 million votes to Labour's 11.5 million (translating to a reduced majority of only 21 seats). At the 1993 Conservative Party conference, Major announced a 'Back to Basics' campaign, which was meant to pertain to a wide range of issues including the economy and policing. However, it was interpreted as a kind of return to 1950s morality and the idea of traditional family values. Subsequently, it did not look good when numerous Conservative politicians were exposed in tabloid stories with their trousers down, so to speak. Two of these were Michael Brown and Jerry Hayes. In May 1994 the *News of the World* published photographs of Brown (Conservative, Brigg and Cleethorpes) on holiday in Barbados with a twenty-year-old gay man. Had nobody told him that the age of consent was still 21? The headline was 'Lawmaker as Law Breaker', resulting in Brown resigning as a government whip and coming out as gay. Hayes (Conservative, Harlow) was outed as bisexual by *The Mirror* in January 1997, which reported that he was having a long-term affair with another man. The age of consent for gay men was starting to look rather silly by this point, and Edwina Currie (Conservative, South Derbyshire), who, years earlier, had briskly congratulated Chris Smith on his coming out, tabled an amendment to the Criminal Justice and Public Order Bill in February 1994 to set the age of consent at sixteen for everyone. It was defeated by just 27 votes, although a subsequent amendment reduced the age of consent to eighteen for gay men.

The Tories continued to hold power for almost a decade after Section 28 was implemented. This chapter considers what life was like for people who were affected by the legislation during that decade. We'll cover educational policy and how it was applied to schools, along with the effects that it had on pupils and teachers. Then we'll look at what Section 28 meant for lesbian mothers and the arts, particularly arts groups who relied on funding from council grants. Finally, there's a description of the formation of two groups, Stonewall and OutRage!, both of which had the goal of tackling homophobia in British society, although they went about it in very different ways.

Teaching sex

If homosexuality couldn't be promoted in schools, then where did that leave sex education, particularly at a point where HIV-AIDS therapies were undeveloped and the need for safe sex was paramount? The national curriculum, established by the

Education Reform Act (1988), gave the government centralized control over what could be taught. The Science Curriculum did cover some aspects of sex education, including HIV and AIDS, in a limited way, although this was a requirement of all schools. Sex education beyond this was covered by the Education (No. 2) Act (1986), which left it up to governing bodies to decide, as long as it was carried out with regard to 'moral considerations and the value of family life', whatever that meant, thanks to Lord Buckmaster's intervention in the Education Act, outlined earlier.[1]

A new Education Act in 1993 was more specific, allowing the biological aspects of HIV, AIDS, other sexually transmitted infections and sexual behaviour to be included in the national curriculum. Non-biological aspects (such as discussion of relationships or consent) were not allowed, and parents could withdraw their children from sex education classes if they wished to, without giving a reason. In order to keep Local Education Authorities out of the picture, the actual policy was left to the governors of schools to decide.

Then a circular on sex education was put out by the government in 1994, intended as a replacement for the previous 1987 circular, which had defined homosexual acts as buggery and gross indecency. This new circular still noted that 'buggery' and 'gross indecency' were offences unless carried out by men aged over 21 together and in private (although this would be reduced to eighteen once the Criminal Justice Bill was enacted). Despite the outraged, outdated legal terminology, the circular seemed to be engaging in a bit of damage control regarding the ongoing criticisms of Section 28. It reminded everybody that Section 28 *only* applied to the activities of local authorities as opposed to those of governing bodies and school staff. In terms of making the moral framework for sex education more specific, it had this to say:

> The Secretary of State believes that schools' programmes for sex education should therefore aim to present the facts in an objective, balanced and sensitive manner, set within a clear framework of values, and an awareness of the law on sexual behaviour. Pupils should accordingly be encouraged to appreciate the value of stable family life, marriage and the responsibilities of parenthood. They should be helped to consider the importance of self-restraint, dignity, respect for themselves and others, acceptance of responsibility, sensitivity towards the needs of others, loyalty and fidelity.

Did you clock the word *marriage* halfway through? Although heterosexuality is not mentioned in this framework, the fact that at the time marriage was only allowed for opposite-sex couples strongly implied that the circular wanted everyone to be heterosexual. Elsewhere in the wording, teachers were discouraged from providing specific advice to pupils. It recommended that if an individual pupil approached them to ask for help about contraception or other aspects of sexual behaviour, the teacher should encourage the pupil to seek advice from their parents or a GP or school doctor/nurse if appropriate. If the pupil appeared to be at 'moral or physical risk or in breach of the law' then the head teacher should be notified. It seems sad that the pupil's own choice in who they want to confide in gets completely disregarded. It's likely they will have thought carefully about which adult to approach regarding a possibly embarrassing and confidential matter. If they hadn't already talked to their parents about it, then there was probably a good reason. So to ask a teacher for advice and be told, 'I can't help, see a doctor or nurse' must have seemed like a rejection of trust.

In teaching about HIV and AIDS, schools had to 'aim to offer balanced and factual information and to acknowledge the major moral and ethical issues involved'. Ian McKellen told me, 'Although Section 28 was debated almost entirely in terms of schools, when it was passed it said that it had no jurisdiction over what schools actually did. So it was all a bit of a red herring.' And even though Section 28 specified what local authorities were allowed to do with respect to schools, not schools themselves, the wording was often either interpreted as an implicit message not to discuss homosexuality in schools or misunderstood as a blanket ban on schools discussing homosexuality. The government's circular was too little too late.

School's not out

In the early 1990s a music style called grunge travelled from Seattle, settling for a time in the UK. It was typified by groups such as Nirvana, Pearl Jam and Soundgarden, its uniform charity-shop chic: check shirts and grandad cardigans, topped off with lank, unkempt hair. Grunge had a nihilistic, angsty feel – vocalists mumbled, moaned and screamed their way through songs that had equally traumatic lyrics. Soundgarden wished for a black hole sun to come, while the dark king of grunge, Kurt Cobain, sang that it was fun to lose and to pretend. Tragically, he committed suicide on 5 April 1994. The anguish and alienation of grunge provides a fitting soundtrack for the Section 28 years as the LGBTQ+ youth of the UK suffered needlessly.

Section 28 made school life tense, frustrating and scary for LGBTQ+ teachers. On the face of it, such teachers should have had little to worry about. There was nothing in the section which said that you could be sacked for being openly gay or lesbian. And a legal opinion commissioned from Lord Gifford by the Association of London Authorities and National Council for Civil Liberties had noted that technically, teachers could still protect students against homophobic bullying as they have a duty to protect pupils' welfare.[2] However, the wording of the section made interpretation difficult. What exactly did 'promote homosexuality' mean? Even if being an out gay teacher was not promoting homosexuality, what if it caused pupils to start asking you questions about your life and relationships? At what point does answering such questions start to look as if it could be interpreted as promoting homosexuality? And what if a child comes to you and says, 'I think I might be gay, I'm being bullied by other kids and I feel like I have no one to talk to and I might as well kill myself'? Is reassuring the child along the lines of, 'It's perfectly OK to be gay' promoting homosexuality?

Tim Puntis was a teacher working in state schools in Edinburgh. He described how, due to the ambiguous wording of Section 28, it was open to different interpretations and so school management interpreted it as strongly as possible since nobody wanted to be the test case. This resulted in a lot of self-censorship. Puntis also notes how Section 28 normalized homophobia, stating that after it became law, homophobia in schools reached the worst levels he had known since the passage of the 1967 Sexual Offences Act.[3]

What if teachers fell in love? Nia Griffith taught in a large comprehensive school and was in a relationship with another teacher. She never mentioned anything about her personal life at work and feels ashamed that she did not challenge male teachers in the staffroom when they exchanged homophobic 'banter' since she was already mocked as a 'leftie feminist'. Worse still was the fact that the law instilled a fear in her that made it impossible to challenge homophobic bullying among pupils. She recalls that homophobic language was commonplace in classrooms but she believed that she risked being accused of 'promoting homosexuality' and marched to the headmaster's office if she called it out. The best she felt able to manage was asking such pupils if they thought such language could be a bit hurtful.[4]

There was also the question of what material could be taught. Some teachers were able to find ways to smuggle LGBTQ+ inclusion into the classroom, particularly in English literature and drama lessons, where books or plays containing gay characters could be used in the curriculum. But in the main, there was a risk in using such books, particularly if they presented gay people as sexually active, happy or even ordinary. Sue O'Sullivan, of Sheba Feminist Press, describes how in the mid-1990s she was at a secondary school fair in Stoke Newington, an area which has a large concentration of lesbian mothers. She went to the fair to buy some books on a stall run by her friend, noting that while there were books on black and Jewish history there was nothing on homosexuality.

She asked the friend why this was the case and the friend said that the librarian, who was a lesbian, had said that it was too dangerous 'because of Clause 28'.[5]

And, as an example of how far Section 28 could be extended, consider the case of Calderdale Borough Council in West Yorkshire, which, in 1994, decided to ban its local library from stocking the gay newspaper the *Pink Paper*. The decision was challenged by Barry Winchester, who ran the local AIDS and HIV information group. The council told him that if it allowed the newspaper to appear in the library, then they ran the risk of falling foul of Section 28. It took months of lawyers' letters before the council overturned the ban, although it refused to pay any of the legal costs of the Judicial Review challenge that Winchester brought.[6] Additionally, in 1998 Birmingham City Council stopped the publication of an information booklet aimed at young people that covered a range of topics such as eating disorders, racism and bereavement, because there were sections on sexuality and dealing with prejudice. Gay rights campaigners chalked up a victory, at least, over Shropshire County Council, which had removed funding from a Lesbian and Gay Youth group that provided support and counselling services, getting the money restored.[7]

Not all teachers stayed in the closet, although there were often consequences for this. Sue Sanders says that as a white middle-class woman, she was able to use her privilege to be out as a teacher. If pupils yelled that she was a lesbian, she would say, 'That's not news, why do you feel the need to shout it out?' One day, someone wrote 'Sue Sanders is a lesbian' on the blackboard. Sanders rubbed it off and allowed the class to have a brief chat about it at the end of the class after they had finished their work (they finished their work very quickly that day). However, a parent of one of the students complained about her and she was told by the headteacher that she would not be allowed to teach that student again.[8]

However, if Section 28 made things bad for LGBT teachers, it was even worse for pupils. In 1988, Patrick Strudwick was one of the first children to learn what it meant to be taught under Section 28 legislation. One of his teachers had just shown the class a series of sex education videos, and then asked pupils what they thought about them. Eleven-year-old Patrick put his hand up and (rather bravely) said that the videos had been good but none of them had mentioned gay sex. The teacher responded simply by saying, 'That is not sex.' Strudwick notes the large amount of ignorance surrounding gay sex when he was growing up. He didn't know, for example, that men could have sex in the missionary position or that lubricant greatly improved things. This was during a time when most people in the UK only had access to four television channels and a handful of radio stations. There was no Internet so if you wanted to find something out, your options were much more limited than they currently are.

Although Section 2 of Clause 28 stated that none of the prohibitions on promoting homosexuality would apply if the intention was to prohibit the spread of disease, it is clear that messages about safer sex were absent from the curriculum at Strudwick's school. He wishes that he had been taught how to come out, how to deal with homophobic bullying and how to say no to a man who wanted sex.[9]

What made Clause 28 so cruel for children is that most of them were too young to know that there was something missing and if, like Strudwick, they were aware of the gap, they wouldn't have known why. It is unlikely that most children would have been up to date on the British political and legal history of the recent past so they would have been unaware that a law had been passed banning so-called 'promotion' of homosexuality. And, as Strudwick points out, Section 28 pretty much forbade discussion of itself in a classroom environment. As a nod to the 1990s film *Fight Club*, the first rule of Section 28 is that you don't talk about Section 28.

Kat, who is queer and non-binary, was in school for the entirety of the time that Section 28 was in force. They told me how sex education at their school was sparse at best. There was

absolutely nothing on sexuality outside the bounds of procreative sex within a heterosexual marriage. Not even stuff on consent and talking to a partner about sex, let alone any mention that sexualities other than heterosexuality existed. The worst exercise was finding magazines and cutting out pictures of families from them. Practically all of them were straight, white, nuclear families – mum, dad, a couple of kids – and I remember feeling really alienated from the whole exercise because it didn't reflect my complex Indian kinship network. Naturally it didn't reflect queer families in any way.

In 2019, in the first series of the reality competition TV show *Drag Race UK*, one of the contestants, Divina De Campo, who is gay and non-binary, spoke about being bullied at school and how Section 28 was so damaging:

It just erases gay people completely. There was no discussion around it, so you have no understanding as a gay person that there can be a different way of living, because you never get told that. That never happens, whereas for a straight person, you are constantly fed, 'You are correct, you are right, you are valid.' You don't get that as a gay person . . . Kids in the playground pushing and shoving and calling you a 'fag'. Throwing their drinks on you. Because of Section 28 it meant that a lot of teachers felt like they couldn't step in.

That lack of validation, coupled with bullying, can have consequences throughout a life, just as a stone thrown into a pool of water will inevitably result in ripples outwards. Athlete Beth Fisher has described how she came to hate the word 'lesbian' because for the majority of her life she never heard it used in an affectionate way. 'The word in school was never used in an endearing manner. It was used as a word to purposely offend and humiliate girls who didn't fit in with the norm – those who dared to be a little different or wear something different.' She wonders if without Section 28 she would have been able to come out sooner; perhaps she would have bunked off school less and maybe her schoolwork and exam results would have been better.[10] Politician Liam McClelland was born in 1988, the year the clause became law. He describes how at secondary school he was told that all gay people should be lined up against a wall and shot. Faced with a lack of information and support at school, McClelland went online to find others to talk to, which resulted in him being groomed and sexually abused.

He attempted suicide on several occasions. He attributes the early lack of positive role models and advice as leading him to have unhealthy relationships, which contributed towards a later drug addiction and HIV+ diagnosis.[11]

And while teachers may have felt unable to intervene in cases of homophobic bullying, imagine how it must have been for the recipients of such bullying. The playwright Chris Woodley describes how despite having forward-thinking parents and coming out at fourteen, he faced the five worst years of his life at an all-boys school. 'I was spat at, sworn at, shoved around, belittled, bullied and abused on a regular basis, like so many others. The school did very little.'[12]

Section 28 affected the atmosphere in colleges as well as schools. In January 1989, a young man at Shrewsbury College of Arts and Technology suggested that the students' union start a gay society. Senior staff at the college asked him to leave, citing Section 28 as the reason.[13] And Kat told me about a relationship they had with a girl at sixth form. 'It was incredibly difficult because we were equipped with precisely none of the things we needed to have a caring, fulfilling relationship. We barely had words for what we were, let alone how to see and understand each other. We were ostracized by the rest of sixth form and basically had to choose between acceptance from our peers or being totally shunned.'

Individual examples are useful in that they give a vivid and relatable impression of people's experience, but there's always the possibility that the most shocking cases have been cherry-picked in order to paint an especially awful picture. Combining such cases with larger-scale evidence is more helpful. So how about we consider a few surveys?

In 1999, a study of teachers at 307 secondary schools in England and Wales indicated 'almost universal' awareness of homophobic bullying among pupils, with more than one in four teachers saying they were aware of homophobic physical bullying. Some schools had policies on bullying and confidentiality, but these polices rarely referred to gay and lesbian issues.[14] A study of abusive language was published in 2001. The study asked 377 English and Welsh fourteen- and fifteen-year-olds to list the words 'people at school use for slagging someone off' and then to put a tick next to the ones which the children considered to be the worst. Almost 6,000 terms were reported (that's a lot of slagging off), with 31 per cent of them receiving a tick. The teenagers came up with 590 words that were classed as homophobic. These included terms such as *lez*, *dyke*, *fanny-licker*, *gaylord*, *bender*, *knobsucker*, *poof*, *batty-boy*, *faggot*, *pansy*, *shit-stabber* and *shirt-lifter* (I can almost hear the clang of the school bell calling me back to class when I read them). At 10 per cent of the total set of words, this was fewer than the words classed as sexist (28 per cent) but more than racist words (7 per cent). What stands out for me, though, is the fact that pupils didn't seem to judge the homophobic words as particularly offensive – such words received a tick 28 per cent of the time whereas racist words received a tick 55 per cent of the time.[15]

At this point it's also worth considering a couple of surveys into homophobic bullying in schools that were carried out by Stonewall (described in more detail later in this chapter), one of 1,145 LGBT secondary school students, published in 2007, the other of 2,043 teachers, published in 2009. The study of pupils found that 65 per cent of them had experienced direct bullying, 60 per cent had heard phrases like 'that's so gay' used pejoratively at school, 97 per cent had heard other phrases like *poof, dyke* and *bender* often or frequently, and only 23 per cent had been told that homophobic bullying was wrong at their school.[16]

The study of teachers found that 90 per cent of secondary school teachers and 44 per cent of primary school teachers reported that children and young people regularly experienced homophobic bullying, name calling or harassment, regardless of their sexual orientation. Half of those who were aware of such bullying said the vast majority of incidents went unreported. The only other form of bullying that was more prevalent was due to bullying related to weight. Some 90 per cent of teachers had received no specific training on how to prevent or respond to homophobic bullying and 28 per cent of secondary school staff said they would not be confident in supporting a child who came out to them.[17] Both of these studies took place a few years after Section 28 had been repealed. It is not a stretch to imagine that the situation would have been even worse before that.

Using the word *gay* as an insult was one of the more insidious trends of the Section 28 era, although it was most likely an enthusiastically adopted u.s. import. In the early 2000s, I recall hearing a couple of nice female undergraduate students in the corridor outside my office complaining that an exam timetable was 'gay' (meaning they didn't like the timing of their exams). In the 1970s, people kept banging on about how *gay* used to mean happy and lively but those awful homosexuals had appropriated the word and changed the meaning. Now I was the one complaining about the appropriation of the word. Around the same time, posters appeared around my university declaring, 'Homophobia is gay.' I can see what they were trying to do but it felt like a bit of an own goal.

Pretended family relationships

In 1980s and 1990s Britain, it was pretty much unheard of for two men to raise a child together. Adoption was nigh-on impossible and surrogacy arrangements were rare. If a heterosexual couple divorced, custody of any children was almost always granted to the woman. So, while Section 28's reference to 'the acceptability of homosexuality as a pretended family relationship' did not specify gender, at the time it usually referred to families where the parenting was carried out by one or two women. In calling such families 'pretended', the idea of a lesbian mother was effectively denied in law.

However, if we accept that gay and lesbian families are real, then the term 'pretended family relationship' gives Section 28 a bizarre meaning – that the law was made to stop cases where, say, two lesbians who don't even like each other very much adopt a child and pretend to be a family, perhaps so one of them can inherit money from a wealthy aunt who has stipulated that such a family must exist. It sounds like the premise of an especially corny sitcom (and of course, in the last episode the women would end up falling in love anyway).

Sue Sanders and Gill Spraggs, writing just after the passage of Section 28 into law, noted that there were indications that judges were becoming hostile in their attitudes towards lesbian mothers in custody cases and that such women were likely to conceal their sexuality and relationships out of fear of losing their children or having their children victimized at school.[18] Jill Butler, a lawyer specializing in lesbian custody cases, had voiced her concern over Section 28 in April 1988: 'I think undoubtedly anything which contributes to a climate of bigotry will hinder lesbians from getting custody. Anything which singles out a minority also legitimizes prejudice. It is a dangerous law.' Butler describes how one judge had said homosexuality was not natural and animals didn't do it, forbidding the claimant from meeting other lesbians.[19] In December 1990, Butler was quoted as saying that she'd never had a case where a lesbian mother hadn't been asked questions in detail about her sex life. Typical questions included 'Will you have sex in front of the children?', 'Do you make a noise when you have sex?' and 'Do you use appliances?' In answer to the latter, the witness reportedly replied, 'We've got a Hoover.'[20]

In April 1988, a woman called Judith was quoted in *The Guardian*, describing how she was treated in court when she tried to get a restraining order against her violent estranged husband. When she said that she was a lesbian, the focus shifted onto her sexual identity and current relationship rather than the husband's violence. She said, 'It was amazing how all the men in the court, whatever their age or their position, were united against lesbianism. My husband and the judge were on the same side.' She was accused of feminizing her son by dressing him in girls' clothing and was even banned for fifteen months from having any sort of contact with her partner, despite the fact that the two women worked together. The custody case lasted five years, resulting in Judith and her husband getting joint custody.[21]

And in August 1990, the *Daily Mail* reported on a custody battle for a six-year-old girl between a father and 'his lesbian ex-wife' with one of the judges, Lord Justice Glidewell, quoted as saying 'A lesbian relationship is an unusual background in which to bring up a child . . . It is undesirable that this child should learn or understand at an early age the nature of her mother's relationship.'[22]

Sue O'Sullivan has spoken of another effect of the wording 'pretended families'. During the protests around Section 28, efforts were made to support and protect the rights of lesbian mothers to have and look after children; in other words, to say that lesbian mothers *were* part of a real family. However, Sue points out that 'some of the more radical or critical feminist positions on the normal family, the accepted family, were muted because you had to say, well, we're not a pretended family, we're a real family. The discussion wasn't all one way or the other, but there was a slight problem.'[23]

Arts attack

The effects of Clause 28 were already beginning to show for those involved in the arts, even before the legislation had passed. In *EastEnders*, the relationship between Colin and Barry ended in 1987 on New Year's Eve. Gary Hailes, who played Barry, later claimed that 'there was a whole load of storylines that were dropped because of Clause 28 . . . The BBC found themselves in a very difficult position . . . It got cut because it didn't fit within the realms of Clause 28 so they changed it and replaced it with something else. And that put the brakes on what they could do with the characters. There was a point where Barry became straight and got a girlfriend.'[24] I asked Michael Cashman, who played Colin, whether that had been his impression. He said that studio bosses never told him to 'calm it down, stop giving interviews, stop going on marches' and he wonders if instead Barry's return to the closet was in fact more a reflection of what was happening in the lives of some working-class young men around this time, with homophobia at its peak. Whatever the reason, the writers were certainly cognizant of Section 28. When filming one episode, Colin walked into the Queen Vic (the pub in *EastEnders*), and the actor Mike Reid ad-libbed, 'Here he comes, Clause 28!' The line was allowed to stay in.[25] I admitted to Michael Cashman that I had been upset when Colin left *EastEnders* in 1989 (the writers had given him multiple sclerosis and he didn't even get to walk off with a boyfriend). But he reminded me that the character eventually got a happy ending, returning in 2016 to invite his friend Dot Cotton to his wedding.

The BBC had a headache around the screening of a television play by Leslie Stewart called *Two of Us*. Produced and directed by Roger Tonge, the play was a love story between two working-class boys of school-leaving age, Matthew (played by Jason Rush) and Phil (Lee Whitlock). It was meant to be shown on BBC Two as part of the schools' 'Daytime on Two' slot but nervous executives pulled it, then decided that it would air on 25 March 1988 at the much later time of 11.30 p.m. *The Sun* was not happy: 'it is wildly irresponsible for the BBC to screen the play. It will be irresponsible for any teacher to show it to his pupils . . . They should ensure that any videos stay where they belong. Locked away in the closet.'[26]

Luckily, the media furore meant that *this* pupil had caught wind of the play and so I stayed up to watch it downstairs on the living-room TV while my parents slept upstairs. I loved it. It was the first realistic depiction I had seen of the kind of relationship I desperately wanted to have. There were longing looks at the local swimming baths, some camp comic relief provided by Kathy Burke in an early role, a holiday to the coastal resort of Seaford, lots of 1980s saxophone/synthesizer music and then, an oddly jarring ending. Phil's girlfriend Sharon shows up at the beach and the two of them go off together, leaving Matthew alone.

Later, I learned that the ending had been hastily changed. In the original version, Phil takes Sharon back to the train station, sees her on the train and runs back to the beach to be with Matthew (romantically calling 'Oi, Maff-you!' from a cliff-top). So not only was *Two of Us* shown at practically midnight, it had been altered so one boy magically becomes heterosexual and gets a happy ending, and the remaining gay one gets a whole lot of nothing. At least the original ending was restored for a broadcast that occurred two years later on 2 February 1990, by which time Auntie Beeb was a bit less antsy about Section 28.

If there was confusion at the BBC, the situation in theatres was worse. Gay Sweatshop had held a meeting after Christmas 1987 to discuss Clause 28 and, as a result, a group called the Arts Lobby was formed in early 1988 to campaign on attacks on freedoms restricted by Section 28. Michael Cashman told me, 'When you accept that local authorities have concert halls and theatres and libraries, to suggest, without giving a definition of promotion, that a local authority couldn't do that, suggests that there could be censorship and that's what also brought out a large number of people who might perhaps not otherwise have come out.'

On 25 January 1988, the Arts Lobby held a memorable and well-attended press conference at the Playhouse Theatre, organized by Ian McKellen and Michael Cashman as well as the playwright Martin Sherman and the director Sean Mathias. Members of the House of Lords were bussed there from Parliament. Michael remembers a wonderful designer who stupefied them all when he took out a cast of Michelangelo's David and said, 'This would be the effect of Section 28.' He then produced a mallet and smashed it. The press and photographers loved it but most of them hadn't realized what was going to happen so had missed the photo opportunity. Cannily, the designer said, 'Don't worry, I've got another one, I'll do it again.' The Arts Lobby won the support of numerous prominent figures in the arts. Its achievements involved campaigning to support the rights of lesbian and gay students at a music college and winning back funding for a gay play that had been threatened.[27]

But perhaps its most high-profile work involved the organization of a gala benefit at Piccadilly Theatre on 5 June 1988 called 'Before the Act'. It was produced by a lesbian theatre group called 20th Century Vixen, run by Wendy Martin and Trina Cornwell. Michael Cashman told me that they'd introduced themselves to him at the Never Going Underground demonstration in Manchester and that it had been the start of a fruitful collaboration: 'It was a pretty important day in terms of forming relationships that would go on to lead to bigger and greater change.' The benefit was directed by Richard Eyre and devised by Michael Cashman, Ian McKellen, Martin Sherman, Sean Mathias and the composer Stephen Oliver.[28]

Ian McKellen explained to me that the gala's concept was

that all the material in the show would have been written by a gay person. So we did Tchaikovsky, poetry by Sappho, extracts from plays by Orton and Wilde. Lots to choose from. And it's the most distinguished group of performers ever assembled I think for any charity. The spirit was just overwhelming. It was easy for people in the arts to latch on to because they could feel, straight or not, that they were being attacked by Section 28.

Katrina Buchanan, from the Hot Doris Band, a four-woman a cappella group that opened the show, described how Alan Bennett had been approached to ask if they could use some of his work. In relation to his sexuality he apparently said, 'In my time I've had a little bit of both and not enough of either.'[29] Stifyn Parri, who also performed in the benefit, told me that he was starstruck by his co-stars: 'I was working with all sorts of people, Dames, Pet Shop Boys, Harold Pinter, Derek Jacobi. I remember sitting in a rehearsal in the stalls with Ian McKellen. The Pet Shop Boys were sound checking and I said to Ian, "I will never forget this."'

It was the worst of times to come out, so not everyone wanted to be involved. Michael Cashman describes how 'a raft of "known-to-be-gay" performers were suddenly "unavailable" or heading "out of town" for the weekend.' He and fellow organizers joked that there must be one bus going around collecting them all. And the lyricist and composer Stephen Sondheim refused to give his consent to use his lyrics due to the 'exclusivity of the evening'.[30] But despite the absence of some notable names, the line-up was dazzling and Michael Cashman recalls that Ian McKellen 'certainly used his Filofax – there's an old expression – to get people there'. Among the 320 performers were Peggy Ashcroft, Jane Asher, Vanessa Redgrave, Alan Bates, Judi Dench, Hugh Quarshie, Miranda Richardson, Timothy West, Rupert Graves, Patrick Stewart, Sheila Hancock, Joan Plowright and Stephen Fry. Performances included a sketch written by the co-creator of *EastEnders*, Tony Holland, featuring stars from both *EastEnders* and *Brookside*, and there were scenes from the plays *Bent*, *Entertaining Mr Sloane* and *Hands across the Sea*. The second half opened with the first ever live performance by the Pet Shop Boys, while the Medici String Quartet performed music by Cole Porter, Tchaikovsky, Leonard Bernstein, Peter Maxwell Davies, Francis Poulenc and Benjamin Britten. There was a dance performance from the group DV8, and one part of the evening involved an anthology of love poetry, which included work by Oscar Wilde, Sappho, Tennessee Williams and Carol Ann Duffy.

Some of those present made impassioned speeches about the effects of Section 28. Journalist and broadcaster Anna Raeburn said, 'I'm here because I oppose Section 28. I oppose it for everything that it stands for and everything that it opens the doors to.' Richard Sandells of Gay Sweatshop said, 'This is primarily an attack on the civil liberties of individual men and women. It's a threat to the happiness and dignity of every lesbian and gay man in the country. If any of you have listened to any of the debates of Parliament you'll know that this is nothing less than parliamentary queer-bashing.'

At the end of the benefit, the entire cast came on stage and threw pink roses into the audience. Michael Cashman proudly remembers how 'people just rose to their feet and cheered and cheered and cheered. It was very special.' The benefit raised £15,107 to counter the effects of Section 28.[31] If I had a time machine, I'd set the dials to 5 June 1988 so I could be in the audience.

There had been concern that Section 28 would not only apply to schools but would restrict galleries and theatres that received council funding. In April 1988, one of OLGA's founders, Eric Presland, reported how the name of his theatre company, Homo Promos, was deemed to be problematic. The Oval House Arts Centre had agreed to host a production of the company's new comedy, *Double Vision*. However, the name of the group just wouldn't do, and he was told he could change it to 'Not Homo Promos'. Eric, faced with little choice, made the change before it was done for him.[32]

In the ensuing weeks, some theatres responded with defiance. For example, in June 1988, Newham Council supported the staging of a play called *The Public* at the Theatre Royal Stratford East. The play, which had sexual themes, was written by the Spanish writer Federico García Lorca, a gay man who had been murdered by supporters of Franco in the Spanish Civil War.[33] The performance was viewed as something of a test case to see whether Section 28 legislation would be applied to theatrical performances (it wasn't). The same month there was controversy around a gay and lesbian exhibition at the New Victoria Theatre Newcastle (Staffordshire), organized by the group Stoke-on-Trent Repeal Section 28. Local Conservative politician Roger Ibbs threatened to petition the council to axe grants for the theatre.[34]

In the same way that performers came together for the 'Before the Act' gala benefit, Section 28 also united comic book artists who collaborated on an anthology called AARGH! (Artists against Rampant Government Homophobia!) which was published in October 1988. AARGH! was organized by Alan Moore, who formed the publishing company Mad Love to release it, and the book featured 33 comic strips from artists including Robert Crumb, Posy Simmonds, Alexei Sayle, David Shenton and Neil Gaiman. They included a Section 28 trivia quiz, a parody of the 'Protect and Survive' Nuclear War government advice campaign, a children's storybook and a superhero comic strip. Proceeds went to the Organisation for Lesbian and Gay Action.

Another example of fightback occurred the following January, courtesy of a relatively new television channel called Channel 4, which has been mentioned briefly in previous chapters. While the BBC was initially cowed by Section 28, trendy, bolshy Channel 4 thumbed its nose at it. It commissioned a new series called *Out on Tuesday*, which was fittingly scheduled to air its first episode on Valentine's Day. Its editor, Mandy Merck, was quoted as saying that if young people are watching and want to learn about gay lifestyles,

then they will find out! . . . The question we are asking is can homosexuality be 'promoted'? It is patterned so strongly in childhood that I don't think any amount of advertising could influence sexuality to that extent. The House of Commons, by any stretch of the imagination, is not expert on sexual orientation. MPs take up these causes to add a bit of prestige to their name.

But I hope that eventually this clause will be shown to be illegal and against the Bill of Human Rights. As a lesbian myself, I am outraged by it and most thinking people would agree with that.[35]

Out on Tuesday connects to other aspects of our story. The producer for the first series of the programme was Clare Bevan, who had been the picture and music researcher for the award-winning (and controversial) experimental film *Framed Youth*.[36] And the production company that created content for *Out on Tuesday* was called Abseil. For the first two years that it ran, the programme ended with Abseil's logo – a silhouette of a woman sliding down a rope, a not so subtle nod to the women who had invaded the House of Lords.[37]

Prior to coming out to my parents, I'd watched *Out on Tuesday* on my new portable television in my bedroom, sitting as close as I could to the screen with the volume at whisper level. Since its creation in 1982, Channel 4 had initially been aimed at a fringe audience with some programmes appearing left-leaning politically while other shows were intellectually demanding compared to the light-hearted fare on other channels. *The Sun* initially labelled it Channel Swore but after the novelty had worn off some journalists called it Channel Bore. I have to admit that quite a lot of *Out on Tuesday* went over my head due to its highbrow content. My favourite piece was about the appeal of the sitcom *The Golden Girls* to gay men, while a few years later there was an episode that looked at gay history and had some bona fide sketches of people speaking in the secret language Polari throughout the twentieth century. Those sketches helped to inspire me to research Polari as a

PhD topic, which eventually resulted in me writing a sort of prequel to this book called *Fabulosa!*

In the summer of 1989, four of the London councils (Camden, Hackney, Haringey and Islington – the ones normally labelled as 'loony left') pledged support for the Lesbian and Gay Pride Festival. They stumped up £20,000 between them to help stage over fifty events for LGBTQ+ communities in June of that year to celebrate the twentieth anniversary of the riots that took place in 1969 when police raided the Stonewall Inn, a gay bar in Greenwich Village, New York. The Equal Opportunities policies of these councils were cited as a loophole to allow them to claim that they were discouraging discrimination by supporting the event.[38] By the end of June, there were reports that a Conservative councillor at Haringey, Jim Buckley, was threatening legal action. He told *The Stage* that 'legal advisors had said they had a good case to proceed with action, although finding the cash to do so was the main obstacle.'[39] This threat did not put off the councils from continuing with the remaining events and a Haringey Labour councillor called Vince Gillespie said, 'If we are challenged on Section 28, we will challenge it in court.'[40]

But not every funding source was as bold as those London councils. The Glyndebourne Schools Festival was faced with a difficult choice in May 1989 when the local council intervened and told organizers that they would have to change the programme. A performance of Benjamin Britten's opera *Death in Venice* was meant to have been held but because of its gay content it was cancelled. The schools' officer for Kent had denied that Section 28 was behind the decision but instead said that most of the audience (aged thirteen to eighteen) wouldn't understand the opera's themes. One of the organizers offered to restrict the performance to sixth-formers (sixteen- to eighteen-year-olds) but this was still not seen as acceptable. Eventually a kind of compromise was reached where *Death in Venice* was staged as a separate performance not linked to the festival.[41]

In October 1989, the Bristol-based Avon Touring Theatre was forced to close after it lost its funding. The company had come under scrutiny the previous year when it had been banned from performing a play called *Trapped in Time* at a local school due to the fact that it contained a gay character coming out to his friends. The school in question paid the theatre group £70 in compensation but the company's administrator, Cathy Smith, was reported as saying, 'We put responsibility on the government for introducing such an ineffectual law, which makes it impossible for anyone to sort out where they stand. This is just the beginning. It will be an ongoing battle. The law is so ambiguous it will definitely remain a problem.' Then, the Arts Council, which had been financing the company to the tune of £80,000 a year (amounting to two-thirds of its annual income), withdrew all the funding, meaning that the company had to be disbanded.[42]

In 1990, the artist Sunil Gupta created a set of images called the *'Pretended' Family Relationships* series. The title acknowledged that controversial piece of wording within the Section 28 legislation, and the art comprised a series of colour photographs showing gay and lesbian couples, juxtaposed with different sections of a poem that Gupta's partner Stephen Dodd had written. On the right side of each piece of art was a cutaway section of a photograph in black and white showing anti-Section 28 demonstrations. Gupta didn't want

Round moon; disk
light thinner
than city winter

lamps through
which we drive

My favourite of the *'Pretended' Family Relationships* series
of photographs by Sunil Gupta.

to idealize same-sex partnerships or show them in a uniform
way, so some of the images depict couples in a home environment while others imply street cruising or unfulfilled longing.
My favourite shows two young women standing face to face,
close together in Piccadilly Circus, with the statue of Anteros
(usually referred to as Eros) framed in the background between
them. To the left, an older woman in a sensible overcoat with
a handbag over her shoulder is looking towards the camera.

However, Gupta has described how Section 28 scuppered
another exhibition he had created that year with Tessa Boffin.
It was a project based around the representation of AIDS in the
UK called 'Ecstatic Antibodies' that had been due to take place
in Salford at the Viewpoint Photography Gallery the same year.
Contracts had been signed and educational material had been
created. So it was very late in the day when the booking was

abruptly withdrawn. Gupta says that officials at the Town Hall came to the acting director's office and removed her file relating to the exhibition. They told her that if she spoke to the press about it she would lose her job.[43] While it was claimed that the cancellation of the exhibition was due to some of the works being pornographic, the *Pink Paper* reported that in the same year an exhibition of lesbian erotica at the Young Unknowns Gallery in Waterloo went ahead without problem, even noting that the 'Lesbian Erotica slaps the face of Section 28 with its daring audacity'.[44] The lack of a single set of centralized rules or guidelines about what was acceptable meant that Section 28 emboldened people who were looking for an excuse to censor. As a result, nobody knew where they stood.

Gay Sweatshop, which had helped form the Arts Lobby, was feeling the cold. Its last performance was of a play called *Kitchen Matters* in December 1990 in Manchester. Ironically, the play was about the problems of putting on a show with project funding. The Sweatshop had submitted an application to the Arts Council asking for a grant for three more years. The council turned them down but stressed that homophobia was not the reason, citing the fact that their own Drama Officer had had one of his plays produced by Gay Sweatshop in the past.[45] However, Gay Sweatshop's artistic director, David Benedict, claimed that the funding was pulled due to covert discrimination as a result of Clause 28, saying, 'We have definitely lost bookings. But no one will quote Clause 28 to you because they are afraid of court action.'[46]

It's clear that funders wouldn't have wanted to mention Clause 28 as the reason for banning a production or withdrawing money, and this can make it difficult to fully know if there were other factors at work. A study by Cardiff Law School published at the end of 1990 surveyed feedback from 348 local councils, noting that only 37 had sought legal advice regarding Section 28 and 41 had prepared their own guidelines. Just five councils had cited Section 28 as a reason for refusing funds. On the surface, then, it appeared that Section 28 had failed to have had much of an impact. However, the authors of the study, Philip Thomas and Ruth Costigan, warned that the section could encourage a hidden agenda of anti-gay prejudice and prevented an adequate response to the problems posed by AIDS.[47] And a report by the National Campaign for the Arts in 1997 by Jennifer Edwards concluded that theatre-in-education companies had avoided work by gay writers or plays that featured gay characters. In other words, a decade of self-censorship had occurred.[48]

Lobbying versus zapping

Rebecca Flemming, one of the organizers of the 'Stop the Section' campaign, which was active in the late 1980s, said that while it was created for a specific reason, its underlying purpose was to encourage the formation of other groups and continuing activity rather than last as a movement.[49] She saw Stop the Section as trying to bring together large numbers of people who were coming from quite different ideological perspectives at times, and therefore there were differences of opinion. For example, some people believed that it was physically impossible to promote homosexuality while others believed the opposite: that homosexuality could and should be promoted, and as often as possible.[50] The Stop the Section campaign was focused on opposing Section 28 rather than trying to encourage or resolve these kinds of debates (I'm not sure they *are* resolvable) and as the months passed it was clear that people wanted to go their separate ways. Similarly, OLGA was not destined to last much longer – it was disbanded in 1990 after issues around funding. Lisa Power was critical of both campaigns: 'We cocked it up really badly. We fought against ourselves as much as the clause. OLGA and Stop the Clause were both trying to run it and no one in the groups would talk to the Tories. But it was a Tory majority in the Commons and the Lords. Without speaking to them we were never going to make a dent.'[51]

Michael Cashman recalls visiting Ian McKellen one Sunday morning and telling him that they needed to form an organization to ensure that another Section 28 would never happen again. A week later McKellen and Cashman met with

Stonewall (some of the original cast members, including Ian McKellen and Michael Cashman at the front), 1990.

Douglas Slater, their mole in the government Whips' Office of the House of Lords. Slater had had a similar idea about creating a lobbying organization.[52] And so, on 24 May 1989, a year on from the passage of Section 28 into law, a new organization, Stonewall Equality Limited (usually abbreviated to Stonewall), was formed. It was named after the Stonewall riots described earlier. The link to American rights movements was also evident in the fact that Stonewall was modelled on two U.S. campaigns, the Human Rights Campaign and the National Gay and Lesbian Task Force.[53] There were fourteen founders: Peter Ashman, Deborah Ballard, Duncan Campbell, Olivette Cole-Wilson, Michael Cashman, Pam St Clement, Simon Fanshawe, Dorian Jabri, Ian McKellen, Matthew Parris, Lisa Power, Fiona Cunningham Reid, Peter Rivas and Jennie Wilson.

Simon Fanshawe, writing about Stonewall's formation, described how its aim was 'to bring the issues [of gay and lesbian equality] into the general political agenda' and to create 'a behind-the-scenes establishment group to negotiate the settlement of the issue'.[54] The significance of these early meetings taking place at McKellen's home in Limehouse was not lost on him. Some 140 years ago, Dr Thomas John Barnardo had opened his first East End Juvenile Mission to rescue children from the streets (the charity Barnardo's thrives today). Now Limehouse was home to the birth of a second organization, this time aimed at saving children from the damage that Section 28 inflicted.

The group was announced by Michael Cashman at the closing concert of the 1989 European Lesbian and Gay Festival of Song at Sadler's Wells Theatre in Clerkenwell on 14 May.[55] An associated charity called the Iris Trust was also set up. Michael Cashman explains how the thinking behind this was twofold.

First, gay people who were not out would be less willing to support Stonewall, although they might be more inclined to donate money to Iris. Also, charities could not work for political change, whereas Stonewall could.[56]

Lisa Power notes that the coalition consisted of people who had been involved in political rights movements for a long time and were realizing that the tactics they were using on Section 28 were not affecting the legislation despite mobilizing the community, along with people who had never been politicized before Section 28.[57] Stonewall was therefore formed as a lobbying group that aimed to change legislation around rights for LGBT people. Its formation attracted a bit of criticism. For example, a letter to *Gay Times* in July 1989 claimed, 'I fear the Group will prove "tragic" *and* "toothless".'[58] Michael Cashman remembered that the attacks came from all sides, including the gay media. He told me that when people claimed that Stonewall comprised a self-selecting, self-serving elite, his view was, 'Yeah, you're absolutely right, we're trying to get equality and if people want to opt into it, fine. If they want to opt out, fine. We don't have elections, we're pulling together a group of people, we don't have a membership because we're going to service the arguments for change, not service the internal machinations and splits that had occurred within activist organizations around LGBT issues.'

Then there was disapproval from some people who didn't want to rock the boat too much. Ian McKellen described to me how one of his friends, a closeted man who was high up in the arts at the BBC, had been appalled by the idea of Stonewall, telling him, 'Don't cause a fuss, dear. And if you've got to do it, if you want to get anywhere, what I recommend to you, get a leader who is a woman and is straight, you want a mother figure in there.'

Some of the early meetings took place in the gay night-club Heaven. Ian McKellen recalls that 'it was owned then by Richard Branson. We told him what we were up to and he let us have the bar there. We had our two-hour meeting in there and then at eleven o'clock all the people came in to party and we went home. Well, not all of us.' The government felt comfortable talking to Stonewall, and the group was able to trade on its appearance of respectability to get the attention of politicians: 'They saw Stonewall, who turned up to meetings in ties and jackets and had all been to university: "it's our sort of person."' However, this was all carried out in a distinctly low-tech way. As McKellen notes, 'We did it before there was such a thing as the Internet, the only technology we had to hand was the fax machine. There was no just pressing a button and contacting a thousand people to turn up on a march, it was all done on the phone and in person.'

While there was certainly a need for a lobbying organization like Stonewall, other activists were considering alternative methods. After Section 28 passed, Peter Tatchell describes how he had felt 'totally and utterly betrayed by democracy'. He says that there had been a sense that there needed to be a 'different style of campaigning, by all means lets have the orthodox lobbying, let's write to MPs, let's all lobby ministers, but in addition many of us felt we had to do much more'.[59]

Then, on the night of 30 April 1990, a 48-year-old man called Michael Boothe walked home past Elthorne Park in Hanwell, west London. The park housed a cottage (a public toilet where men had sex) and there were a group of six men waiting around outside. The men pushed Boothe to the ground, kicking and stamping on him. He was discovered by a couple who called an ambulance but he died of internal bleeding in hospital. This form of violence was so common that it had its own name: 'queer-bashing'. It was not, let's say, a type of crime that was particularly high priority for the constabulary, who were instead more interested in entrapping gay men for engaging in consensual sex in cruising areas, sometimes deploying 'pretty police': young, attractive plain-clothes officers who would hang around a public loo and act as if they were interested in sex.

Michael's killers were never found and the case was closed. A review by the London Metropolitan Police implied that it was his own fault, concluding that his lifestyle was 'destined to bring him into contact with his murderers'. However, a report by the Independent Lesbian Gay Bisexual Transgender Advisory Group, carried out in 2007, concluded that killings might not have occurred if previous attacks had been 'investigated seriously'.[60]

Michael's death provoked grief, horror and anger among the gay community. And so, on 10 May 1990, around fifty activists attended a meeting and decided to form a group. Modelled on another American organization, Queer Nation, its founders included Keith Alcorn, Peter Tatchell, Simon Watney and Chris Woods. At a second meeting, held in public two weeks later, Keith Alcorn came up with the name OutRage! and Peter Tatchell produced a draft 'Statement of Aims'. The group was given office space at the London Lesbian and Gay Centre by OLGA. Peter Tatchell has described how

OutRage! partly came into existence to fill a gap created by all the things Stonewall wasn't. OutRage! had
an agenda beyond equality . . . Equal rights within
straight society means equality on heterosexual terms.
We conform to their agenda. OutRage! has always
sought to articulate a post-equality agenda which
seeks to renegotiate the values, institutions and laws of
straight culture, challenging not just the homophobia
but the authoritarian and puritanical stance of social
institutions.[61]

On 7 June, OutRage! activists demonstrated outside public
toilets at Hyde Park to protest against police entrapment of
men cruising. This was the start of a concerted campaign to
change this kind of police activity, with activists carrying out
direct action at police stations, publicly identifying the 'pretty
police' and using leaflets and stickers to warn men who were
cruising.[62] Another early high-profile demonstration involved
a kiss-in at Piccadilly Circus on 5 September. Gay Sweatshop's
Richard Sandells, looking dashing in denim, climbed onto the
statue of Anteros and kissed it. He told me, 'Once I'd had the
idea of climbing Eros I don't remember thinking much about
the risk involved, either to one of London's most iconic land-
marks or to my own health or subsequent liberty! It was only
when I was up there with him that I realised not only that he's
totally to human scale but is also, genuinely, incredibly beautiful
– to kiss him seemed just the most completely natural thing to
do.' Lisa Power recalls, 'I remember the actor, Richard, climbing
up Eros – the bloody thing swayed! . . . Even the police said,
"Bloody hell".'[63]

One of the more controversial activities that OutRage! was involved in was the 'outing' of closeted public figures who were deemed hypocritical, being gay in private and homophobic in public. There was no consensus in the group so an offshoot was formed called FROCS (Faggots Rooting Out Closeted Sexuality) with Peter Tatchell acting as spokesperson. In November 1994, FROCS famously named ten bishops at the General Synod of the Church of England, urging them to 'tell the truth'. Two bishops (who were not on the list) came out. In the weeks that followed it appears that the Anglican Church signalled a change of policy, with the Archbishop of Canterbury stating that lesbians and gays were 'made in the likeness of God' and that society must 'reject homophobia'.[64] Another goal was to expose the hypocrisy of newspapers who had outed people but instead I think the press loved the idea of outing: they were able to have their cake and eat it – blaming OutRage! for exposing people's private lives while raking in readers by reporting on who had been outed. It was a toxic relationship, resulting in tragically unintended consequences when a couple of months later, members of FROCS privately sent letters to twenty MPs inviting them to come out. One of these was James Kilfedder (Ulster Unionist Party, North Down). The year before, Kilfedder had voted to keep the age of consent for gay men at 21. Peter Tatchell had said that although the group had been approached by journalists to out a Unionist MP, they had refused but this was enough for journalists to telephone Kilfedder's office, incorrectly suggesting that OutRage! were going to reveal that he was gay. On 20 March, the *Belfast Telegraph* carried a story that said that an Ulster MP had been targeted by OutRage! Kilfedder apparently learnt of the news and while travelling by train from Gatwick into London he had a heart attack and died. Edwina Currie was quoted in *The Times* as calling the outing campaign cruel, wicked and evil.[65]

Another form of protest that OutRage! used was the zap. The term comes from protest groups in the USA, with the Gay Activists Alliance popularizing the phrase in the 1970s. A zap is a public demonstration that intends to draw attention to lesbian and gay rights and is sometimes aimed at embarrassing a public figure. They can be carefully planned or spontaneous. Of course, Peter Tatchell had been zapping since 1971 when the GLF had released mice into Methodist Central Hall during a Nationwide Festival of Light rally.

One OutRage! zap involved an ad hoc protest against high-profile Nationwide Festival of Light member Cliff Richard on 11 March 1991. Members of OutRage! had appeared in the Derek Jarman film *Edward II*, and during filming Jarman told them that he'd seen Cliff 'looking like a chestnut' in the canteen and mischievously suggested that they pay him a visit as he was rehearsing in a nearby studio. The ensuing zap involved thirty men dressed as nuns blowing trumpets and shouting 'Come out of the closet Cliff and declare yourself a full blown homosexual!'[66] Some activists covered his white Rolls-Royce in stickers, which said 'It's cool to be queer.'[67] In his 2008 autobiography, Cliff revealed that he had struck up a close friendship with a man who was a former Roman Catholic priest. 'He has become a companion, which is great because I don't like living alone.'[68]

OutRage! was split into groups that concentrated on different aspects of queer rights. The groups were known by provocative acronyms, so the Policing Intelligence Group was called PIG, Perverts Undermining State Scrutiny were PUSSY, Lesbians Answer Back in Anger were called LABIA and Sex Information for School Students and Youth went by the name of SISSY. It was SISSY that tackled Section 28, with one form of protest being the distribution of leaflets about homosexuality outside schools. During lunch hour on 27 November 1991, members of OutRage! handed out leaflets to pupils at Haverstock Secondary School in the Chalk Farm area of London. Labour's Education Secretary Jack Straw was reported as condemning the group for 'embroiling' young children in their views, while Stonewall also criticized the action.[69]

And on 30 April 1992, OutRage! carried out a zap on the Conservative Central Office to mark the fourth anniversary of Section 28. As members of staff watched from upstairs windows, about thirty members of OutRage! offered a 'free trial of queer sex' by kissing on the pavement outside, calling on the onlookers to join in. Peter Tatchell dubbed the Central Office the 'Headquarters of Homophobia'.[70] SISSY later changed its name to YOUTH and continued leafleting schools. On 22 January 1992, the group were contacted by a gay teacher at the Sacred Heart School in Camberwell who suggested they might want to campaign there. During the leafleting, one of the members of OutRage!, Alan Jarman, recalled how a woman came up to him and threw purple liquid in his face: 'I was completely horrified, thinking "Shit someone's killed me with acid" and it turned out to be vinegar.' Another member, Nick Cave, reported that the action resulted in a lot of interest from other schools, which kept phoning up to ask for copies of the leaflet.[71]

Ten years after Section 28 came into law, OutRage! protested outside the London Oratory School, accusing it of

OutRage! offer additional reading suggestions to pupils at Haverstock school, Camden, 1991.

homophobia. The London Oratory School is a Catholic secondary school in Fulham. It has been described as an elitist or 'old school tie' school: two of former prime minister Tony Blair's sons attended it, as well as ex Lib-Dem leader Nick Clegg's son.[72] OutRage! accused the school of censoring gay issues. At 8.15 a.m. on 28 May 1998, fourteen members of OutRage! stood outside, holding placards that read 'Teach lesbian and gay sex ed too'. They handed out leaflets to teachers that featured photographs of gay couples kissing and stated 'Heterosexuality, homosexuality and bisexuality are equally valid . . . If you are not sure about your sexuality, it's okay to experiment. Don't knock it till you've tried it!' Phone numbers for gay helplines were also given. The demonstrators were met with hostility from some teachers, with one defending the right of teachers to be homophobic, while some pupils shouted abuse at the protesters.

I asked Michael Cashman what he'd made of OutRage! and whether he'd ever been tempted to join in. He admitted that at the time he had been diametrically opposed to them. 'I didn't have the good sense to realize that we were the perfect Blitzkrieg. I remember being on *Question Time* with Peter Tatchell and disagreeing about outing. Me saying, "Absolutely not, you're using it as a negative instrument".' However, he thinks that 'without them, in conjunction with Stonewall, we wouldn't have achieved equality as quickly as we did.'

Another group that protested against Section 28 in the 1990s was the London chapter of the Lesbian Avengers (that's a comic book series that needs creating), a pressure group to promote lesbian visibility and rights that had begun in New York in 1992 (the London group was set up in 1994). The mid-1990s had begun to see a tiny amount of mainstream media representation of lesbian identities. *Brookside*, ahead of the curve as usual, had broadcast a kiss between two women, Beth Jordache and Margaret Clemence, the first one that had occurred before the '9 p.m. watershed' when children are meant to be in bed, in January 1994, while the crime noir film *Bound* featured a lesbian relationship between Jennifer Tilly and Gina Gershon. However, there was still censorship and some representations were aimed at titillating straight male audiences, with terms like 'lipstick lesbian' and 'lesbian chic' indicating a kind of frivolous, sexualized, non-committal representation. The Avengers aimed to combat the notion of lesbian chic and to fight for equal rights for gay partners, healthcare, parenting and fostering rights and education. The London group was founded in part by ex-members of OutRage! and employed similar zap-like tactics. Their first action took place in August 1994 with around forty women invading the Queen Victoria monument near Buckingham Palace. Clad in black-and-white T-shirts they banged on drums and held up signs that read 'Lesbian Avengers say: we are not amused', 'Visible and Victoria's lesbians' and 'Lesbian Avengers: out for power'.

In June 1995, to mark seven years of Section 28, around fifty Avengers toured the West End of London in an open-top bus, addressing members of the public with a megaphone: 'Yes, you in the brown coat, hello, we're lesbians . . . we can spot your homophobia.' The bus made several stops, including at the Tate, where a kiss-in occurred by Rodin's *The Kiss*, at a branch of Laura Ashley, where the dresses were made fun of, and even at Marks & Spencer, where they 'mucked around' with the underwear in the lingerie department and thrust leaf-lets on customers and staff, who, according to Avenger Lynn Sutcliff, 'loved it, they were very friendly. We were posing with the models and showing people we buy pants here too.'[73]

So, as the 1990s progressed, two models of activism for gay and lesbian rights became firmly established – a softly-softly approach that sought dialogue and consensus through incre-mental changes to the law and a loudly-loudly one that aimed for shock, embarrassment and laughter. It probably wasn't a conscious strategy but it was a good one – as noted earlier, an enemy is harder to defeat if it is multifaceted and the differ-ent approaches allowed more people to participate. Perhaps it was simply best to accept the fracture and acknowledge the common goal after all.

SECTION 28 APPLIED only to local authorities. It did not relate to television stations or publicly funded bodies such as the Arts Council, or directly to teachers. However, there was confusion around what it meant – this all happened before the Internet made information instantly available. You couldn't just Google 'Section 28' and bring up the wording. And even if you could get a copy of Section 28, it was written in legalese, which made it hard to follow, while phrases like 'promote homosexuality' were open to interpretation. So it was unsurprising that many people who had heard about Section 28 overextended its remit. To add to that, the homophobic climate of the time meant that it could be misused by people who perhaps wanted to silence gay and lesbian voices anyway.

I don't think that all the homophobia in schools after 23 May 1988 can be blamed on Section 28. There was already plenty of it around anyway, and it could be argued that the law was really an expression of existing homophobia, which would have occurred whether Section 28 happened or not. But Section 28 certainly made things worse. It made it difficult for teachers to talk about homosexuality, to tackle homophobic bullying or to be openly gay or lesbian. And it legally sanctioned homophobia – in classrooms and staffrooms, in assembly halls and sports halls across the country. Its effect on children was damaging. Designed to protect them, the law failed them, often when they needed support the most. Section 28 made things worse for families with two gay parents, a reminder that this kind of family was deemed 'pretended', making it difficult for children of such families to be open about their home set-up with friends. And for queer people involved with the arts in the late 1980s and 1990s, the effect was devastating as sources of funding dried up.

Perhaps none of this was intended. Perhaps it was the fault of the wording. There had been plenty of warning during the parliamentary debates about the ambiguous language of Clause

28 but MPs had gone round in circles, barely improving on it. From reading the debates, I get the impression some of them didn't really care; they just wanted any sort of anti-gay legislation passed. It was all a bit of a mess really, but instead of making those pesky gays and lesbians shut up and go away, it had had the opposite effect. They kept coming out of the closet and going on marches or staging mass kissing sessions in public.

As the country plodded on towards the end of the millennium, the Conservative Party was getting tired. It had held on to power since 1979 and, while there had been economic recovery and falling unemployment after a recession in the early 1990s, within the party there had been fights around membership of the European Union. They were also dogged by allegations of sleaze, which continued to make them unpopular. Meanwhile, Labour had made some major changes, altering its policy on nuclear disarmament and abandoning its commitment to mass nationalization of industry. When Labour came to power in 1997, many LGBTQ+ people across the country gave a sigh of relief. Surely, *they* would prioritize putting an end to the awful, hated Section 28, wouldn't they?

6

The Rocky Road to Repeal

Despite not being the sort of person who enjoys going on marches (they make me terribly self-conscious), I did get involved in the protests against Section 28 that continued through the 1990s, although it was in a peripheral sort of way, standing on some Town Hall steps at a local demonstration. However, I felt I was better suited to sitting in a cold, dark room on my own so I joined my local Lesbian and Gay Switchboard and for a few years spent Friday evenings in a dilapidated basement answering calls. There were people who were moving to the area and wondered whether it was friendly, people who were coming for a few days and wanted to know where to go, people with complex relationship problems (far beyond anything I had experienced and all I could do was provide a sympathetic ear really), children who wanted to prank us (possibly for complicated reasons) and people who viewed the phone service as a kind of sexual outlet. I was at least doing something for gay rights in my quiet little way but I felt it wasn't enough, so I contributed a couple of articles to a gay website about Section 28. In those days there were only about three hundred websites in existence so I like to think that people stumbled across it eventually because there was not much else to look at, and perhaps I inspired some of them to write to their MP or support a gay rights group.

Speaking of letter writing, remember Dame Elaine Kellett-Bowman from Chapter Three? She was the MP who said that it was quite right that there should be intolerance of evil after the arson attack on *Capital Gay*'s offices. Once I'd settled down into homo-domesticity it came to my attention that she was now my local MP. So I wrote to her, asking her to support gay rights. I didn't expect her to reply but to her credit she did. A few days later an official-looking letter arrived in the post. It was handwritten, quite long and signed by Dame Elaine. In it she spelled out her views on homosexuality and why she *wasn't* going to vote for any sort of equality. I got the impression she'd rather enjoyed writing it.

My parents, on the other hand, had been impressed at a talk by a smart barrister who was Labour MP for Sedgefield, which adjoined their constituency, Easington. As a student he had been in a rock band called Ugly Rumours. 'He's marvellous!' my mother told me during one of her phone calls in 1994. 'He's going to be our next prime minister.' I'd never heard of him so wasn't especially convinced. But then, Labour's leader, John Smith, died suddenly and the Ugly Rumours singer took his place, going on to win the 1997 election for Labour.

'See!' said my mother.

A light shines

In the late 1990s, Britain felt Great again, for a short time at least. The phrase 'Cool Britannia' was all over the place and Britpop bands such as The Stone Roses, Elastica, Suede, Echobelly, Happy Mondays, Oasis, Blur and Pulp celebrated 'youthful exuberance and desire for recognition',[1] offering a British, working-class, laddish alternative to angsty American grunge. Britpop was cheeky, observational and wry. Irony was the order of the day and the catchy, upbeat tunes disguised more profound lyrics about class, gender, ethnicity and nationality. This was a recognizably self-possessed sound; it knew it was onto something good and it didn't mind whether you liked it or not.

The day after Tony Blair's 'New' Labour Party won the general election on 2 May 1997, there was a completely unexpected coincidence. The UK won the Eurovision Song Contest with a song called 'Love Shine a Light'. The last time this had happened was in 1981. At the time of writing, we have not won since. There was a sense of confidence about the direction in which the country was heading and, increasingly, politically, a feeling of consensus. It wasn't just in the UK. For a short time there was a sense that Western liberal democracy was going to be the final form of government for all nations. A book was even written about this called *The End of History and the Last Man*.

Accordingly, Blair's party was a shift away from the left and towards the political centre. No wonder that Labour won 43.2 per cent of the vote and 418 seats (a landslide) compared to the Conservatives' 30.7 per cent and 165 seats. New Labour was modernizing, more socially liberal than the Conservatives and kinder to needier members of society, although keen to keep the rich and powerful on side too. Tax rates did not increase in Blair's first term and even the right-wing tabloids seemed to be prepared to put up with Labour for now. It might be expected that Section 28 – almost a decade old by this point and still the target of equality campaigners – would be one of the first laws to be overturned, especially with that massive majority of Labour MPs to vote it out.

However, as the weeks turned into months, the new government did not seem to be making a move. Towards the end of May 1998, to mark Section 28's tenth anniversary, frustrated campaigners from the gay rights group YouthSpeak delivered a 25,000-signature petition to 10 Downing Street. Their chair, Chris Morris, said 'Labour have made lots of promises on this issue. Promises do not change the lives of young people – we want some action.'[2]

There was dissatisfaction within the Labour party, too. Chris Smith had kept his seat and told me of his frustration that so little progress was being made on getting Section 28 repealed.

When we came in in 1997 there were a number of us, people like Michael Cashman and Waheed Alli and myself, who were trying to persuade Number 10 that we needed to get moving on the LGBT agenda, and Blair's office was really nervous at the outset, it sort of reflected back in the same way that Jack Cunningham and people had been nervous back in the day with Section 28 itself. We got things from Blair's office like 'We're very worried about what our pensioner voters are going to think if we start doing stuff on this.' And they were worried about the *Daily Mail* and *The Sun* and the tabloids.

'The great heroine':
Angela Mason, former
Chief Executive of
Stonewall.

Some campaigners viewed the campaign to repeal Section 28 as a bit of a distraction anyway. On 14 May 1999 Peter Tatchell of OutRage! argued that Section 28 didn't prevent schools from talking about gay issues and repealing it would not stop homophobia in classrooms. He said that the only positive benefit of getting rid of it would be to debunk the idea that it prevents discussion of gay issues. In addition, he noted the importance of a new legal obligation to stamp out homophobic bullying in schools, promoting students' under-standing and acceptance of gay people and ensuring that sex education and AIDS awareness lessons provide information about homosexuality and safe sex for queer kids.[3]

Since Labour had come to power, Stonewall had been powering up. Angela Mason, formerly of the Gay Liberation

Front, had been the Chief Executive of Stonewall since 1992. She'd applied for the job after the first CE, Tim Barnett, had moved to New Zealand. She hadn't expected to get it, telling me, 'It was rather surprising really as I was considered a bit of a lefty.' It was a role that she found hugely inspiring. 'The most exciting thing was that there was the possibility of great change.' But there were also challenges, the shoestring budget, the fact that they didn't always succeed and then the disagreements within. 'Everybody had an interest in change and they had different views and perspectives. It was a big party but hard sometimes to keep consensus and keep going forward and not get distracted by conflicts and differences.' She certainly impressed Ian McKellen, who described her to me as 'the great heroine who knew exactly how the law worked'. Michael Cashman was equally admiring: 'A brilliant strategist. Her success – she gave to other people. She wasn't interested in owning it. She was on to the next step.' Angela Mason recalled the substantial opposition to Section 28 across the country: 'I remember sitting on the Tube and there were people sitting with Stop the Clause badges and me thinking "My God, there are a lot of us." So it really brought everybody out. That was the platform on which Stonewall could build and do its more detailed lobbying and networking work.' There was still political will to get the law changed outside of Westminster – when Stonewall held meetings in towns across the UK, two hundred or so people attended each one. And Section 28 was continuing to have a negative effect on children. Mason pointed to the large amount of evidence Stonewall had amassed about homophobic bullying in schools that went unchallenged because teachers were frightened to do so.[4]

I asked her what lobbying actually involved and she explained that essentially it was about people making their voices heard. Their reasoning was that 'about half the MPs never answered anything, but all MPs can count. And they really notice if you're speaking on behalf of a significant number of people, especially if those people are trying to talk directly to them. And it also humanizes the whole process. The most powerful thing that a lobbyist can do is tell their story. That creates compassion and understanding and support.' It wasn't just speaking to the party in power though. 'We had to establish good relationships with all the political parties and crucially with those sections of civil society that were willing to support change.' Getting the support of all the children's organizations was crucial. Also, they got the nation's Agony Aunts on board, a group who had a considerable amount of secular influence over the morals of the nation.

However, the repeal of Clause 28 was just one item on a shopping list of legal changes for queer people. The age of consent for gay men stood at eighteen while it was sixteen for everyone else, and lesbians and gay men could not serve in the armed forces, adopt or foster children or marry one another. Then there were all sorts of protections relating to homophobia in the workplace, provision of goods and services, violence and abuse, and enabling trans people to legally change their gender. Around the same time that the government tried to repeal Section 28, there were campaigns to equalize the age of consent for gay men and remove the armed forces ban. On behalf of several members of the forces who had been dismissed, Stonewall went to the High Court and then the Court of Appeal, where judges had to admit that the ban was not justified but they could not overturn it. However, Stonewall had an ace up its sleeve – the European Court of Human Rights. Housed in a building that looks like a spaceship that has been grounded in Strasbourg, the court was one of the bêtes noires of the right-wing press. It ruled in favour of the plaintiffs, and the armed-forces ban was overturned on 12 January 2000.

There had been a similar success story for the age of consent, with the European Commission of Human Rights finding against the UK's discriminatory age of consent on 1 July 1997. The government signalled that it would propose a bill to reduce the age of homosexual consent from eighteen to sixteen. What followed was (in my opinion) one of the nastiest sets of parliamentary debates in British history, especially when it got to the House of Lords. On 13 April 1999, Baroness Young, whose eminent proclamations we will hear more of shortly, said, 'As regards human rights, I do not believe that there is any human right to commit buggery,' while on 22 July 1998, Lord Longford expressed concern about young men (but not young women) getting 'ruined for life' if they were seduced by older men: 'A girl is not ruined for life by being seduced. A young fellow is. That is the distinction.' The Lords voted the legislation down three times. As a result, the government invoked the little-used Parliament Act to override the Lords and get the measure onto the statute books anyway, so there!

Chris Smith told me that after the age of consent was equalized, 'the wonderful thing of course was, there was no outcry, the pensioners weren't upset, everyone thought this was a good thing and it was celebrated rather than denigrated. The tabloids didn't go berserk and after that it became much easier sailing, for getting other things done.' Still, these Lords were getting to be a pain for Labour and something had to be done about them. The Upper House skewed decidedly to the Tories, particularly among the hereditary peers whose views were thought to be out of touch with those of ordinary people in modern society. Blair's government had suffered more defeats in the Lords during the 1997–8 session than any government since 1979–80 when Mrs Thatcher became prime minister.[5] So on 11 November 1999, the government saw to it that more than six hundred hereditary peers lost their right to sit and vote. Ninety-two of them were allowed to remain, although, similar to *Big Brother*, the television reality show that would absorb the nation's attention a few months later, their fate was in the hands of their 'housemates', who got to vote on the matter. Hilariously, each Lord had to write a 75-word 'manifesto' to help their fellow Lords decide who should stay and who should go. Baroness Strange (who had complained about misuse of the word 'gay' in one of the earlier Clause 28 debates) wrote in her manifesto that 'I bring flowers every week to this House from my castle in Perthshire.' She got to stay! Meanwhile, poor old Lord Monckton of Brenchley used his 75 words to argue the case for muzzling cats to stop 'the agonising torture of mice and small birds' but that wasn't good enough and he got the boot.[6] Perhaps this reformed, chastened House of Lords would make the removal of Section 28 more likely – that's if the government ever got round to giving it a go.

Saving PHACE

Despite being reactionary, poorly worded and mean-minded, in the 1990s Section 28 hadn't really resulted in court cases due to people self-censoring. However, at the start of the year

2000, that was to change. On 4 January, a young man called Charlie McMillan started a new job – he was Chief Executive of PHACE (Project for HIV and AIDS Care and Education) West, which was based in Glasgow. Before he'd even had a chance to settle into his office the phones were ringing with members of the press getting in touch over a breaking story – a group called the Christian Institute were taking Glasgow City Council to court for providing PHACE West with funding when it allegedly provided explicit sexual material.

PHACE West ran the website of a related youth group called Bi-G-Les (ahem). Considering that the group's website had to provide material for people as young as twelve and as old as 25, and that it was essential to give safe-sex advice during a time when combination therapies were only just starting to extend the lives of people who were HIV+, there was a dilemma about what sort of information to include on it.

So the website provided links to other sites that contained online versions of three publications, one by Stonewall and Gay Men's Health called *Coming Out – A Guide for Young Men*, which was aimed at 'the younger age-group', another by the Terrence Higgins Trust called *True Colours – Choices for Young Men Coming Out* and a third, written by PHACE West in conjunction with a group called Healthy Gay Scotland, called *Gay Sex Now* which the Bi-G-Les website described as 'a more general booklet for gay men covering sexual health in more detail'. As noted in the description, the third booklet was intended for gay *men* and it covered various aspects of sexual acts, sexual health and relationships. The booklet takes a non-judgemental, sex-positive position. It *is* explicit – there is advice on scat (don't get it in your eyes), a quote from a man who likes cruising for sex in parks – 'it's the best buzz there is' – as well as sections on S&M, water sports, negotiating safe sex, combination therapies, contact ads, hepatitis and how to put a condom on.

When the Christian Institute got wind of *Gay Sex Now* they were outraged. They backed a nurse called Sheena Strain, who sought an interim interdict to prevent funding of a number of groups. So, in March, rather than getting caught up in months of legal wrangling, Glasgow City Council decided to suspend funding to four agencies that provided HIV/AIDS services: Body Positive Strathclyde, the Strathclyde HIV & AIDS Carers & Family Support Group, Strathclyde Lesbian and Gay Switchboard and PHACE West. The suspension was to last until a judicial review, which had to occur within six weeks.[7]

In July, Sheena Strain took the fight to the Court of Session in Edinburgh, claiming that the website run by PHACE West contained pornographic material and that, by giving the group funds, the council were in breach of Section 2A (as Section 28 was known in Scotland). She called *Gay Sex Now* a pornographic booklet.[8] As I've noted, it was explicit, but I wouldn't call it pornographic – the aim of porn is to sexually arouse its readers. The challenge with safe-sex information is in making it accessible and interesting to those who are likely to benefit most from it, and sometimes this requires the use of eye-catching images and plain language. But primarily, the booklet was aimed at educating, keeping people safe and preventing them from catching sexually transmitted infections. I think the title of the leaflet appears purposefully ambiguous – it could be interpreted as 'What gay sex is like nowadays' or 'Come and have gay sex now.' Also, perhaps the links section of the Bi-G-Les website could have done more to highlight the fact that the link to *Gay Sex Now* was not intended for younger viewers. However, the case raises the issue of how difficult it is to make websites age-appropriate. The site creators could have required people to go through some sort of age verification system to access *Gay Sex Now* but that might have resulted in people being reluctant to give their details.

The case was finally dropped after solicitors working for both sides drafted a covering letter that was to be applied to any future grants given out by the council. The letter stated: 'You will not spend these monies for the purpose of promoting homosexuality nor shall they be used for the publication of any material which promotes homosexuality.' At the time Charlie McMillan was quoted as saying, 'Mrs Strain has completely backed off and walked away from a case she knew she could not win. It is outrageous we have had to go through this process. We have been vindicated because the letter that was agreed is nothing that we don't do already.'[9] Sheena Strain had to pay costs of £7,000, a sign perhaps that her arguments had not impressed the judge. The Christian Institute made the best of it, putting out a press release on 6 July which was headed, 'Glasgow forced not to promote homosexuality,' claiming that the council-backed groups 'made no secret of the fact that an explicit booklet, Gay Sex Now, was available at a youth group and that children as young as 12 had attended.'[10]

I had to know more so I contacted Charlie McMillan to ask him what he could recall about the PHACE West case and whether twelve-year-old children had actually attended the youth group. He told me that

my view is and always has been that the allegations
were tosh. *Gay Sex Now* was a bona fide sexual health
resource which had been carefully researched and considered in terms of trying to convey an HIV safer sex
message for a specific audience of people. We benefited
greatly from the fact that Stonewall was in the process
of opening up an office in Scotland and they agreed to
cover our legal costs and advice and guidance on how
to deal with this from a very early stage. Another key
point for me is the fact that the case was based on a
story that was only half-true and was a mix of this half-
truth and a huge amount of conjecture and prejudice.
Our resource *Gay Sex Now* was aimed at gay men –
true; we facilitated Bi-G-Les Youth Group – true; did
the two ever 'meet' – who knows but probably; was the
group attended by the mythical twelve-year-old – who
knows, but I doubt it. That line was taken from some
PR material and was there to show that someone as
young as twelve might need support with their sexual
health or sexuality. That's what PHACE Scotland was
all about – we were clear that people needed support
and information to make the right choices for themselves, so they could live the life they wanted and be as
safe as possible, despite the widespread prejudice and
discrimination that was – is – around. We had all lived
through it ourselves and were dealing with the long-
term consequences of growing up LGBT in Scotland.

Events in Scotland are about to get even more exciting.
I've reserved you a place on Brian Souter's big bus tour of the

Lowlands and Highlands – as long as you're willing to put a few hundred thousand envelopes through letterboxes along the route. But we're going to take a detour first, back to London, where Labour are coming down from their Millennium Party hangover and are getting serious about waving goodbye to Section 28, while the Tories have a new leader and are trying to rebuild their party.

Quite simply, sickening

After seventeen years, the Tories were out of power. John Major had resigned, paving the way for a relatively young (36-year-old) new leader, William Hague. Would he signal a change of thinking from Major's discredited 'Back to Basics' campaign? Not really. An early sign of how things were going involved Hague's decision, in 1999, to sack one of his front benchers (the spokesman on London, Shaun Woodward) because he supported the repeal of Section 28, a view that was still very much against Tory party policy.[11] Woodward was director of the charity Childline, which had received the proceeds from the sales of songs by Wet Wet Wet and others that had topped the charts the day that Section 28 had passed into law all those years earlier. As a result, he had become concerned about the effects of Section 28 on bullying in schools. Angela Mason viewed Shaun's support as 'a great turning point. We'd done this major piece of research about homophobic bullying in schools. Shaun Woodward was very engaged in the whole thing and he was raising questions in the Conservative Party. Then he was thrown out and that made him less powerful as an advocate for that particular time.'

Woodward's sacking resulted in criticism of Hague from other Conservative MPs, and Woodward defected to the Labour party. At the following election, Hague had to choose someone else to run for Woodward's old seat at Witney. On 4 April 2000, he picked another man in his mid-thirties, David Cameron, who walked it with 45 per cent of the votes, compared to Labour's 28.8 per cent. Cameron had been hoping to stand for election since 1997 but had missed out on selection on several occasions. And of course, this is the David Cameron who would later go on to lead the Tories back to power in 2010, legalize same-sex marriage and then in 2016, for his next trick, ask the whole country to vote on whether it should leave the European Union, resulting in the unexpected answer 'yes' by a narrow margin. Fans of the concept of the Butterfly Effect could have a lot of fun with Section 28's role in what would later be known as Brexit.

In their own way, the Tories had acknowledged that Section 28 was problematic, attempting to clarify and update the legislation around sex education in the years that followed. As noted in the previous chapter, the Education Act (1993) had put the biological aspects of sex education policy in the hands of school governors while the Education Act (1996) extended this to headteachers. Those terms like 'promoting homosexuality' and 'pretended family relationship' still hung around like a bad smell, though, and by the turn of the century Section 28 was seen as a symbolic example of egregious homophobia.

However, repeal was not necessarily the view of the public at large. Between 25 and 27 January 2000, a poll of 1,007 adults by Ipsos MORI took the pulse of the nation on Section 28. Some 54 per cent of respondents said that the ban should remain while 39 per cent wanted it to end (7 per cent didn't know, poor things). So much for Cool Britannia – the poll seemed to indicate that most of the country was still trapped in the Victorian era. However, we should be mindful that a poll's wording can affect its outcome. The first option read, 'The ban should remain and schools should not be allowed to promote homosexuality,' while the second option stated, 'The ban should end and schools should be free to decide whether to promote homosexuality.' The poll used the contested wording from Section 28 which assumed that homosexuality *could* be promoted, also raising the possibility that some schools would immediately try to do so. If the poll had explained that Section 28 was being misinterpreted, resulting in bullying, and then asked whether it should be replaced by legislation that allows information about homosexuality to be taught in a non-judgemental and age-appropriate way, there may have been a different result.

Despite these figures, an MP called Maria Fyfe (Labour, Glasgow, Maryhill) had tabled an Early Day Motion on 1 November 1999 that called for the repeal of Section 28 on the grounds that it discriminated against homosexuals and was especially harmful to youngsters who risked being bullied. Subsequently, this formed part of the Local Government Bill (1999–2000) that was introduced in the House of Lords on 25 November 1999, where it received its first reading. The day before, at a special panel on Section 28 that had been held by the Institute of Historical Research, Angela Mason warned that 'the bad news is that even with a reformed House of Lords it's going to be very very hard I think to get . . . the Lords to pass the repeal of Section 28.'[12] She was right. The hatred towards gay people during this Lords debate was set to 'rabid level', to say the least. During the second reading on 6 December 1999, Lady Saltoun of Abernethy asked, 'why do homosexuals proselytise?' and went on to provide an answer: 'I think it is rather in the same way that drunks try to persuade everyone round them to drink too – because they feel more comfortable if all around are the same as them. If I were purple with orange spots, I should probably want every one of your Lordships to become purple with orange spots, so that I should feel at home.' Baroness Knight (inaccurately, see earlier) referred to 'The Playbook for Kids about Sex in which brightly coloured pictures of little stick men showed all about homosexuality and how it was done. That book was for children as young as five.' Meanwhile Lord Waddington asked, 'How can the Government countenance young children being taught that it is alright to indulge in homosexual activity, and promiscuous homosexual acts at that,' going on to say that 'sodomy is not the moral equivalent of sexual intercourse between a man and a wife.'

However, the most fervent champion of Section 28 was Baroness Young, who had been the first female leader of the House of Lords (from 1981 to 1983). She'd kept a low profile during the original debates in the late 1980s, but now she was going to have her say. And the way that Baroness Young spoke about Section 28, it seemed that she *loved* it with every bone in her body. She called the provision to remove Section 28 'nasty', referred to taxpayers' money being wasted on teaching children about homosexuality, said it would 'open the floodgates to very unsuitable material appearing in schools', baldly stated that a homosexual relationship is *not* the same as a heterosexual one, and then crowed about being intolerant: 'I am always intolerant when I believe that anyone is playing politics with children.' If Section 28 was a pantomime, as Ian McKellen had once joked, then Baroness Young would appear in the second half, amid lots of black smoke and a thundercrack, and we'd all be encouraged to shout, 'She's behind you!' whenever she came onstage.

Angela Mason remembers Baroness Young well: 'We were continually blocked by the House of Lords and that's what happened the first time round with Section 28, particularly the opposition of Janet Young. And they were all terrified of her. She was very effective. I remember once [Earl] Conrad Russell tried to organize a tea with Janet Young – a rapprochement. But she was quite a difficult person – so this tea didn't work terribly well.'

There were a few defenders of the repeal. Lord Lipsey called Section 28 'a little sop before the 1987 general election to the closet homophobes of the golf club bar and the regimental dinner'. And Lord Whitty said that Section 28

allows more homophobic bullying in our schools, not because it directly causes that bullying but because teachers and others in authority are more inhibited than they should be about doing something about it. That is why, without ascribing any malign motivation, I believe that in effect it has become a pernicious piece of legislation. The number of assaults, self-inflicted wounds and suicide attempts among young gay people . . . bears witness to that.

Yet on 7 February 2000, at committee stage, the Lords voted by 210 to 165 to essentially keep Section 28 in place but with some extra wording that would mean that governing bodies of schools, head teachers and teachers should not be prevented from taking steps to stop any form of bullying. Fifteen Labour peers voted for this, despite a three-line whip to vote against it. One amendment, tabled by the Bishop of Rochester, said that nothing in the wording should 'prevent the provision of a comprehensive and ethically-based curriculum on sex education'. This amendment is of particular interest to me due to the startling reaction it produced from Lord Randolph Quirk, an academic who was one of the forefathers of something called corpus linguistics – which involves using computer software to analyse real-life uses of language. It's a method I've used a lot in my own research, and the chap who gave me my first academic job was one of Lord Quirk's PhD students. So on the one hand he's a bit of a hero to me. On the other . . .

Lord Quirk had already shown his opposition to homosexuality in the debates around equalizing the age of consent, where he focused his argument around the 'terrible risks' of anal sex. In this later debate he made a speech that could perhaps be described as 'trolling' in today's parlance. Typically for a linguist, he based his attack on the meaning of the word 'comprehensive' in the bishop's proposed amendment, beginning by saying that the bishop had used it to mean 'the forms of sexuality with which children are likely to come in contact in the course of their lives'. Quirk went on to ask, 'Those would presumably include sado-masochism, bisexuality, paedophilia and even perhaps bestiality. Necrophilia has also been mentioned during this debate. Is it my understanding that the right reverend Prelate would want a sex education that was comprehensive plus or minus some or more of those things, but that the only form of sexuality that was to be forbidden was homosexuality?'

That list of sexual practices brings to mind the old 'guilt by association' strategy which I'd noted was used by homophobic MPs earlier. Lord Lester of Herne Hill called Quirk out on this. 'Perhaps I may say this to the noble Lord, Lord Quirk. Homosexuality is not to be equated with bestiality or necrophilia, if that was the burden of his remarks.' Lord Quirk played daft laddie, replying, 'I did not say anything to equate them. I was simply teasing out from the right reverend Prelate what would be covered by his comprehensive sex education.'

Teasing indeed.

Baroness Young was in a pensive mood when she took her turn, complaining about intolerance (of those who disagreed with her). 'I have been called a number of names,' she bemoaned. But she was determined to put a brave face on it, finding solace in *Hamlet*. 'In politics one expects "to suffer the slings and arrows of outrageous fortune" and I do not complain.' However, the 7 February debate was also remarkable because it contained four mentions of the word *Internet* – a term that had not appeared up to now since, for most of the 1990s, using the Internet had been a minority pastime. But by 2000, 25 per cent of the UK population were online (in 2020 it was 96 per cent).[13] Earl Russell (who'd had the awkward tea with Baroness Young) noted that sex education is not done in a vacuum – children obtain information from a variety of sources, including pornography on the Internet, and it is those children who must be helped. Baroness Hamwee and Lord Whitty made similar points. Since the enactment of the Obscene Publications Act in 1959, the UK had had some of the most restrictive laws in Europe around access to depictions of sex. However, in the year 2000 this was to change. A test case to ban seven 'extremely explicit videos' (titles included *Horny Catbabe* and *Nympho Nurse Nancy*) brought by the British Board of Film Classification had failed, effectively legalizing hardcore pornography, subject to certain conditions.[14]

It seemed that the whole country had suddenly liberalized – as mentioned earlier, in 2000 the age of consent for gay men was reduced to sixteen (seventeen in Northern Ireland) and, in the summer, on a trip to London, I had been taken round Soho by friends, surprised to see what was now displayed for sale in shops. Accordingly, the music of this era feels more sexualized and materialistic than earlier fare. Since the 1990s, gangsta rap had largely concerned the violent and impoverished lives of black Americans living in inner-cities – by the 2000s this form of music had become commercially successful. Hip hop music was in its 'bling' or 'jiggy' era – with rappers showing off expensive jewellery and extravagantly decorated homes. It could be argued that this form of music did not represent women well. For example, one song by Jay Z in 2002 was called 'Bitches and Sisters'. The performers often peppered their lyrics with parody and irony, and there were attempts by female performers to reclaim terms such as 'bitch', but I am not sure that audiences were always in on this. The UK's best-selling song in 2000 was 'Who Let the Dogs Out?' by Baha Men. The 'dogs' in the song were actually meant to be badly behaved men, although many listeners interpreted the song to mean that the group were talking about ugly women.

Meanwhile, female performers were increasingly objectified. In September 2000, eighteen-year-old Britney Spears performed her hit, 'Oops! . . . I Did It Again' at the MTV Music Awards. About a minute into her act she ripped off her black suit to display a revealing flesh-coloured outfit with strategically placed sequins. And a study of *Rolling Stone* magazine covers found that in the 1960s, 11 per cent of men and 44 per cent of women were sexualized in some way (for example, partially clad, naked or the surrounding text was sexually explicit). These figures were 17 per cent and 89 per cent in the 2000s.[15] The debate in the Lords touched on these issues – with a society that was becoming increasingly sexualized and so much explicit content becoming available online, the idea of protecting children from finding out about different forms of sexuality was starting to look quaintly foolish. Elsewhere, it was increasingly argued that sex and relationship education ought to help children to navigate an adult world that was often motivated by commercial interests and did not depict sex and related issues such as consent and body image in realistic or sensible ways. This applied to both gay and straight contexts. For better or worse, the country had changed. But would politicians acknowledge this?

After the 7 February debate, the chances of repealing Section 28 were not looking good and Blair was concerned enough to try to fend off accusations that Labour were planning to replace it with gay sex lessons in class. During a visit to Scotland in March before a by-election in Ayr, he made the following speech:

I've just seen the posters here in Scotland. I don't think I've ever seen a more astonishing campaign in all my born days. People are being told their children will have to play – what was it? – homosexual role playing in school. No wonder parents are concerned. It's nonsense. No child is going to be given gay sex lessons in school. Not under this Government now. Not ever.

The government were realizing that repealing Section 28 was not going to be easy, so as a kind of compromise, they suggested an amendment to another bill, the Learning and Skills Act (2000), which would give schools the duty of following statutory guidance on sex and relationships education. This was defeated, however, and instead, after its third reading in the Lords on 23 March 2000, the Learning and Skills Act would emphasize that pupils should be taught the importance of marriage for family life and bringing up children, and that 'they are protected from teaching and materials which are inappropriate having regard to the age and the religious and cultural background of the pupils concerned.'

Baroness Young resumed her position as chief defender of Section 28, saying 'I know that I am speaking for the overwhelming majority of the population which does not want the promotion of homosexuality in schools. I have had some 4,000 letters begging me to stand firm; letters from teachers, doctors, nurses, social workers, hundreds of church-goers, parents, grandparents and even a few homosexuals.' She also spoke of an exhibition she had arranged of sex education material, claiming that 'the books which were produced for use in primary schools were, quite simply, sickening.' One of the pieces in the exhibition was a teachers' pack that had been created in 1999 by a group called Freedom Youth, paid for by the Health Promotion Service in Avon, intended for use with teenagers. It was called *'Beyond a Phase': A Practical Guide to Challenging Homophobia in Schools* and consisted of a booklet and a fourteen-minute video. The video contains interviews with members of Freedom Youth, talking about their experiences and how homophobic bullying impacted on them. At one point a young man called Karl suggests 'experimenting with both boys and girls to see who you're most comfortable with'. It was an ill-judged inclusion in the video, easy to pick on as encouraging secondary schoolchildren to have sex before it was legal as well as potentially pushing them into situations that could result in complicated, embarrassing outcomes.

The pack also contained a scenario about a fifteen-year-old called Michael who wants to have sex with his boyfriend but is nervous. 'Michael knows he should use a condom but doesn't know where to go for help. What should he do? Consider . . . what might you do?' I'm less concerned about this part. Asking children to see things from someone else's perspective isn't the same as instructing them to be like that person. Some teenagers, gay and straight, do have sex before the age of sixteen and alongside issues of STIs, there is the risk of pregnancy, so it's important to teach them about safe sex, contraception and consent.

The written materials in *Beyond a Phase* also get students to role play different characters, including a married man who has sex with other men in secret, a female sex industry worker and a transvestite cabaret artist. As a result of this kind of content, the pack had been targeted by the Christian Institute, which had claimed that it had been purchased by Fife Education Authority and a school in Inverness, resulting in coverage in the national press and denials from Scottish school board associations that schools would be allowed to use them.[16]

In the 30 March debate in the Commons Desmond Swayne (Conservative, New Forest West) brought along the notorious lesson plan and read out a list of fifteen different characters that children were asked to role play in 'Extra lesson (1)'. As well as those listed above, it included a black disabled lesbian who is also a wheelchair user, a bisexual fourteen-year-old young woman and a Chinese bisexual fifteen-year-old young man. Well-meaning the teaching pack might have been, but this part reads like the sort of thing that a right-wing newspaper would invent if it wished to caricature the 'loony left'. Swayne sarcastically said, 'One is tempted to ask: what of the needs of the Aztec community in South Nerdley? Why has it been omitted from this litany of roles? Extra lesson plan II adds, for spice, a man "done for cottaging" – whatever cottaging may be – a "Bisexual Granny" and an "S&M Heterosexual Woman".' He referred to the material as 'filth and nonsense'. The pack also contained facts, figures and testimonies about the extent of homophobic bullying in the 1980s and '90s, which it could be argued are much more shocking, but these were not mentioned in the debates.

Gerald Howarth (Conservative, Aldershot) also noted some draft guidance distributed by the Secretary of State, relating to sex education. He picked on the *Gay Sex Now* leaflet that had been causing so much excitement in Scotland, calling it 'quite disgusting' and noting that it had 'been published with £50,000 of public money'. Shadow Education Minister and future prime minister Theresa May also spoke out against the proposed repeal, claiming that the government were 'acting against the wishes of the many parents who want to ensure the protection of children in schools and other local authority institutions'.

On 16 July, a private memo from Blair, written on 29 April, was printed in *The Times* and *The Sun*. In it, he warned that Labour were seen as 'weak' on gay issues and indicated a perception that he and his government were 'out of touch with gut British instincts'.[17] As well as being an embarrassment, the leaked memo called into question the extent that Labour was committed to repealing Section 28.[18] Baroness Blatch used the memo as ammunition, archly referring to it during consideration of the amendments to the Learning and Skills Act on 24 July, saying that it 'is very revealing of so much'. The bill came under attack from other quarters. Baroness Young cautioned that the amendments only concerned sex education in schools but did not apply to youth groups or children's homes. She also noted that she'd now had 5,000 supportive letters from members of the public (in case you weren't keeping count, that's an extra 1,000 since her last tally four months earlier) and urged the Lords to continue to support Section 28. As with earlier debates, the Lords were keen to put in wording that protected children from bullying but voted against adding anything which might undermine Section 28.

And so, the government backed down – they wanted to get the Local Government Bill through, with or without Section 28, and they didn't want to risk the Lords scuppering it altogether. They couldn't even use the Parliament Act to overrule the Lords this time because the bill had started off in the Lords, and the

Parliament Act applies only to bills introduced in the Commons. Labour were disappointed but seemed undeterred. William Hague couldn't resist a bit of gloating. On 26 July, during Prime Minister's Questions, he gently mocked Blair, asking if he agreed that the House of Lords had 'more accurately reflected public feeling than the House of Commons'. Despite the implicit reference to the dratted memo, Blair responded firmly in the negative. 'I believe that Clause 28 is a piece of prejudice. It is right to remove it and I remain committed to removing it.' But a few minutes later, the leader of the Liberal Democrats, Charles Kennedy, asked Blair *when* he proposed to repeal it. Blair wouldn't give a timeframe, saying, 'We will declare our position at a later time,' while Tory MPs apparently jeered him.[19] Theresa May, who was Shadow Education Secretary at the time, called the defeat 'a victory for common sense' and urged the government not to bring the legislation back.[20]

Around this time another future prime minister, Boris Johnson, who in those days was the editor of *The Spectator*, wrote of 'Labour's appalling agenda, encouraging the teaching of homosexuality in schools, and all the rest of it'.[21] However, Johnson's opinion seems to have been rather malleable. The author, scriptwriter and political campaigner John O'Farrell describes how he would sometimes appear on panel shows alongside Boris Johnson, with Johnson asking O'Farrell to tell him what his opinion on Section 28 should be. O'Farrell convinced Johnson that he should be against it and felt quite pleased with himself until later he heard him opposing Labour's repeal.[22]

Even with a Labour majority and a reduced Lords, Section 28 had been reprieved. When, if ever, would it be taken off the law books?

The Scottish question

Scotland also had to abide by Section 28, or Section 2A as it was referred to north of the border. A charity called Equality Network had been founded in 1997, which campaigned to have Section 2A repealed in Scotland. Campaigners were right to be hopeful – the political landscape in Scotland had completely changed that year. The country had been directly governed by the Parliament of Great Britain for the last three hundred years, but this did not sit well with some. There had been suggestions to 'devolve' before 1914 but the First World War had put things on hold. However, support for 'home rule' had been growing since the 1960s, particularly with the discovery of oil in the North Sea, and then all those years of Conservative government in the 1980s and '90s. On 11 September 1997, just a few months after Tony Blair won the UK election, the Scottish electorate voted for devolution, resulting in Scotland having its first election to fill 129 seats on 6 May 1999. Labour won 56 of them but were 9 short of a majority so they formed a coalition with the Liberal Democrats, who had 17. The new Scottish Executive, led by its First Minister Donald Dewar (Labour), held its first meeting in the General Assembly Hall of the Church of Scotland in Edinburgh on 12 May 1999. With no Lords to get in the way, one of the first policies of this new Parliament was to abolish Section 2A. It was going to be easy-peasy and Scotland would show those Sassenachs how to get it done. But then along came Brian.

Brian Souter was one of the richest men in Scotland. He had been employed as a bus conductor when he was eighteen and had worked his way up, founding the Stagecoach Group,

Scotland's largest privately owned public transport company. Concerned about the repeal of Section 2A, an organization called Keep the Clause had been formed with Brian as its most high-profile supporter. Remember the Ayr by-election that had occasioned Tony Blair to denounce gay role-playing in schools? It had been a safe Conservative seat for practically a century until New Labour had snatched it away in 1997. However, in the 1999 Scottish parliamentary election, Labour had only won by 25 votes, prompting two recounts. The winner, Ian Welsh, a professional footballer, had suddenly resigned after just 230 days in office, returning to his post as Chief Executive of Kilmarnock Football Club. Subsequently, at the by-election on 16 March, the seat went to John Scott (Conservative). Keep the Clause backed him, putting up billboards in the area and chalking up the win to their campaign. Souter was quoted as saying 'There is no doubt this was the "keep the clause" by-election. The party that fought repeal won. The major parties who supported repeal lost.'[23]

Another prominent supporter of Keep the Clause was Cardinal Thomas Winning, head of the Roman Catholic Church of Scotland. Illustrative quote: 'I deplore homosexual acts. I hesitate to use the word perversion, but let's face up to the truth.' In January 2000, Winning had made a speech in Malta, warning that Europe's pro-gay activists were 'pushing for greater power' and claiming that 'the threat to the Christian family is very real. I would ask you to cast your minds back to the dark days of the Second World War. The parallels with today are striking. In place of the bombs of 50 years ago you find yourselves bombarded with images, values and ideas which are utterly alien.'[24] He hadn't actually

Protect our children
KEEP THE CLAUSE! 28

Memories of Scotland in 2000: the Keep the Clause! logo.

said that gay people were Nazis, but you don't need a PhD in discourse analysis to see how it was pretty much implied. This fighting talk was enough to bring him to the attention of OutRage!, which has been rather well-behaved in this chapter until now. On 7 March, its supporters decided to pay Cardinal Winning a visit. He happened to be giving a lecture at the time at St Mary's Catholic Church Hall in Croydon, so was quite surprised when Peter Tatchell called out from the audience, 'Why don't you respect gay people?' Then six members of the group walked onto the platform where Winning was standing, surrounding him and holding up placards that read 'Stop Crucifying Queers' and 'Apologize for Church Homophobia'. I think he got off lightly – no stink bombs, mice or dancing nuns were involved. One member of OutRage! was arrested but later released without charge.[25]

Meanwhile, Keep the Clause came up with an audacious scheme. Confident that they had public support, they would ask *everyone* of voting age in Scotland if they wanted Section 2A to remain as law. They asked the Electoral Reform Ballot Services (ERBS) to organize the poll but the ERBS refused, saying they didn't feel it would be a 'legitimate democratic exercise'. I can see why – it could end up with people demanding public votes on every change to the law that they didn't like. But Keep the Clause supporters were not impressed. One of their spokespeople, Jack Irvine, said, 'I have seldom come across a more gutless, spineless bunch of people in my life. We're utterly appalled by their decision, we think it's an affront to democracy. The society's mission statement says they give effective representation to all significant points of view within the electorate. Well, they've got a very funny way of showing it.'[26]

With or without the help of the ERBS, Keep the Clause was going to have its ballot. So Brian Souter reportedly used £1 million of his own money to pay the company Vote It to run things. Rather than using polling stations, they set up a postal vote based on a voting register from 1999. This resulted in some irregularities. There were reports that many voters, especially eighteen- and nineteen-year-olds, had not received a paper, others had received multiple copies and thousands had been sent out to people who were dead.

The ballot form had two options: 'I vote to *retain* Clause 28 (Section 2A)' and 'I vote to *repeal* Clause 28 (Section 2A)'. Almost 4 million ballot papers were sent out (3,970,712 in total) with 31.8 per cent of them returned – not great, being lower than the turnout for any Scottish national election. It was reported that Members of the Scottish Parliament such as Tommy Sheridan and Bishop Richard Holloway ripped up their ballot papers while some people burned them in the street.

Others posted the prepaid envelope with nothing inside it, incurring wasted expenditure for the poll organizers.[27] Of those papers that did make it back to Vote It, 86.8 per cent of them were to retain Section 2A and 13.2 per cent were for repeal. Souter called it a 'tremendous result', noting that the number of people who had voted to keep the clause was higher than the number of votes cast for any single political party in Scotland at any election in the previous decade. Others were not convinced. Wendy Alexander, the Communities Minister, noted that two out of three voters 'rejected or binned or simply ignored this glorified opinion poll'.[28] Ipsos MORI, which knows a thing or two about opinion polls, leapt in to say that no, actually, it wasn't an opinion poll because it wasn't a representative sample of the population, and it wasn't a referendum because there had not been a full-scale campaign with both sides given the chance to put forward their views in a balanced way.[29] Peter

Brian Souter's 'tremendous result' for the Keep the Clause campaign
(bearing in mind that only 31.8 per cent of votes were returned).

Tatchell was even less impressed, calling Souter's support for Section 2A 'the moral equivalent of the business-funded campaign to maintain racial segregation in the Deep South of the USA in the 1950s'.[30]

Remember the London Lesbian Avengers who had shouted provocative things from the top of a London bus in the last chapter? The group had been 'resting' for a number of years but Souter's support of Section 2A inspired them to re-form. A double-decker bus was also going to feature prominently in this next action – it was a Stagecoach bus and it didn't stand a chance. On a rainy day a group of Avengers surrounded a number 15 as it passed Piccadilly Circus. Armed with buckets and brushes, they coated the whole bus, windows and all, in pink paint. A pink banner was stretched from a lamp-post to the statue of Anteros (still blushing from having been kissed by Richard Sandells a decade ago). The banner read 'Let There Be Love!' For the pièce de résistance, two women climbed on top of the bus and held up another, enormous, banner which simply stated, 'Repeal Section 28'. Seven Avengers were arrested although two had their charges dropped. Subsequently, on 12 June 2000, the Pink Bus Five appeared in court. Their magistrate, a Mr Pratt, was not impressed, ordering them to pay £2,000 for criminal damage and to carry out community service.[31] However, he evidently had a secret sense of humour because they were sent to paint schools.

It was not a very pleasant time for LGBT+ people in Scotland. One of my Scottish friends, Iain, remembers, 'The billboards were everywhere. Big on the red print to hammer home the danger. My boyfriend Lee and I were in Glasgow and we came across some Keep the Clause campaigners. Lee approached them and one woman said to him, "Well are *you* gay?" and when he said "yes" she flat out said to his face, "Well I want you to know that I think you are disgusting."' Charming.

But it was not a good time for Stagecoach either. Souter's stance brought the company a lot of bad publicity. Its Chief Executive, Mike Kinski, resigned in February, a decision that some newspapers claimed was to do with Souter's Section 2A support, although this was denied by Stagecoach. After Stagecoach sold off Porterbrook, a train-leasing business, its shares had tumbled in price to 63 pence compared against a twelve-month high of 233 pence.[32] Souter had to wait until Labour were out of power to receive a knighthood. After accepting the award at Buckingham Palace on 11 November 2011, he said, 'This is a proud day, not just for myself, my wife, Betty, and my family, but for all of the unsung people who have supported me in my business ventures and charitable work . . . I hope this honour sparks the drive in others to start their own business and help other people.'[33]

As for the Scottish Executive, they paid absolutely no heed to the Keep the Clause campaign and on 21 June 2000 they passed the Ethical Standards in Public Life Act, which repealed Section 2A. The debate that took place within the Scottish Parliament itself was relatively calm, compared to the World Wrestling Federation atmosphere at Westminster whenever anything involving Section 28 came up. Even the public gallery was described as 'strangely quiet', with no activists or demonstrators from either side.[34] In case you're wondering how MSPs voted, it was 99 to repeal, 17 against and 2 abstentions.

David explains everything

Scotland had led the way, distinguishing itself from Westminster as being more modern and forward-thinking. However, the success in overturning the repeal there gave New Labour confidence to keep trying. Michael Cashman summed up the continuing frustration with the government, 'I was arguing that it was totemic, it needed to be dealt with and indeed, it was on that basis that it took us until 2003, after the Scottish Parliament had repealed it, that I was able to go to Tony Blair and say, "Look, there's a lot of work to be done on reassuring the LGB community, therefore will you bring forward the Civil Partnership Act?" And it was on that basis that we moved forward.'

Then Section 28 lost one of its most enthusiastic supporters – Janet Young. The Baroness died on 6 September 2002 at the age of 75. She had kept up her opposition to gay rights to the end, leading the dissent against the Adoption and Children Bill that would allow unmarried couples (gay or straight) to adopt. Speaking from recent experience, it *is* difficult, getting older and seeing the world change all around you and not liking it. How sad it must be to know that the political tide has changed and as you continue to stand against it, one by one, your allies pass away. That soon you will be gone too, and that those who remain will get to decide how you will be remembered. In her obituary, published in *The Independent*, Margaret Thatcher called Baroness Young a good friend, courageous and an effective politician, while Peter Tatchell was quoted as saying that she had 'poisoned society with prejudice and intolerance' and that 'future historians will rank her alongside the defenders of apartheid.'[35]

Even so, the government did not seem especially keen on being front and centre this time. At the start of 2003, it was reported that it had not planned any new legislation to repeal Section 28 but that it was prepared for a backbencher to sponsor the change.[36] And so, an amendment to abolish Section 28 was added to a Local Government Bill by backbench MPs. Reassuringly, it was a cross-party effort introduced by Ed Davey (Liberal Democrat, Kingston and Surbiton) with assistance from Kali Mountford (Labour, Colne Valley) and John Bercow (Conservative, Buckingham). This was a sensible strategy – if members of all parties were behind it, then that had to raise its chances of passing.

The clause to repeal Section 28 went to committee stage on 13 February, debated by only a couple of dozen MPs. Just two of them voted against the amendment, Desmond Swayne (Conservative, New Forest West) and Andrew Turner (Conservative, Isle of Wight). Neither had much to say, although Mr Swayne reminded the House of the *Beyond a Phase* pack, referring to it as 'the sort of filth being peddled in schools'. Mr Turner made one of my favourite contributions. Kali Mountford recounted a letter she had received about a young man who had died and his school had been prevented from putting on a display of his artwork because he was gay. Turner interjected with 'That is bonkers.' Only Alan Partridge could have said it better.

Just as Labour had tried to use so-called 'wrecking amendments' to mitigate the effects of Section 28, now it was the Conservatives' turn. One Tory amendment asked for 'an appropriate mechanism . . . for consulting parents of registered pupils by ballot about the contents of any written statement made in pursuance of section 401(1)(A) of that Act'. This would essentially create local referendums about sex education at schools throughout the country. In response, Ed Davey said 'In a liberal democracy, the need to protect minorities properly sometimes means that protection cannot be achieved through the ballot box and that some things are not appropriate for a vote.'

The Commons debated Clause 11 relating to the repeal of Section 28 on 10 March 2003. Clause 11 required monitoring of the effect of the repeal of Section 28, for example, to see if schools made their policies on sex education available to parents, and to determine how many parents had withdrawn their children from such lessons. The vote to read that clause a second time resulted in 127 Ayes and 356 Noes. The Tories were still 'officially' opposed to any sort of repeal, having included the line 'We will retain Section 28 of the Local Government Act' in their 2001 manifesto. However, since then, William Hague had been replaced by Iain Duncan Smith as leader of the party. Duncan Smith decided to give his MPs a free vote on whether to repeal Section 28. This essentially meant they could vote how they pleased, rather than being 'whipped' into voting along party lines.[37] This was announced by the new Shadow Minister for Local and Devolved Government Affairs, Geoffrey Clifton-Brown (Conservative, Cotswold), who began the debate with, 'Let me say at the outset that the Conservative party regards these as matters of conscience. We will therefore have completely free votes on the whole of this part of the Bill.'

Clifton-Brown did not especially want to repeal Section 28 himself though. He brought up the by-now-notorious *Gay Sex Now* pamphlet: 'I shall not subject the House to its contents except to say that it refers to practices called rimming and scat

– I do not know what they mean.' Despite claiming ignorance of these practices, he knew enough to determine that the material was 'inappropriate for children'. He referred to another booklet, produced by Avon health authority (probably *Beyond a Phase*), as 'a nasty little document' of which he promised to 'spare the House the gory details'. As in previous debates, gay sex was characterized as disgusting and unspeakable.

Again, there were several Tory-led amendments and additional clauses that were designed to compromise or wreck matters, depending on your point of view. There was the amendment discussed at committee stage, which gave parents in schools the power to vote on sex education. Ed Davey was still having none of it, calling it 'one of the most odious amendments to come before the House in a long time'. He warned that 'there would be ballot after ballot led by homophobes trying to change the sex education policy of school after school.' Another was to insert a new clause that did not refer to sexuality but required 'a balanced presentation of opposing views' on 'issues relating to the morality of sex outside marriage'. Chris Bryant (Labour, Rhondda) called that one a 'smokescreen'. But the masterwork was a set of amendments by Ann Widdecombe (Conservative, Maidstone and the Weald) and Edward Leigh (Conservative, Gainsborough), who had come up with a cunning plan to essentially save Clause 28 by removing Clause 119, which removed Clause 28 (still with me)? Perhaps they were hoping that MPs would get confused and vote for it by accident. However, it only received 77 yes votes and 368 no votes despite Duncan Smith setting the example by leading the shadow cabinet ministers into the lobbies to vote for it. Even Clifton-Brown abstained when it came to this vote, saying he was doing it 'to demonstrate strict neutrality', regardless of the shocked looks this earned him.

This debate is also notable for the return of David Wilshire, who had proposed the original amendment that got Section 28 passed into law all those years ago. Having held a sphinx-like silence over his role in the legislature, he felt that the House deserved an insight into the workings of his mind at the time. Will this be the moment in our story when there's an unexpected twist and everything we thought we knew is suddenly thrown up in the air? Hansard sadly does not record the appearance of wavy lines then everything being bathed in sepia but it does reveal the story of an eager new MP, having slogged it out for eleven years in local government, proudly now taking his seat at Westminster but feeling shy and inadequate amid glamorous types like Norman Tebbit or intellectuals like Jill Knight. He had been 'unceremoniously dumped' on to a Standing Committee and nobody had told him that backbenchers 'are not supposed to say or do anything'. Most people, when they make a mistake in a new job in the first few days, usually just break the photocopier or accidentally upset the person in the next cubicle, but David Wilshire invented Section 28. He claimed that he had only introduced the amendment because he had been concerned about councils wasting large sums of public money to achieve social change that people did not want. This innocent goal had resulted in him being pushed, unwillingly, into the limelight. He referred to the hate mail he had received and the unflattering publicity. The abseiling incident even got a look-in as Wilshire lamented that he had been 'blamed for a siege of Parliament'. It was a full-on flashback, reminding me of when Davina McCall used to show the 'best bits' to evicted housemates in *Big Brother*. My favourite part of this fifteen-years-overdue piece of exposition was when Wilshire attempted to put to bed the idea that he was a bigot once and for all by quoting from an interview he had given to *Capital Gay* that was published on 5 February 1988: 'David Wilshire – the man who introduced Clause 28 into Parliament – is not a bigot. Confused, ignorant and illogical – Yes. Stupid, even. But bigoted he is not.' So the Big Twist was apparently that Section 28 had happened because a new MP didn't know what he was doing. Oh David, you mean we could have been friends all this time?

Repeal had got through the Commons, with even some Tory MPs voting for it. But what would happen in the Lords?

The last shout

The Lords had the second reading of the act on 3 April 2003. Baroness Young may no longer have been with us but Section 28 had a new defender, Baroness Blatch. A staunch champion of traditional methods of teaching, Blatch was one of those people who wanted kids to learn about Shakespeare, not soap operas. She had complained that children were being taught to look for the meanings of words rather than how to spell them, how to use a calculator rather than to add up, and that they were being told they had achieved something rather than the difference between right and wrong.[38] Baroness Blatch had made a few contributions to the initial debates in 1988 and had spoken up for Section 28 in the 7 February 2000 debate in the Lords. But it was in this last set of debates that she would really come into her own.

Shakespeare not soaps: Baroness Blatch, one of the last defenders of Section 28.

First though, there were signs that even the Lords affiliated with the Church, who could usually be relied on to say something homophobic, were starting to come round to the concept of gay people. The Lord Bishop of Guildford made a statement calling Section 28 discriminatory, then arguing for the importance of marriage, but rather than using that to exclude and denigrate gay people, he said that marriage was 'good for people who are gay or straight'. He didn't go as far as saying that gay people should be allowed to marry but it could have been interpreted that way.

Waheed Alli, a media entrepreneur who had received a life peerage in 1998, and was the first openly gay peer, also spoke in support of gay rights. He called Section 28 'completely redundant' due to the Education Act (1996) and other guidelines on sex education. However, perhaps as an indication of the lesser amount of controversy around the topic, Section 28 got sidelined a bit, while other Lords got caught up in discussion of Business Improvement Districts and council tax. At 7.12 p.m.

Baroness Blatch tried her best to shock everyone with a long speech that involved partner swapping, anal sex and tying people up, all from a resource pack for teachers called *Taking Sex Seriously*, but she couldn't sustain enough interest to keep the subject in the air and by 7.35 p.m. Lord Smith of Leigh got everyone back to council tax.

On 10 July 2003, the Lords debated Section 28 again. Baroness Blatch was in a foul mood due to a rogue briefing paper about the bill that had been sent round in advance. The briefing paper looked official enough – it was even written on Local Government Association (LGA) headed notepaper. However, when the Baroness had contacted the Chief Executive of the LGA, he had pretty much claimed no knowledge of it. What was in this briefing paper that was so offensive? Well, it 'contained inaccuracies' but worst of all, it criticized Baroness Blatch by name. And to her fury, she'd heard that the person who'd written the brief was phoning people up, looking for material to strengthen it. They'd even said, 'We are doing a job on Lady Blatch.' Who would *dare* to do such a thing? Baroness Blatch knew the answer and was happy to share it with the shocked House.

'The noble Lord, Lord Alli, did so, using House of Lords facilities and its materials.'

There was no love lost between the two. According to Stonewall's Chief Executive Ben Summerskill, when Waheed Alli had first been appointed to the Lords, Baroness Blatch had apparently sniffed to a pal, 'He's as queer as the ace of spades, you know.'[39] Lord Alli tried to explain but Baroness Blatch was having none of it, going on to speak at length about her amendments to the bill. These would only allow the law to be repealed when arrangements were put in place to give parents the right to view sex education materials in their children's school. Parents were also to be consulted when schools set a policy on the use of non-teachers to take sex education lessons. And schools would be allowed to carry out polls of parents regarding sex education. It was pretty much a rehash of the Commons amendments, in other words.

When Lord Alli got the chance, he apologized, saying he'd circulated the briefing by mistake, not realizing it was meant only for him. He went on to express dismay at the purposefully divisive nature of Section 28, producing what is one of my favourite lines from any of the debates: 'We all take our predictable paths. It is bit like a bad soap opera – we deliver our lines, and in some cases we play to the camera.' Then Baroness Richardson of Calow gave a rundown of last night's television, which included *Sex Tips for Girls*, *Sex Toys* and something simply called *Undressing*. These programmes were cited in order to argue that Section 28 was akin to closing the door after the horse had bolted. Baroness Richardson explained, 'It is ludicrous to suggest that children and young people are waiting for local authorities to produce sexually explicit material with which to corrupt them. Such material is readily available. What young people need is to be taught how to respond to the material thrust at them from all sources.'

Towards the end, Earl Russell spoke. The earl had been the Chief Executive of Childline, and said that last year the charity had counselled 16,000 children who were confused about their sexuality. He gave the example of a boy called Bill who had experienced homophobic bullying at school. Bill's teacher had told him to speak to his father, who had beaten him. Lord

Russell warned that such children can run away from home and end up in the sex industry.

But before the vote could take place, Baroness Blatch decided to rely on a well-worn strategy. She got out her (by now well-thumbed) copy of *Taking Sex Seriously* and performed a final encore from it. You may be doubtful that there'd be anything left in this unfortunate text that the Lords hadn't already been required to express shock at, and indeed, her final choice did not appear to arouse the feelings of horror that she might have been hoping for. The teaching instructions she alighted upon asked children to think about the sexual activities that two people can do together. They were allowed to write them down in whatever language they liked, 'for example, rather than just "oral sex" they might put "sucking a man's penis" or "licking a woman's clitoris".' To emphasize that audience members were meant to find this disgusting, Baroness Blatch told them, 'I stand here as a mother and simply say that for 11 pluses in schools that is outrageous.' It was a noble effort but perhaps by this point the Lords and Ladies had become desensitized, having had so many examples of disgusting and outrageous pieces of sex education advice read out to them over the years.

The debate ended and the House voted on Baroness Blatch's amendment. A total of 130 were for it but 180 were against. The Lords had changed direction. I think by this point the defenders of Section 28 knew that the jig was up. They'd lost their numbers. They'd lost Baroness Young. The government had already equalized the age of consent and allowed gay people to serve in the armed forces and the sky hadn't fallen in. Even some Tory MPs were now voting to repeal it. And if

Blair's government failed again, it might pull the Parliament Act or the European Court of Human Rights out of its bag of tricks. Worst of all, the British public were changing their views. Remember that British Social Attitudes Survey carried out in 1987, which had reported that 64 per cent of people said that 'relations between two adults of the same sex' was always wrong? When the same question was put again in 2003 this figure was 31 per cent. The Lords couldn't convincingly argue that Section 28 was what the public wanted any more.

I don't think there was any single reason for the change in public attitudes; rather, it was the gradual effect of a range of factors – increased visibility of LGBTQ+ people in the media, the work of the equality movements, and the fact that more people were starting to come out to their family and friends. Rates of HIV infection had stayed low due to the fact that so many gay men practised safe sex in the 1990s, while anti-viral drugs were lengthening the lives of those who were HIV+. Under such circumstances it was harder for the press to continue a hate campaign against gay people. People were becoming better educated about sex and sexuality in any case – to an extent the threat of HIV had broken the taboo around discussion of sex and as noted earlier, the UK was becoming a lot less uptight about sex itself.

On 10 September, there was a somewhat half-hearted last-ditch attempt to get another amendment into the bill, this time by Lord Brightman. It said, 'Subject to the general principle that the institution of marriage is to be supported, a local authority shall not encourage, or publish material intended to encourage, the adoption of any particular sexual lifestyle.' The amendment would not apply to sexual health risks. But there was little will left. Only half an hour was devoted to its discussion and the Lords rejected it by an even greater number: 100 to 25.

The Local Government Act (2003) received royal assent on 18 September. The part that referred to Section 28 was tucked away, right at the end of Part 8 in a section called 'Miscellaneous and General'. Before you get to the bit about Section 28, there are sections relating to fixed penalties for litter and dog fouling offences, regulation of cosmetic piercing and skin-colouring businesses and schemes for establishing fire brigades. Then, almost as an afterthought, there is something called Section 122. Unlike the section that it removes, it is short and to the point.

122 Repeal of prohibition on promotion
   of homosexuality
Section 2A of the Local Government Act 1986 (c. 10)
   (local authorities prohibited from promoting
   homosexuality) ceases to have effect.

On 17 November, Stonewall hosted a 'Kiss Section 28 Goodbye' party at the London nightclub G-A-Y.[40] Those present included Ben Bradshaw (Labour, Exeter), the *EastEnders* actress Michelle Collins and the original Smalltown Boy, Jimmy Somerville, who was quoted as saying that Section 28 had forced him to become political.

The following day, the repeal of Section 28 came into effect. Ben Summerskill was reported as saying, 'This unnecessary clause only served to spread confusion and fear. It will now be consigned to where it belongs – onto the legal rubbish heap of hatred and bigotry.'[41] Funnily enough, the change to the law did not receive much attention outside the lesbian and gay press. While *The Guardian* did have an article about Section 28 on page 6, the national newspapers generally did not applaud or decry its demise. Instead, they mainly ignored it in favour of reporting on President George Bush, who was making a controversial visit to the UK, just six months after the U.S.-led attacks on Iraq. His visit resulted in protests across the country and attendant column inches. Meanwhile, on the front page of the *Daily Express* that day, readers were urged to drop two dress sizes. British people got up and went about their business. Children went to school as usual. It was just another ordinary day.

But after fifteen years, five months and twenty-five days, Section 28 was history.

7

A Legacy Is Etched

In 2019, much of Westminster looks pretty similar to what it was like in 1988. But it feels like a completely different place. I have signed up to go on a ninety-minute LGBTQ+ history tour of Parliament, a recently installed option amid the various tours you can attend. The tour guide introduces himself as Felix, impressing me because he doesn't need a script to refer to the numerous facts he imparts. Towards the end we are led into the House of Lords – it is the first time I've been there and it feels strange standing among all this red leather and polished wood panelling on a Saturday afternoon while the chamber is bereft of its pontificating peers. I wonder if I put my ear to one of the benches I will hear a ghostly echo of Lord Longford proclaiming that homosexuals are disabled people. Felix points to the balcony where 31 years ago a few fearless young women outraged and amused those in the chamber below by climbing over the balcony and sailing down lengths of clothesline that they had brought with them from Clapham Market. He tells us that after the abseiling event, apparently one of the Lords asked Baroness Elizabeth Barker (Liberal Democrat) if she was going to come into the chamber the usual way or over the balcony

(Barker revealed that she was in a same-sex relationship in a speech to the Lords in 2013). The House of Lords is a much friendlier place for LGBTQ+ people nowadays – there are now 22 'out' lords and ladies, including Lord (Chris) Smith and Lord (Michael) Cashman. The existence of the LGBTQ+ history tour makes me happy – haven't we all come such a long way and all that. It also makes me realize that 1988 is now considered history. It's so long ago that there's enough emotional distance for us to talk of these things without anyone getting upset. It's like when we say that someone famous died a long time ago. But to me, 1988 isn't that long ago.

For others, the ideology of Section 28 was so deeply embedded that it is still 1988.

A study carried out by Catherine Lee, published in 2019, found that LGBTQ+ teachers who had taught under Section 28 were still adversely affected by the experience. Compared to those who had trained after 2003, they were less likely to be open about their sexuality (20 per cent versus 88 per cent). A total of 60 per cent said they never took their partner to school events (no teachers who had trained after 2003 said this), and they were more likely to see their teacher and sexual identities as incompatible (40 per cent versus 13 per cent). One teacher was quoted as saying, 'Sometimes when I'm teaching, I find myself stopping mid-sentence to check that what I'm planning to say isn't going to out me to the kids. I must appear very strange to them sometimes.' Another teacher said, 'I keep myself to myself at school. In the early days, I used to make up girlfriends but now I can't be bothered to lie so I don't tell anybody anything about my life outside school.'[1] I get it. Sometimes I wonder if I'd be more relaxed generally if I hadn't been gay in the 1980s.

At least when Section 28 does get mentioned these days, it is almost always as a mistake, a piece of homophobic legislation or, as Tristan Garel-Jones, the deputy chief whip for the Conservatives, apparently called it, a piece of meat thrown by Mrs Thatcher to her right-wing wolves.[2] Ironically, Section 28 itself is used to educate younger LGBTQ+ people about the history of the equality movement. The anniversaries of its passage and repeal are usually marked by a slew of news articles and it has been the subject of numerous exhibitions. For example, one on stories from the LGBTQ+ community at the Museum of Liverpool in 2017 contained protest material relating to Section 28 while in 2018, during LGBTQ+ history month, Staffordshire University put on another to commemorate thirty years since its introduction. The same year the University of Sussex held an event called 'What Section 28 Did to Me'.

And as we learn about Section 28, we can even laugh at it. The law is already well on its way to becoming a cultural artefact, a piece of political ignominy, which, along with Cabbage Patch Kids and asymmetrical hair, is a kitsch relic of the 1980s. In 2013, the play *Margaret Thatcher Queen of Soho* imagined what would have happened if, on the eve of a crucial vote about Section 28, Maggie had got lost in Soho and accidentally become a cabaret superstar. Written by Jon Brittain and Matt Telford (the latter also played Mrs Thatcher), the play blends its serious message about homophobia and censorship with one-liners, dance numbers and the PM in a feather boa. In 2015, another play that combines comedy and drama, *Next Lesson*, by Chris Woodley, told the semi-autobiographical story of a fourteen-year-old called Michael, who comes out at school in 1988, then returns years later as a teacher. Considering the censorship that Section 28 caused in the theatre, it is nicely ironic that it is now acting as a muse to playwrights. And perhaps the ultimate example of how times have changed is the 2019 publication of a children's book by author Olly Pike called *Kenny Lives with Erica and Martina*. Unlike *Jenny Lives with Eric and Martin*, this book features cartoon characters rather than photographs of actual people. However, it echoes the themes of diversity and equality in the original by having Kenny live in a world where everything is coloured grey until two neighbours appear, bringing colour to everyone's lives. While Jenny was pilloried, Kenny is having a much nicer time. On 1 June 2020, Deliveroo announced it was partnering with food chain Leon so that when someone ordered food from its app, the order would come with a free copy of either that book or another one, *Prince Henry*, which has a similar message. Would you like your burger with a side of diversity?

The hardest word

What did the architects and supporters of Section 28 make of its repeal, in the months and years that followed? Those people are now thought of as being on the wrong side of history. How did they account for their actions, if at all? And did they ever try to apologize?

One of the first people to address Section 28 was Michael Howard, who gave an interview to the gay magazine *Attitude* in 2005. By this point Howard was leader of the Conservative Party and this was an election year. With their equal age of consent and right to serve in the armed forces, gay people were on their way to becoming first-class citizens so could now be respectably courted for votes. As Minister for Local Government in 1988, Howard had been one of the people responsible for pushing Clause 28 through. In the interview he didn't apologize but said that Section 28

> was brought in to deal with what was seen to be a specific problem at the time. The problem was the kind of literature that was being used in some schools and distributed to very young children that was seen to promote homosexuality . . . I thought, rightly or wrongly, that there was a problem in those days. That problem simply doesn't exist now. Nobody's fussed about those issues anymore. It's not a problem, so the law shouldn't be hanging around on the statute book.

Rightly or wrongly – that's a step towards admitting you got it wrong. He lost the election and Tony Blair swept in for a third and final term.

The Tories went a step further on 9 February 2006, when Conservative Party chair Francis Maude was interviewed for the website *PinkNews*, saying that Section 28 (which he had voted for) had been wrong and was a mistake.[3] Then in June 2009, the leader of the Conservative Party, David Cameron, made a speech apologizing for Section 28 at a Tory fundraising event for Gay Pride (both the apology and the event itself would have been unthinkable twenty years previously). Cameron admitted that he did not have the perfect record on gay rights. Stonewall described the speech as 'historic . . . We have heard the leader of the Conservative party say the words "Section 28" and "sorry".'[4]

However, some of the principal actors in the Section 28 drama were unrepentant until the end. Not all of them lived to see the law repealed, which was probably just as well for them. As noted earlier, Baroness Young ('I do not believe that there is any human right to commit buggery') died in September 2002 while Nicholas Fairbairn (who called homosexuality a 'morbid squint') died in February 1995. The Earl of Halsbury, who had kicked it all off back in 1986 with his Private Peers Bill ('they act as reservoirs of venereal diseases'), died in 2000, while Lord Longford ('all homosexual activity . . . is morally wrong') died in 2001. Others lived past the section's repeal but do not appear to have expressed any regret for their role in the debate. Cardinal Winning died in 2001, only months after Section 2A was repealed in Scotland, Baroness Blatch died in 2005, just two years after she led the last stand for Section 28 in the Lords and Elaine Kellett-Bowman ('quite right that there should be an intolerance of evil') died in July 2014.

Margaret Thatcher died at the Ritz Hotel in London in April 2013. She had been given a life peerage in 1992, although by the time of the 2003 debates she had suffered several small strokes and cancelled all speaking engagements. Her visits to the House of Lords had become less common, although she found time to attend the debates on repealing Section 28 on 23 March and 24 July in 2000 and on 10 July 2003. Ian McKellen told me how he had been present during one of these debates too. 'Voting there, right to the end, in the House of Lords to retain it, sitting with Jill Knight, was Margaret Thatcher. It was one of the last things she did as a politician, to vote to retain Section 28. It would be my principal argument for saying that she shouldn't have a state funeral and of course she did.'

And what of Jill Knight? In May 2018, the peer who had
been at the centre of the Section 28 debate gamely consented to
be interviewed by the writer and long-term editor of *Attitude*
magazine, Matthew Todd, for *Newsnight*. She said that 'the
intention was the well-being of children. And, if I got that
wrong, well, I'm sorry. I'd have welcomed a letter from you
– someone who knew what that legislation was actually feeling like.' Todd managed to find some common ground with
Baroness Knight by noting the negative portrayals of gay people
at the time, saying if there had been more honest representations, perhaps she wouldn't have felt she needed to do what she
did. Baroness Knight mentioned letters she'd received from the
public and then reiterated that she was 'sorry if anything I did
upset you'. Not everyone was convinced by the apology, due
to her use of the conditional *if*, which rendered it a pseudo-
apology because it didn't fully acknowledge that the hurt
occurred. But perhaps her apology was better than nothing.

A more carefully worded apology was produced on 2 July
2018 when Prime Minister Theresa May spoke to ITV at a
Downing Street LGBTQ+ reception. Eighteen years ago, May
had called the retention of Section 28 a victory for common
sense. Now she said, 'There's some things I've voted for in the
past that I shouldn't have done and I've said sorry. Section
28 obviously would have been one of those things . . . I hope
people will see the fact I recognize that I shouldn't have taken
that view on Section 28. I have developed my views. I want
to be seen as an ally of the LGBT community here in the UK.'[5]
And in January 2020, after the 'yuppie poofs' article about
the gay kiss between Colin and Guido in *EastEnders* was
shared on the social media platform Twitter, its author, Piers

Morgan, responded by writing 'I'm ashamed of some of the inappropriate language I used in *The Sun* 30 years ago about gay stars. They were different times, but that's no excuse – it was offensive, it was wrong, and I apologize for it.' This resulted in a mixed response, with some people being supportive, while others angrily insulted him or brought up his more recent views on trans people. I asked Michael Cashman whether he had forgiven Morgan and he replied, 'I can forgive the fact that he wrote what he thought people wanted him to write. But I can't forget it, because to forget it allows such actions to be repeated when a different political environment deems it so.'

Brian Souter hasn't apologized, although in an interview he gave in 2014 he said he supported the traditional marriage-based family and that stance sometimes gets interpreted as homophobic. He also said he had gay friends and wouldn't mind if one of his children was gay.[6] His role in trying to block the repeal of Section 2A in Scotland continues to haunt Stagecoach. In 2019, the Turner Prize ended its sponsorship with Stagecoach South East the day its shortlist had been announced at a press conference, where someone had asked whether the choice of sponsor was a bad idea.[7]

I'm not sure whether it's useful to try to determine whether the apologies of those responsible for Section 28 were in earnest or not. Even the ones that sound sincere might just be because the person apologizing knows how to craft contrition. Even putting aside the issue of whether the apologizer truly means it or is just going along with the majority view, it can sometimes feel like it's too little, too late. With that said, refusing to apologize feels worse than apologizing, and for some people an apology, even decades later, can feel like a step towards closure. Ultimately, I'd be more interested in looking at how such people live their lives in the present day. Are they acting with kindness and respect towards others? Are they quick to judge those who are different from them? Do they court controversy and conflict? Do they give others the benefit of the doubt? Angela Mason had this to say on the matter: 'People do move on and we have to create the space for people to change. That's the generous and the politically effective thing to do.'

Although the 1980s (sort of) look modern, it *was* a different time and many of the people who argued for Section 28 had been around since the Second World War. In turn, they'd been taught and influenced by people even older than them. Looking back on the twentieth century, the amount of social change is dizzying – male homosexuality was only (partially) decriminalized in 1967. Some people can adjust easily, meeting each fresh trend with continued enthusiasm, others can't – and it tends to get harder to keep up, the older you get. I also wonder if some of the Lords had been involved in coercive sexual experiences at boarding school that may have left them feeling guilty or traumatized. And then there's religion, ironically something that often gets 'promoted' to us when we're children and haven't developed the critical faculties to decide for ourselves. Some of the proponents were acting on longstanding religious beliefs that cannot be easily reasoned away because they are based on faith. On the other hand, I don't think everyone should get a free pass, particularly the journalists who stirred the pot and the politicians who thought it would help their career or damage their opponents. Section 28 wasn't a game but at times it felt like some of those involved thought it was. Still, there is something to be said for being gracious in victory. Not forgetting but moving on all the same.

All happy now

It is May 2017 and I am getting hitched to my man, Tony, for the third time. With both sets of families present, we'd first had a 'blessing' at the Manchester Metropolitan Church in 1999, which had no legal status whatsoever. 'Don't throw confetti,' begged our vicar. 'I'll be on my knees picking it up for ages after you've all gone home!' Then we had a low-key civil partnership in Bristol in 2005 (we went to a fish and chip shop afterwards). Appropriately, this third ceremony (to change the civil partnership to a marriage) takes place within the jurisdiction of one of those 'loony left' councils, at Camden Town Hall. Tony is jet-lagged after a long-haul flight and we are a bit scared of our officiator as she gives the couple before us a telling-off for not filling in their form properly. When it is our turn, we sit meekly in her office while she keys in our information. The computer keeps crashing and she gets more and more frustrated as she has to keep going back to the start. Then she can't get the printer to do our certificate so we are sent to sit on a bench in the corridor while she harangues someone from IT over the phone. 'I've got the public outside! This is unacceptable!' we hear her tell them. It is quite a long wait and when I look across to Tony, he's dropped off to sleep. I don't have the heart to wake him up. Instead I think, 'Elton John would be disgusted at us.'

Afterwards we share a piece of cake at a café down the road and I announce our marriage to my 105 Facebook friends by posting a selfie of us smiling. It doesn't feel like a big deal although it's the culmination of decades of campaigning and hard work by numerous people, and we are privileged to hold a legally meaningful piece of paper that would be unthinkable in many other parts of the world. It is funny, really, how the importance of a stable married family life kept coming up in those debates over Section 28 and sex education. Now we are married. Did we win or did they win? And if both sides won, did anyone lose?

The Marriage (Same Sex Couples) Act (2013) legalized 'gay marriage'. It had been pushed through by David Cameron, who led a coalition Conservative–Lib-Dem government. While fewer than half of his MPs backed him over it, I recall arguments from friends at the time that, actually, marriage was a key part of the establishment and by letting gay men and lesbians get married, they were simply being allowed in, helping to swell its numbers and ultimately support the status quo. Rather than undermining marriage, as detractors of the new law had argued, letting us marry would result in more people getting hitched, with the concept of marriage becoming stronger and fewer people likely to consider alternative ways of conducting relationships. I'd thought at the time, 'Well, no one's *forcing* anyone to get married and it's nice to have the *choice*.' But then I remembered back to my time at Lesbian and Gay Switchboard when I'd heard from callers who were in romantic and sexual relationships that did not involve loving commitment or just two people. It feels a bit like society has said, 'Well, we like the nice gays who get mortgages together and shop at IKEA, so they can join the club, but the rest are still perverts.' Perhaps the goalposts have just shifted, then. And perhaps that'll be as good as it gets.

Juliet Jacques, an author and journalist whose memoir *Trans* was published in 2015, has written about how she interviewed people who were involved in organizing the historic march to protest against Section 28 that took place in Manchester on 20 February 1988. She highlights how two decisions were made about the march, revealing further fractures in our story. The first was a motion to support Viraj Mendis, a Sri Lankan national who had come to the UK in 1973 on a student visa and had then claimed asylum in Manchester in the 1980s. Mendis claimed that, as a supporter of the Tamils, his life would have been in danger if he had returned to Sri Lanka. His claim was rejected and so, to avoid being deported, he ran into the Church of Ascension in Hulme, staying there for two years. He was eventually arrested in 1989 during a police raid of the church and deported. He was not killed and claimed that his case had received so much publicity that the Sir Lankan government did not dare harm him. The proposal to explicitly support Mendis was apparently rejected by the march organizers because it might confuse things, although despite this, photographs taken on the day show that some marchers carried banners labelled 'Viraj Mendis Will Stay' and 'Viraj Mendis Defence Campaign'.

The second decision involved whether two performers, Andy Bell (of Erasure) and Jimmy Somerville (from Bronski Beat and The Communards), should perform in drag during the music festival that took place after the march. This was also rejected, as some of those involved with the march believed that it would confuse issues around sexuality or be demeaning to women.[8]

The first decision raises a question about whether it is more important for a range of disparate cases of oppression to indicate solidarity with one another by sharing the same platform or whether there are times when different issues ought to be addressed singly. The second comes back to the issue of respectable versus outrageous protest. I'm not sure these issues can be easily resolved. For me, they show that even in groupings that aim to overthrow oppression, there can still be feelings that some voices can dominate while others do not get heard for a range of reasons.

It is a point made by the genderqueer artist Del LaGrace Volcano, who was one of the participants at the seminar about Section 28 and queer politics that took place on 24 November 1999 at Senate House in London. Volcano raised the issue of the people who are excluded when we talk about a gay and lesbian community, noting that 98 per cent of the people in the room consisted of 'white, probably middle class, lesbian and gay people'. They noted the absence of trans, intersex, black, Asian and disabled people, suggesting that even if they had been invited 'they didn't come, and nobody ever looks at the reason why those people do not feel included.' Volcano called 'for a queer politics that doesn't actually focus on who you have sex with and will become more inclusive'.[9] Are we there yet?

Stonewall, which was founded on the back of Section 28, began a campaign called 'Education for All' in 2005, implicitly acknowledging that the repeal of Section 28 did not magic away homophobia overnight. The campaign was supported by over seventy organizations. I recall seeing the slogan 'Some people are gay, get over it!' on posters on buses. And since then, Stonewall has changed its policy on a number of issues – it was initially not in favour of supporting same-sex marriage, for example. And it did not directly campaign for trans people, although this has since changed and, on 16 February 2015, the charity announced that after a consultation with over seven hundred trans people it planned to campaign for trans equality.

Trans visibility and awareness of issues that trans people face has increased since 2015, although with it has come an ugly backlash, a lot of it from online sources, some suspiciously anonymous, some from more high-profile feminists, sometimes referred to as TERFS (trans exclusionary radical feminists) by those who disagree with their views. Just as large sections of the British press did not do much to help gay men and lesbians during the 1980s, the picture is similar for the last decade when it comes to trans people. A report I produced for the charity Mermaids in 2019 noted some improvement – a shift in terminology had occurred between 2012 and 2019, with joking language and use of terms like *tranny* much reduced. Instead, there was more recognition of transphobia and inclusivity. But not all of this was well-intentioned. About half of the time the term *transphobia* was written about in ways that questioned whether it actually occurred or even existed, while trans people were often characterized as demanding and aggressive or having a propensity to be overly offended. At times, it is hard to characterize discussion over the rights of trans people as even constituting a debate, since the level of discourse is so poisonous, especially on social media, which favours quick-fire short responses that can often serve to make people feel more distant from one another.

So, while I feel that equality has been mostly achieved for me, a gay, white, [latterly] middle-class cisgender man, this is not the case for everyone. It's as if people who sound and look like me got to be at the front of the queue when it came to getting equality. We have a duty to those who are still in the queue.

Section 28 – the sequel

In 2011, one of my nephew's classmates called him gay. My nephew said, matter-of-factly, 'My uncles are gay and there's nothing wrong with it.' And that was the end of that. I took it as an example of how homophobia can and is being countered by openness and a refusal to participate in shame. Similarly, Kat, whose own school experiences I wrote about earlier, told me 'a couple of years ago a friend and I were invited to talk to some young trans people through an LGBTQ+ youth group, mostly just to show them that trans people grow up. They were mostly aged between 12 and 15, and they were absolutely astonishing. Confident, smart, curious and open-minded . . . they had this extraordinary level of self-awareness and self-possession.' Perhaps the kids are alright now? However, there are indications that in some quarters the values of Section 28 are creeping back in, or in some cases, never really went away.

In 2011, the Conservative government changed its guidance on relationship education in schools. They added a clause to a model funding agreement that academies and free schools are beholden to, if they decide to opt out of local authority control. Previously, the guidance had emphasized that care should be taken to avoid stigmatization of children based on home circumstances. The new guidance stipulated that the benefits of marriage should be taught in schools and that schools should avoid using 'inappropriate teaching materials' for sex and relationship education, whatever that meant.[10] Perhaps it was coincidence, but the clause that this appeared in was number 28.[11]

Academies had been established under the Learning and Skills Act (2000) by Tony Blair's government. Free schools are a type of academy that had been established under David Cameron's government in 2011; they can be run by parents, education charities or religious groups. There have been concerns that despite the overturn of Section 28 and the model funding agreements that stipulate what should be taught, some of these schools have managed to retain a homophobic ideology. In August 2013, LGBTQ+ activists, working with the British Humanist Society, identified twenty schools that had sex and relationship policies that replicated the language of Section 28, a further 22 that implied that Section 28 was still in force and three that were otherwise vague.[12] For example, Colston's Girls' School's policy stated, 'The Governing Body will not permit the promotion of homosexuality' (they removed the policy when contacted by activists). Other schools included the Evelyn Grace Academy chain of faith schools, and the Northumberland Church of England Academy and Tasker-Milward V.C. School. Subsequently, the Department for Education conducted an investigation and stated that schools were prohibited under DfE guidance from discriminating on the basis of sexual orientation.

Despite this, the issue of teaching sexuality continues to cause controversy. Andrew Moffat is the same age as me and would have turned sixteen around the same time that Section 28 came into law. His descriptions of school life ring true: 'I knew I was gay by the time I was 13 or 14, and I couldn't tell anybody until I was 27 . . . School was brutal really in the eighties. Virtually every gay person who grew up in the era

No Outsiders: Andrew Moffat (in T-shirt) at Birmingham Pride, 2019.

has the same story about being bullied . . . I don't want any child to go through that lying, the shame, the self-hatred.'[13] In 2007 Moffat developed a teaching resource called *Challenging Homophobia in Primary Schools*, which he used to train teachers to manage homophobic bullying. While working at Chilwell Croft Academy in Birmingham, Moffat came out as gay in a school assembly. After this, some parents complained that they were not happy with their children learning that it is OK to be gay. Moffat resigned, taking up a new position at Parkfield Community School in Saltley, Birmingham. He implemented a programme he had developed called No Outsiders, which promoted inclusivity and tolerance. His work earned him an MBE for services to equality and diversity in education and, in 2019, having taught No Outsiders for four years, he was a finalist for the Global Teacher Prize.

However, the same year parents withdrew about six hundred children from the school for a day and crowds of protesters gathered outside the school gates, chanting, 'Get Mr Moffat out.'[14] The school sent a letter to parents telling them that they would not be teaching No Outsiders lessons for the rest of the term, although this was due to the fact that the curriculum had already been blocked for religious education.[15] However, the protests spread to other schools, including a primary school in the Sparkhill area of Birmingham called Anderton Park, which had an 'Educate and Celebrate' diversity programme that used teaching materials which featured same-sex families. One of the books was *And Tango Makes Three*, a children's book published in 2005 that tells the story of a couple of male penguins called Roy and Silo who fall in love, unsuccessfully try to hatch a stone and are then given an actual egg by their zookeeper. They call the resulting baby penguin Tango.

I knew about *And Tango Makes Three* because one of my students, Mark McGlashan, had based his PhD on studying the language used in a collection of children's books that contained same-sex families, including the one that kicked it all off – *Jenny Lives with Eric and Martin*. He'd collected a whole bookshelf of them – 72 that were published before 2012 when he did his research. *And Tango Makes Three* was typical of the more recent crop that tended to include cute cartoon animal families. Mark had identified how the concept of love was central to many of these books, often demonstrated by the little phrase 'love each other'. For example, in *Jenny Lives with Eric and Martin* there's the text '"We do love each other – even if we argue sometimes," says Eric, looking at Martin.' Appearing alongside these three words there are often images of same-sex parent families embracing or hugging one another. That's what these books are about – love, not sex. The protesters might at least take solace in the fact that *Jenny Lives with Eric and Martin* is unlikely to be part of these teaching packages – its notoriety means that, at the time of writing, second-hand copies go for over £1,000.

During 2019, Anderton Park was regularly surrounded by protesters – parents and others who disapproved of the Educate and Celebrate programme, as well as LGBTQ+ activists and their supporters, who agreed with the school's policy. Sparkhill is an inner-city area of the Sparkbrook ward of Birmingham. In the 2011 census, 70.2 per cent of the residents of Sparkbrook gave their religion as Islam and about half the teachers at the school are Muslims. Some protesters had guarded the roads leading to the school, telling parents, 'If you take your kids to school today you're not a Muslim and you'll burn in hell.'[16] Some 21 teachers at the school were treated for stress while, as usual, children were caught up in the middle of a row that was about them but which they had no control over. On 26 November, a High Court Judge ruled to permanently ban protests outside the school.

It is inaccurate to view the conflict as Muslims versus gay people – Muslims were represented on both sides. Muslim activist Saima Razzaq, a representative of a group called Supporting Education of Equality and Diversity in Schools, has said that 'the answers have to come from within our community . . . It has to be done sensitively, and we have to have those conversations as Muslims, British Pakistanis, as people from Birmingham. It can't be done through the white saviours who are holding counter-protests at the school. That's not helping, it reeks of a colonial mindset to me.'[17] There have been also been claims that those who are at the front of the protests are pawns or are doing it to launch a political career. Angela Mason told me that it was crucial to continue to negotiate differences in society: 'If we don't heal and build bridges, our enemies, and we do have enemies still, will use it to divide us and it will be worse for everyone.'

A 2021 study by Cibyl on behalf of the young people's charity Just Like Us found that LGBTQ+ school children are twice as likely than other children to be bullied, contemplate suicide and feel lonely on a daily basis. Half of them had heard little to zero positive messaging about being LGBTQ+ in school in the last twelve months and 91 per cent had heard negative language about being LGBTQ+ in that period.[18]

So we should not assume that repealing Section 28 has resulted in a consensus about how homosexuality should be taught in schools. It hasn't. Likewise, we should be wary of only looking inwardly at our own society while ignoring what is happening elsewhere in the world.

Hate in a cold climate

Do you recall the throwaway remark I made at the start of the last chapter about how in the 1990s people thought that Western liberal democracy was going to sweep through the nations of the world and it was the end of history? Since then, history has shown itself to be in rude health while Western liberal democracy isn't having as much fun as it thought it was going to in this shiny new millennium. Although the UK may be (mostly) tolerant of its LGBTQ+ citizens, things are not going as well in other parts of the world. Take Russia, for example. On 30 June 2013, a law 'for the Purpose of Protecting Children from Information Advocating for a Denial of Traditional Family Values' (I think something got lost in the translation) was signed into law by President Vladimir Putin. It criminalized the distribution of 'propaganda of non-traditional sexual relationships' among children. Like Section 28 in the UK, it is so broadly written that it has far-reaching effects. It becomes difficult to hold a gay pride march, for example, because children could see it. Kiss a same-sex partner in public? Crime! Hold up a sign saying, 'Being gay and loving gays is normal'? Crime! Display a rainbow flag? Crime! Crime! Crime! Despite the repeal of a law criminalizing gay sex in 1993, and the declassification of homosexuality as a mental illness in 1999, since then the tone in Russia has been increasingly homophobic. In 2012, Moscow's top court upheld a ban on gay pride marches for the next one hundred years while 2017 saw reports of arrests, torture and killings of gay men in the republic of Chechnya. In 2020, voters backed amendments to the constitution that effectively placed a ban on same-sex marriage.

Similarly, opposition to homosexuality is increasing in Poland, with most of the southeast of the country declaring itself an 'LGBT-free zone' and the newspaper *Gazeta Polska* giving out stickers that declare this to be the case. In November 2018, Andrzej Duda, the president of Poland, said he would support a 'homosexual propaganda' ban: 'I think that this kind of propaganda should not take place in schools, it has to be calmly and consistently opposed . . . if such a law was created and would be well written, I do not exclude that I would approach it seriously.'[19] Such a law would violate both the

Polish constitution and the European Convention on Human Rights (ECHR). The ECHR helped to put the kibosh on a similar law in the Ukraine that had received its second reading in October 2012. It would have made it against the law to talk about homosexuality in public or the media or to import, distribute or broadcast anything that 'encourages homosexuality'. After the draft law was condemned by Amnesty International, the European Union and the United Nations, it was eventually removed from the agenda.[20] Along similar lines, in November 2016, a village in Hungary called Ásotthalom passed a law banning 'gay propaganda' along with the Islamic call to prayer and Muslim dress. The law was struck down by the Constitutional Court in April 2017.[21] However, in June 2021 Hungary's parliament passed a law that banned gay people from appearing in school educational materials or TV aimed at people aged under 18.[22] A book called *Wonderland Is for Everyone* seems to have acted as Hungary's *Jenny Lives with Eric and Martin*. And so it starts all over again.

China doesn't have a 'gay propaganda' law, but in 2017 a United States Department of State report found that 'References to homosexuality and the scientifically accurate words for genitalia were also banned. Writers who cover lesbian, gay, bisexual, transgender, and intersex; gender; and youth health issues expressed concern over how to proceed without being shut down.'[23] And it seems petty to talk about censorship laws in the many countries around the world where homosexuality itself is illegal – at least seven states in Oceania, nine in the Americas, 23 in Asia and the Middle East and 33 in Africa.[24]

Opposition to homosexuality is sometimes linked to nationalism, particularly as some advocates of these 'propaganda bans' try to position themselves as different from and thus better than the values of 'the West'. For example, at a Moscow rally in February 2015, which protested against the new government in the Ukraine, a popular slogan translated to 'We don't need Western ideology and gay parades.'[25] Ironically, some of the countries that have anti-gay laws initially had similar laws imposed on them by Western colonizers. And it shouldn't be assumed that everyone in 'the West' is LGBTQ+-friendly anyway. Conservative media in the U.S. regularly complain about the 'indoctrination' of schoolchildren. For example, in 2018, Fox News pundit Todd Starnes, in response to the news that parents in Orange County, California, cannot opt their children out of lessons related to gender identity or sexual orientation, wrote on his website, 'Our nation's public schools have been turned into indoctrination centers by a gang of radical, sex and gender revolutionaries.'[26]

It is a depressing catalogue of ignorance, intolerance and ultimately brutality. And the more it happens, the more likely it is that LGBTQ+ people will go into hiding so the lies don't get countered and the supposed threat from queer people becomes abstracted, making it easier for people to hate what they don't know. It is frustrating, too, that it feels like there's so little that can be done about it. Attempts at intervention can come across as hectoring, no matter how well-intentioned, and I take note of how some of the protesters outside Birmingham schools were characterized as 'white saviours'. But sitting back and doing nothing can come across as complacent and uncaring. I try to think how I'd feel if I was in a homophobic country – what would I want to hear from those in more tolerant places? What *did* I want to hear, back in 1988? Messages of love, hope and support, perhaps. Practical advice from those who've gone through similar things, definitely. Michael Cashman had this to say: 'Don't give up hope because it may take a while. But remember you're not alone. That what happens to you does matter to other people. That *you* matter to other people. It will get better because in the end, decency and justice always prevail. And those of us outside those countries need to ensure that those multinational companies operating in Russia and elsewhere continue to make the point about inclusivity.' It was one of the issues he emphasized in his role as a Member of the European Parliament when considering applications from new countries to join: 'I insisted that the issues around equality, the equal age of consent, non-discriminatory criminal law, were not add-ons, they were essentials.'

Be sure – those hateful laws won't be around forever. And after they've gone and histories are written, how will those who put them in place be remembered? How is Baroness Young remembered? Of course, those who are doing it due to deep-seated religious beliefs are unlikely to be persuaded by such considerations, but those who are in it for short-term political advantage should take heed – the stain will remain.

So have courage. As this book shows, there's more than one way to protest against a homophobic law. Not all of them may be as easy to implement outside a relatively democratic and liberal country like the UK (the bold women who invaded the BBC and the House of Lords were given cups of tea and freed with no charge after a few hours) but there are always ways, small and large. We can't and won't be regulated away.

And finally

On 1 September 2020, new regulations came into place with the Children and Social Work Act, which made relationships and sex education compulsory in all state-funded secondary schools in England. Relationship education became compulsory in primary schools, although sex education was optional at primary level. Additionally, parents could request to the head teacher that their children are withdrawn from sex education, whether they are at primary or secondary school. Only children who were three terms away from the age of sixteen could attend without parental consent (I'm not sure if that would work in reality). The draft guidance to the act expects 'all pupils to have been taught LGBT content at a timely point' and that 'they should ensure that this content is fully integrated into their programmes of study for this area of the curriculum rather than delivered as a standalone unit or lesson.'[27] However, it is up to schools to decide when the 'timely point' is, and the regulations also stipulate that the teaching needs to take into account the religious background of people, which may call for 'a differentiated curriculum'. Groups like Humanists UK have cautiously welcomed the regulations although have warned about the religious-based exemptions.[28] While the regulations will ensure that most children will receive some sort of sensible message about homosexuality from a teacher, I am not sure that *all* of them will, and perhaps those who could benefit from it the most will continue to miss out. As events in Birmingham and abroad indicate, Section 28's legacy lives on in numerous contexts.

Further guidance published by the Department for Education in 2019 has focused on how schools can ensure that pupils understand how to stay safe and behave online as part of existing curriculum requirements.[29] I think back to Baroness Richardson of Calow's remarks about how easy it was to access explicit sexual material via the media during the 10 July 2003 debate. When I was at school, my extracurricular sex education amounted to finding a few copies of soft porn magazines that someone had dumped in some woodland near my street. The Internet was barely in existence then and I look back on my childhood as one that was relatively innocent. I would not change that. It is naive to think that many children do not learn about sex from the Internet and even those whose parents have the strictest of parental controls are likely to find out things from less regulated classmates. Internet pornography is easily accessible and while it provides accounts of the biological aspects in high definition, it offers unrealistic expectations as well as normalizing unsafe or violent practices and the routine objectification of sexual partners. The task of teaching sex and relationship education is made all the more complex and necessary by this – the dangers of failing our children in this area were never so real.

Will homosexuality be promoted in schools? It depends on your definition of the word and whether you think it is possible to promote it. For me, telling children that homosexuality exists and there's nothing wrong with it isn't promotion. Advertisers spend billions of pounds each year trying to think up ways to get people to change their behaviour by promoting things. I can't imagine that an advert which said 'Product x exists and there's nothing wrong with it' would impress many people.

I want to end the story of Section 28 by emphasizing that, for me, it is a story of good coming out of bad. It's also a story of heroism and humour. The people I interviewed for this book were all very modest and I think I caused some embarrassment when I thanked them for the hard work they did and for putting themselves in the public eye during those homophobic years. Ian McKellen said, 'Don't overestimate what I did, I was scarcely one of a team. I was just there to marvel at what they were doing and occasionally wheeled out to shake someone's hand.' And while I doubt they knew it at the time, for some of the people who spoke out against Section 28, their activism set their careers in new directions. For others, it was something they did but then they went on with their lives. Many of the women who were involved in the House of Lords and BBC News invasions made their mark and then walked off into the sunset as the credits played. Susannah Bowyer told me, 'There's something very cool about that disappearing. And within the group now, people have different takes, some are clear that for them the action stands for itself and they don't want to take part in interviews etc. The fact we did disappear was part of it, so I've got a lot of sympathy with that.' I think the UK would be a worse place without these activists and campaigners. And there are also the thousands of people across the whole country who played their part, organizing, marching, lobbying, donating and zapping. They came together when they had to. As a result, Section 28 was one step back, but it resulted in many steps forward. I'm grateful to all of you.

Chris Smith believes that good came out of Section 28. 'Because it was so egregious and so extreme, I think it helped in one really important way. It helped to change social attitudes. It actually meant that lots of ordinary decent non-LGBT people up and down the country thought these people don't deserve this sort of opprobrium.' In addition, he noted 'the rather wonderful way which the LGBT community did mobilize outside Parliament. The rallies, the demonstrations, the marches. There was one good thing that did emerge out of it all.' Michael Cashman views the fight 'as a connection with strangers – between us we lost the battle for Section 28 but we won the war for equality. And it was the moment I became my father's son – that if you didn't stand up for what you believed in then you couldn't believe in yourself. It was that moment that led me to where I am now.'

Angela Mason described her time in Stonewall as 'the most exciting thing I've ever done in my life. There was wonderful comradeship with everybody who was involved in the struggle. I remember everybody with deep affection.' And despite the fractures, despite the disagreements on how to get things done, despite the fact that there were all these different forms of protest, what they all had in common was a non-violent approach. At the end of my interview with Ian McKellen he simply said, 'The revolution, that was huge, and let's hope permanent, happened without a single brick being thrown, without anyone being hurt. There were no riots in the streets, there were occasional disturbances, but we won the argument and politics is all about that, so there we go.'

So there we go. When I began writing this book I wasn't at all sure that I would enjoy telling the story of Section 28 as on the surface it appeared to be such a depressing topic. But I hope I've shown that it is actually a story of courage and determination in the face of adversity. And ultimately, it is a story that we can be proud of.

References

1 Welcome to Smalltown

1 Paul Baker, *American and British English* (Cambridge, 2017).

2 Fractures in Society

1 See https://ctntp.uk/background, accessed 12 May 2021.
2 Gay Liberation Front, *Manifesto* [1971] (London, 1978).
3 Robert Greenfield, 'Freaking London's Jesus Festival', *Rolling Stone* (11 November 1971).
4 'The Origins of the Gay Liberation Front . . . and Disrupting the "Festival of Light" – UK 1960s', https://libcom.org, accessed 12 May 2021.
5 Peter Tatchell, 'Idealism, Pride and Anger: The Beginnings of Lesbian and Gay Liberation in Britain', www.petertatchell. net, accessed 12 May 2021.
6 Basil Gingell, 'Uproar at Central Hall as Demonstrators Threaten to Halt Festival of Light', *The Times* (10 September 1971), p. 14.
7 Martin Roger Corbett obituary, OutRage! archives (11 July 1996), http://rosecottage.me.uk.
8 Nicholas Timmins, *The Five Giants: A Biography of the Welfare State* (London, 1995).
9 John Davis, 'The Inner London Education Authority and the William Tyndale Junior School Affair, 1974–1976', *Oxford Review of Education*, XXVIII/2–3, A Century of Local Education Authorities (June–September 2002), pp. 275–98.

10 'What's New?', *The Guardian* (16 October 2001), www.theguardian.com.

11 Robert Peal, 'Islington: Children as Guinea Pigs of the Left', *Standpoint* (28 April 2014), https://standpointmag.co.uk.

12 Terry Ellis et al., *William Tyndale: The Teachers' Story* (Tiptree, 1976), pp. 51, 150.

13 James Callaghan, 'A Rational Debate Based on the Facts', speech made at Ruskin College, Oxford (18 October 1976), www.educationengland.org.uk.

14 Damian Barr, *Maggie and Me* (London, 2013).

15 Richard Ford, 'GLC Leader Defends Gay Rights', *The Times* (19 August 1981), p. 2.

16 *The School Curriculum 1981*, Department of Education and Science, Welsh Office, www.educationengland.org.uk/documents/des/schoolcurric.html, accessed 11 June 2021.

17 Ibid.

18 'Global Health Observatory Data: HIV/AIDS', World Health Organization, www.who.int/data/gho/data/themes/hiv-aids, accessed 14 June 2021.

19 Chris Godfrey, '"My Life Is Not Over. But It Feels Like It Is Sometimes": The Rev Richard Coles on Losing His Partner', *The Guardian* (9 March 2020).

20 Tim Jonze, '"It Was a Life-and-Death Situation. Wards Were Full of Young Men Dying": How We Made the Don't Die of Ignorance Campaign', *The Guardian* (4 September 2017).

21 Paul Baker, *Public Discourses of Gay Men* (London, 2005).

22 Peter Tatchell, *London Labour Briefing*, November 1981. https://quotes.yourdictionary.com/author/peter-tatchell/110828, accessed 14 June 2021.

23 Andy McSmith, *No Such Thing as Society: A History of Britain in the 1980s* (London, 2010).

24 'The Battle for Bermondsey', *Southwark News* (4 March 2015).

25 'They Fought and Lost', *The Westminster Hour*, BBC Radio 4 (January/February 2003).

26 Benjamin Cohen, 'Simon Hughes Apologises for Homophobic Smears in 1982', *Pink Paper* (24 January 2006).

27 'Tatchell Backs Simon Hughes', 25 January 2006,

https://archive.is/20120906014023; www.petertatchell.net/
politics/simonhughes.htm.

28 Sheila Jeffreys, 'Political Lesbianism in the UK',
Lesbian History Group (23 January 2017),
https://lesbianhistorygroup.wordpress.com.

29 'Harassment of Lesbians and Gay Men . . . and how
to challenge it at the GLC', GLC leaflet (1985).

30 GLC Women's Committee, *Tackling Heterosexism:
A Handbook of Lesbian Rights* (1986), pp. 5–7.

31 'Equality. It's about Time', www.fawcettsociety.org.uk,
accessed 14 June 2021.

32 London Gay Teenage Group, *Talking about Young Lesbians*,
ed. Lorraine Trenchard (London, 1984), p. 29.

33 Onlywomen Press Collective, *Love Your Enemy? The Debate
between Heterosexual Feminism and Political Lesbianism*
(London, 1981).

34 Beatrix Campbell and Lynne Segal cited in *Women of the
Revolution: Forty Years of Feminism*, ed. Kira Cochrane
(London, 2010), p. 352.

35 Julie Bindel, 'My Sexual Revolution', ibid., p. 354.

3 An Uncivil Debate

1 Susanne Bösche, 'Jenny, Eric, Martin . . . and Me', *The
Guardian* (31 January 2000).

2 Adam Mars-Jones, 'The Book That Launched Clause 28',
Index on Censorship, VIII (September, 1988), pp. 37–40.

3 'In Living Memory – Jenny Lives with Eric and Martin',
BBC Archive (broadcast on BBC Radio 4 on 5 August 2009).

4 John Izbicki, 'Modern Danish Invasion', *Daily Telegraph*
(5 December 1983), p. 25.

5 Roald Dahl, 'Tales We Mustn't Tell Our Children', *Daily
Mail* (4 May 1984), p. 6.

6 'Baker Acts over Gay Schoolbook', *Daily Mail*
(16 September 1986), p. 5.

7 '"Intolerant and Lunatic Libraries" Attacked', *The Times*
(19 September 1986), p. 5.

8 'Baa Baa, Green Sheep!', *Daily Mail* (9 October 1986),
p. 13; 'Comment – Green Sheep – a Red Herring', *Irish Voice*,

Haringey IBRG's Community Magazine (Christmas 1986), pp. 4–5, at http://repository.londonmet.ac.uk/2743/1/ AIB.IBRG.Z.9.1986.pdf.

9 'Schools: Investment in Education and Science' parliamentary debate (7 May 1986), https://hansard.parliament.uk.

10 'In Living Memory'.

11 Ibid.

12 'Upside Down Idiocy', *Daily Mail* (9 July 1986), p. 7.

13 'Bizarre Truth about "Happy Family" in the Gay Schoolbook', *Daily Mail* (22 September 1986), p. 3.

14 'Assault on the Young', *Daily Telegraph* (6 October 1986), p. 16.

15 David Mallen, 'Foreword', in *Positive Images*, ILEA Learning Resources Branch (September 1986), p. v.

16 Ibid.

17 Stuart Lansley, Sue Goss and Christian Wolmar, *Councils in Conflict: The Rise and Fall of the Municipal Left* (Basingstoke, 1989), p. 167.

18 Ibid.

19 'Parents in Clash over Gay Book', *Daily Mail* (1 October 1986), p. 3; Adam Lent and Merl Storr, 'Chronology', in *Section 28 and the Revival of Gay, Lesbian and Queer Politics in Britain*, transcript of seminar held on 24 November 1999, Institute of Contemporary British History, ed. Virginia Preston (2001), p. 13, www.kcl.ac.uk.

20 James Curran, Ivor Gaber and Julian Petley, *Culture Wars: the Media and the British Left* (London, 2018).

21 See www.the-lcva.co.uk.

22 Ibid.

23 Rachel Tingle, 'Ideology of the Gay Liberation Movement' speech (3 June 2004), https://foclonline.org.

24 'Gays "Use Sex Lessons to Promote Their Own Lifestyle"', *Daily Mail* (6 October 1986), p. 9.

25 Kyriacos Spyrou, *Walking after Midnight: Gay Men's Life Stories* (London, 1989).

26 'Pregnant Woman "Punched"', *The Times* (17 March 1987), p. 2.

27 'Handicapped Girls "Saw Lesbian Film"', *Daily Mail* (3 April 1987), p. 9.

28 'Mad Bouncer Killed My Baby', *The Voice* (29 April 1987).
29 'School to Punish "Sexists"', *The Times* (27 July 1987), p. 3.
30 David Rushworth Smith, *Fasting: A Neglected Discipline* (Chichester, 1954), pp. 73–4.
31 'In Living Memory'.
32 'Fly Away Gays – and We Will Pay!' *The Sun* (6 May 1987).
33 Terry Sanderson, *Mediawatch* (London, 1995), p. 68.
34 B. Hansen and P. Patrick, 'Towards Some Understanding of Sexuality Education', in *Adding Value: School's Responsibility for Personal Development of Pupils*, ed. M. Buck and S. Inman (Stoke-on-Trent, 2009), p. 70.
35 Roger Jowell et al., *9th British Social Attitudes Report* (1992: 124), *13th British Social Attitudes Report* (1996: 39), *16th British Social Attitudes Report* (1999: 348) and *17th British Social Attitudes Report* (2000: 112).
36 'In Living Memory'.
37 Martin Durham, *Sex and Politics: Family and Morality in the Thatcher Years* (Basingstoke, 1991), p. 177.
38 Louise Ceroviki, 'Tory Gay-Bashing Charter', *Workers Press* (2 January 1988), p. 13.
39 David M. Rayside, *On the Fringe: Gays and Lesbians in Politics* (Ithaca, NY, and London, 1998), p. 83.
40 'Fire Fund Launched after Arson Attack on Capital Gay', *Gay Times* (January 1988), p. 6.
41 'The Lady's Not Burning for a Witch-Hunt', *Daily Telegraph* (29 January 1988), p. 20.
42 Sue Sanders and Gill Spraggs, 'Section 28 and Education', in *Learning Our Lives: Sexuality and Social Control*, ed. Carol Jones and Pat Mahoney (London, 1989).
43 Ian McKellen cited in *Capital Gay* (23 December 1988).
44 Bösche, 'Jenny, Eric, Martin . . . and Me'.
45 Madeleine Colvin and Jane Hawksley, *Section 28: A Practical Guide to the Law and Its Implications* (London, 1989).

4 The Path of Most Resistance

1 Jennie Wilson, interview transcript (August 2019), Oral History Archive, www.whisper2roar.org.uk.

2 'Songs Produced for the Stop the Clause March', *Gay Scotland*, 9 March 1988, p. 14.

3 'Court Row Erupts over Protest March Arrests', *Gay Times* (February 1988), p. 14; 'Delayed but Charges Dropped', *Pink Paper* (28 January 1988), p. 6.

4 'Clause 28 Meetings This Week', *Pink Paper* (28 January 1988), p. 6.

5 See 'Section 28', www.pinksingers.co.uk, accessed 14 June 2021.

6 'Peregrine Worsthorne: The Oppressive Face of Modern Liberalism', *Sunday Telegraph* (3 January 1988), p. 22.

7 Peregrine Worsthorne, 'Boy Made Man', in *The World of the Public School*, ed. George Macdonald Fraser (London, 1977), pp. 79–96; Peregrine Worsthorne, 'Are Explicit Sex Scenes OK?', *The Spectator* (September 2011).

8 See Ian McKellen, '1988: Ian McKellen, Trainee Activist', https://mckellen.com, accessed 14 June 2021.

9 See Ian McKellen, '1988: Section 28', https://mckellen.com, accessed 14 June 2021.

10 'Remembering the Gay Activists Who Stormed the Six O'Clock News to Protest Section 28', *Attitude* (July 2017); 'You Bigots, Me Jane!', *Pink Paper* (4 February 1988), p. 1.

11 'We Still Have a Long Climb for LGBT Equality, Say 1988 House of Lords Lesbian Abseilers', *Glasgow Times* (15 July 2017).

12 'Remembering the Gay Activists'.

13 Ibid.

14 'Section 28 Protesters 30 Years On: We Were Arrested and Put in a Cell up by Big Ben', *The Guardian* (27 March 2018).

15 'Lord Knows That I Don't Need the Title', *Manchester Evening News* (29 March 2013).

16 'A Jump for Justice', *Diva* (August 1997), p. 29.

17 *Out on Tuesday*, Channel 4 (28 March 1989).

18 Adam Lent and Merl Storr, 'Chronology', in *Section 28 and the Revival of Gay, Lesbian and Queer Politics in Britain*, transcript of seminar held on 24 November 1999, Institute of Contemporary British History, ed. Virginia Preston (2001), p. 13, www.kcl.ac.uk.

19 'Security Row after Gays Abseil into the Lords', *The Times* (3 February 1988).

20 Sarah Green, 'Urban Amazons', *Trouble and Strife*, 35 (1997), p. 52.

21 'Lesbians Abseil into the Lords', *Daily Mail* (3 February 1988), p. 1.

22 BBC *Nine O'Clock News* (2 February 1988).

23 David Mixner and Dennis Bailey, *Brave Journeys: Profiles in Gay and Lesbian Courage* (New York, 2001).

24 'Lesbian Protesters Drop In on Lords', *Daily Telegraph* (3 February 1988), p. 1.

25 *Daily Mirror* (3 February 1988).

26 'Security Row after Gays Abseil into the Lords'.

27 'A Jump for Justice'.

28 Alwyn Turner, *Rejoice! Rejoice! Britain in the 1980s* (London, 2010).

29 'Lord Monkswell: Personal Statement', Hansard, col. 1183 (4 February 1988), https://hansard.parliament.uk.

30 'Apology by Unrepentant Peer Angers the Lords', *The Times* (5 February 1988), p. 1.

31 Ibid.

32 'Gays Pay Rates Too', *Uxbridge and West Drayton Gazette* (9 March 1988).

33 'Gays Hold Rally "Ban"', *Birmingham Evening Mail* (13 February 1988).

34 Lyn David Thomas, interviewed for the Gay Birmingham Remembered Project (2007), www.gaybirminghamremembered.co.uk.

35 'Call to Sack Anderton after Flogging Remark', *Glasgow Herald* (14 December 1987), p. 7.

36 'Lesbian Protest on BBC News', *Witness History* (23 May 2018), www.bbc.co.uk.

37 Samuel Wheeler, 'Never Going Underground: Manchester and Section 28' (19 February 2018), https://confidentials.com.

38 Michael Cashman, *One of Them* (London, 2020), p. 222.

39 Ibid., pp. 226–7.

40 'Filth', *Daily Express* (5 February 1988).

41 Stifyn Parri, *Out with It!* (Llandysul, 2019), p. 50.

42 Jennifer Williams, 'Thirty Years Ago Manchester Held a
    Huge March to Protest against Section 28 – It Would Change
    History', *Manchester Evening Post* (18 February 2018).

43 'Bigotry and Prejudice', *Leeds Other Paper* (5 February
    1988).

44 Rebecca Flemming cited in *Section 28 and the Revival
    of Gay, Lesbian and Queer Politics in Britain*, transcript
    of seminar held on 24 November 1999, Institute of
    Contemporary British History, ed. Virginia Preston (2001),
    pp. 24–7, www.kcl.ac.uk.

45 'Thousands Make Protest March Biggest and Best', *Pink
    Paper* (5 May 1988).

46 'Out and Proud', *Pink Paper* (5 May 1987), p. 1.

47 Ibid.

48 'Boy George Helps', *Daily Mail* (25 April 1984), p. 3.

49 Isabelle Masters and Charlotte Kendal, *If I Can't Dance*,
    short film, www.youtube.com, accessed 14 June 2021.

50 'Gays Throw Smoke Bomb at Royal Car', *Newcastle Evening
    Chronicle* (5 July 1988).

51 David Smith, 'Family Campaigners Demand Ban on Gay
    Magazines', *Gay Times* (August 1990), p. 13.

52 'Princess in Lesbian Demo', *Irish Independent*
    (13 July 1990).

53 'News', *Pink Paper* (24 March 1988), p. 5.

54 'Women Invade Studio', *The Times* (24 May 1988), pp. 1–2.

55 Cliff Joannou, 'Remembering the Gay Activists Who Stormed
    the Six O'Clock News to Protest Section 28', *Attitude*, 286
    (July 2017).

56 'We Still Have a Long Climb for LGBT Equality'.

57 'Cool Sue Keeps Lesbians at Bay', *Daily Mail* (24 May 1988),
    p. 2.

58 'Lesbian Protest on BBC News'.

59 'Remembering the Gay Activists Who Stormed the Six
    O'Clock News to Protest Section 28'.

60 'BBC Six O'Clock News – Section 28 Protesters – with Gallery
    Talk Back', at www.youtube.com.

61 'Women Invade Studio'.

62 *Central Weekend Live* (27 May 1988).

63 'Dykes Penetrate Auntie!', *Pink Paper* (26 May 1988), p. 1.

64 Simon Usborne, 'Nicholas Witchell Has Been Reporting on the Royal Family for 15 Years – Wouldn't He Rather Swap the Palace for the Front Line?', *The Independent* (5 July 2014).

65 Chris Godfrey, 'Section 28 Protesters 30 Years On: "We Were Arrested and Put in a Cell up by Big Ben"', *The Guardian* (27 March 2018).

66 *News at Ten* (23 May 1988), www.youtube.com.

67 'Women Invade Studio'.

68 *News at Ten.*

69 Godfrey, 'Section 28 Protesters 30 Years On'.

70 'Dykes Penetrate Auntie!'.

71 'Lesbian Protest on BBC News'.

72 Ibid.

73 'Dykes Penetrate Auntie!'

74 'Lesbian Protest on BBC News'.

75 Wilson, interview transcript, p. 18.

5 Under the Shadow of Section 28

1 J. Green, 'School Sex Education and Education Policy in England and Wales: The Relationship Examined', *Health Education Research*, XIII/1 (1998), pp. 67–72; p. 69.

2 Sue Sanders and Gill Spraggs, 'Section 28 and Education', in *Learning Our Lives: Sexuality and Social Control*, ed. Carol Jones and Pat Mahoney (London, 1989).

3 'Shadows of Section 28', report on LGBT Health and Wellbeing Event (19 February 2020), www.lgbthealth.org.uk.

4 Nia Griffith, 'I Was a Gay Teacher under Section 28 – Let's Not Go Back There', LabourList (10 June 2019), https://labourlist.org.

5 Sue O'Sullivan cited in *Section 28 and the Revival of Gay, Lesbian and Queer Politics in Britain*, transcript of seminar held on 24 November 1999, Institute of Contemporary British History, ed. Virginia Preston (2001), pp. 32–3, www.kcl.ac.uk.

6 'Calderdale Ordered to Pay Costs of "Section 28" Ban on Gay Paper', *The Guardian* (28 June 1995).

7 'When Gay Became a Four-Letter Word', BBC News, 20 January 2000.

8 Amy Ashenden, 'Exclusive: I Was a Lesbian Teacher under Section 28 and It Was Absolutely Frightening', *PinkNews* (24 May 2018), www.pinknews.co.uk.

9 Patrick Strudwick, '30 Years Ago Teachers Were Banned from Discussing Homosexuality. This Is What I Wish They'd Taught Me', *Buzzfeed* (24 May 2018).

10 Beth Fisher, 'Thanks to Section 28 I'm a Lesbian Who Hates the Word Lesbian. But Now I'm Reclaiming It', *The Independent* (12 November 2018).

11 Liam McClelland, 'Section 28 Was Repealed 15 Years Ago but I Can't Forget the Impact It Had on Me So Easily', *Metro* (17 November 2018).

12 Chris Woodley cited in Daniel Tomlinson-Gray, 'The Soft Subject', LGBTed Blog, www.lgbted.uk, accessed 14 June 2016.

13 'Tragic or Toothless? Section 28 – One Year On', *Gay Times* (June 1989), p. 10.

14 N. Douglas et al., 'Homophobic Bullying in Secondary Schools in England and Wales: Teachers' Experiences', *Health Education*, xcix/2 (1999), pp. 53–60.

15 Crispin Thurlow, 'Naming the "Outsider Within": Homophobic Pejoratives and the Verbal Abuse of Lesbian, Gay and Bisexual Pupils', *Journal of Adolescence*, xxiv/1 (2001), pp. 25–38.

16 Ruth Hunt and Johan Jensen, *The School Report: The Experiences of Young People in Britain's Schools* (London, 2007).

17 April Guasp, *The Teachers Report* (London, 2009), www.educationengland.org.uk.

18 Sanders and Spraggs, 'Section 28 and Education'.

19 'Monday Women: First Comes Prejudice – Lesbian Mothers Fear That Clause 28 Will Make It Harder for Them to Win Custody', *The Guardian* (25 April 1988).

20 'Law: Sex and the Single Parent – Recent Cases Suggest a Shift in Attitudes towards Gay Mothers', *The Guardian* (5 December 1990).

21 'Monday Women: First Comes Prejudice'.

22 'Father Fights to Win Child from Lesbian', *Daily Mail* (25 August 1990), p. 14.

23 O'Sullivan in *Section 28*, p. 32.

24 'EastEnders at 35 – Colin and Barry and the First Gay Kiss in Soap', *Distinct Nostalgia* (27 May 2020), www.distinctnostalgia.com.

25 Michael Cashman, *One of Them* (London, 2020), p. 242.

26 Stephen Griffiths, ed., LGBT *History Month 2018. Section 28: Abseiling Lesbians & Jenny Living with Eric and Martin*, exh. cat., Staffordshire University (Stoke-on-Trent, 2018), p. 4.

27 Philip Osment, *This Island's Mine* (London, 2019).

28 David Mixner and Dennis Bailey, *Brave Journeys: Profiles in Gay and Lesbian Courage* (New York, 2001).

29 Bev Ayre, *Before the Act* podcast, Episode 1, https://beforetheactpodcast.com, accessed 14 June 2021.

30 Cashman, *One of Them*, pp. 243–4.

31 'Before the Act Raises £15,000', *Gay Times* (August 1988), p. 8.

32 'The Oval Arts Centre Afraid of the Implications of Section 28 Has a Theatre Group to Change Its Name So That It Doesn't Risk Flouting the Law', *Pink Paper* (21 April 1988), p. 6.

33 'Public Display to Defy Clause 28', *The Stage* (16 June 1988).

34 'MP Is Urging County Council to Break Law, Claims Tory', *Staffordshire Sentinel* (20 June 1988).

35 'Channel Four Gay Shocker', *Sunday Life* (29 January 1989).

36 Ieuan Franklin, 'Taking Liberties: Framed Youth, Community Video and Channel 4's Remit in Action', in *Queer Youth and Media Cultures*, ed. Christopher Pullen (Basingstoke, 2014), pp. 115–30.

37 Colin Richardson and Paul Burston, eds, *A Queer Romance: Lesbians, Gay Men and Popular Culture* (London, 1995), p. 235.

38 'Gang of Four Attack Clause 28', *The Stage* (8 June 1988).

39 Ibid.

40 'Lesbian and Gay Activists Could Contravene Section 28', *The Stage* (29 June 1989).

41 'Schools Festival Future in Shadow of Censorship', *The Stage* (25 May 1989).

42 'Avon Falls Victim to Clause 28', *The Stage* (19 October 1989).

43 'Sunil Gupta on Clause 28', British Library sound recording (26 January 1994), www.bl.uk.

44 'Lesbian Erotica – for Better or Worse, a Slap in the Face for Section 28', *Pink Paper* (17 November 1990), pp. 10–11.

45 'Arts Council "Regrets" Closure of Sweatshop', *Gay News* (January 1991), p. 12.

46 'Last Push to Save the Gay Sweatshop', *The Stage* (7 February 1991).

47 'Section 28 Has Limited Impact Survey Finds', *Gay News* (January 1991), p. 12.

48 Helen Freshwater, *Theatre Censorship in Britain* (Basingstoke, 2009), p. 108.

49 Rebecca Fleming in *Section 28*, p. 27.

50 Ibid.

51 Sam Gelder, 'Campaigners Recall the Fight against Section 28 at Town Hall Gathering', *Islington Gazette* (25 May 2018).

52 Cashman, *One of Them*, p. 249.

53 Lisa Power in *Section 28*, p. 23.

54 Simon Fanshawe, 'An Ode to Limehouse', *The Guardian* (27 January 2006).

55 See 'Section 28', www.pinksingers.co.uk, accessed 14 June 2021.

56 Cashman, *One of Them*, p. 251.

57 Power in *Section 28*.

58 'Scales Just Fell from My Eyes!', *Gay Times* (July 1989), p. 19.

59 Peter Tatchell in *Section 28*, p. 36.

60 Hugh Muir, 'Officers' Homophobia Hampered Murder Investigations, Says Review', *The Guardian* (15 May 2007).

61 Ian Lucas, *OutRage! An Oral History* (London, 1998), p. 238.

62 'About OutRage!', http://outrage.org.uk/about, accessed 14 June 2021.

63 Lucas, *OutRage!*, p. 33.

64 Marina Cronin, 'Outing Is a Catalyst for Social Change' (1 May 1996), http://outrage.org.uk.

65 'Tatchell's "Fascist Tactics" Attacked by MPs', *The Times* (22 March 1995), p. 2.

66 Lukas Scott, 'St Dezzie Jarman, Fluffy Bunnies and
    Being "Halfway There" to an Equal Age of Consent',
    https://viewfromafridge.wordpress.com, accessed
    14 June 2021.
67 'Derek Jarman's "Queer" Sketchbook', British Library
    collections, www.bl.uk/collection-items/derek-jarmans-
    queer-sketchbook, accessed 14 June 2021.
68 Cliff Richard, *My Life, My Way* (London, 2008).
69 'You're a Queer, a Poof or a Dyke: What School Is Like
    When You're Gay', *The Independent* (25 November 1991);
    Lucas, *OutRage!*, p. 99.
70 'Gay Activists Campaign at Tory Office', *The Guardian*
    (30 April 1992).
71 Lucas, *OutRage!*, pp. 99–100.
72 Melvin J. Lasky, *Media Warfare: The Americanization
    of Language* (New Brunswick, NJ, 2005), p. 103.
73 'Lesbian with a Vengeance', *The Independent* (2 July 1995).

6 The Rocky Road to Repeal

1 See 'Britpop', www.allmusic.com, accessed 14 June 2021.
2 'Gay Campaigners Call for Repeal of Section 28', *The Herald*
   (26 May 1998).
3 Peter Tatchell, 'Stop the Hype on 28', *Metropolis* (14 May
   1998).
4 Angela Mason cited in *Section 28 and the Revival of
   Gay, Lesbian and Queer Politics in Britain*, transcript
   of seminar held on 24 November 1999, Institute of
   Contemporary British History, ed. Virginia Preston (2001),
   p. 45, www.kcl.ac.uk.
5 Richard Cracknell, 'Lords Reform: The Interim House –
   Background Statistics', Research Paper 00/61 (15 June 2000),
   https://commonslibrary.parliament.uk.
6 '75 Words of Tradition', BBC News (5 November 1999), at
   http://news.bbc.co.uk, accessed 14 June 2021.
7 Keith Alcorn, 'HIV Funds Cut in Scottish Storm over Gay
   Rights' (5 March 2001), www.aidsmap.com.
8 'Council Faces Gay Cash Court Battle', BBC News
   (6 July 2000).

9 'Gay Groups Claim Court Victory', BBC News (6 July 2000).

10 'Glasgow Forced Not to Promote Homosexuality', Christian Institute News Release (6 July 2000), www.christian.org.uk.

11 'Tories Split over Gay Rights Sacking', BBC News (3 December 1999), http://news.bbc.co.uk.

12 Angela Mason cited in *Section 28*, p. 44.

13 'Share of Households with Internet Access in the United Kingdom (UK) from 1998 to 2020', www.statista.com, accessed 14 June 2021.

14 'Court Rejects Call for Porn Ban', BBC News (16 May 2000).

15 Erin Hatton and Mary Nell Trautner, 'Equal Opportunity Objectification? The Sexualization of Men and Women on the Cover of *Rolling Stone*', *Sexuality & Culture*, xv/3 (2011), p. 256.

16 *The Case for Keeping Section 28*, Christian Institute (Edinburgh, 2000) p. 10. David Henderson, 'Gay Sex Health Pack Use Denied' (24 December 1999), www.tes.com.

17 'Full Text: We Are Seen as Weak and Soft', *The Guardian* (17 July 2000).

18 'Section 28 Reform to Be Shelved after Lords Defeat', *The Independent* (25 July 2000).

19 'Blair Reaffirms His Pledge over Section 28', *Irish Times* (27 July 2000).

20 'Ministers Back Down on Gay Ban', BBC News (3 December 1999).

21 Boris Johnson, 'One Rule for Bois De Boulogne, Another for Belize', *The Spectator* (15 April 2000), p. 8.

22 John O'Farrell, *Things Can Only Get Worse?* (New York, 2017).

23 'Tories Walking on Ayr', BBC News (17 March 2000).

24 'The Bigots Want a Climate of Fear', *Socialist Worker* (27 January 2000).

25 'Gay Protest Disrupts Cardinal Winning Lecture', press release (12 March 2000), http://outrage.org.uk.

26 'Souter Poll Hits Major Setback', BBC News (31 March 2000).

27 'Scottish Section 28 Vote Descends into Farce', *Gay News* (June 2000), p. 45.

28 'Private Ballot Shows Big Majority in Favour of Retaining Section 28', *Irish Times* (31 May 2000).

29 'Referendum or Opinion Poll?', Ipsos MORI (2 June 2000), www.ipsos.com.

30 Peter Tatchell, 'The Stagecoach Boss Should Rethink His Foolish, Bigoted Million-Pound Campaign in Support of Section 28', www.petertatchell.net.

31 'Lesbian Avengers: Souter's Bus Goes Pink', *Socialist Worker* (1 July 2000).

32 'Stagecoach Out to Calm Investors', *The Times* (11 April 2000).

33 'Sir Brian Souter Receives Knighthood at Buckingham Palace Investiture', Stagecoach press release (18 November 2011), www.stagecoachgroup.com.

34 'Section 28 Falls in Scotland', *Diva* (1 August 2000), p. 16.

35 'Baroness Young, Enemy of Gay Rights, Dies at 75', *The Independent* (7 September 2002).

36 'Section 28 Repeal Back on the Agenda', BBC News (7 January 2003).

37 'Son of Section 28: The Main Players', *The Pink Paper* (14 February 2003), pp. 16–17.

38 'Baroness Blatch: Obituary', *The Independent* (1 June 2005).

39 Ben Summerskill, 'Putting Gay Partnerships on the Map – Why Legal Recognition Matters', *The Guardian* (23 July 2013).

40 'Clubbers "Kiss Off" Section 28', *Diva* (1 January 2004), p. 17.

41 Louise Carolin, 'Section 28 "Consigned to the Legal Rubbish Heap of Hatred and Bigotry"', *Diva* (1 November 2003), p. 18.

7 A Legacy Is Etched

1 Catherine Lee, 'Fifteen Years On: The Legacy of Section 28 for LGBT+ Teachers in English Schools', *Sex Education*, XIX/6 (2019), pp. 675–90.

2 Cited in Ian Mckellen, 'Tribute: Margaret Thatcher (1925–2013)' (15 April 2013), https://mckellen.com.

3 'Tory Chairman Declares His Old Anti-Gay Policies "Immoral"', *PinkNews* (24 July 2010).

4 Nicholas Watt, 'David Cameron Apologises to Gay People for Section 28', *The Guardian* (2 July 2009).

5 'Theresa May Says She "Shouldn't Have" Voted against the Repeal of Section 28', *PinkNews* (3 July 2018).

6 'Michelle Hewitson Interview: Brian Souter', *New Zealand Herald* (31 October 2014).

7 'Turner Prize Deal with Stagecoach Ends after Brian Souter Gay Rights Row', *The Scotsman* (3 May 2019).

8 Juliet Jacques, 'Never Going Underground: The Stop the Clause March, Thirty Years On', *The Comma Press* (12 February 2018), https://thecommapressblog.wordpress.com.

9 Del LaGrace Volcano cited in *Section 28 and the Revival of Gay, Lesbian and Queer Politics in Britain*, transcript of seminar held on 24 November 1999, Institute of Contemporary British History, ed. Virginia Preston (2001), p. 42, www.kcl.ac.uk.

10 'Academies to Teach "Marriage Is Best"', Workers' Liberty (14 December 2011), www.workersliberty.org.

11 Julie Henry, 'Free Schools and Academies Must Promote Marriage', *Daily Telegraph* (3 December 2011).

12 'BHA Identifies 45 Schools That Continue to Have Section 28-Like Policies', Humanists UK (19 August 2013), https://humanism.org.uk.

13 Andrew Moffat cited in Will Hazel, 'School Was Brutal' (27 September 2019), https://inews.co.uk.

14 Simon Rushton, 'School Tells Parents to Stop Holding Weekly Protests outside School over Its LGBT Inclusive Education' (3 March 2019), https://inews.co.uk.

15 Nazia Parveen, 'Birmingham School Stops LGBT Lessons after Parents Protest', *The Guardian* (4 March 2019).

16 See http://sparkbrook.localstats.co.uk; Donna Ferguson, '"We Can't Give In": The Birmingham School on the Frontline of Anti-LGBT Protests', *The Guardian* (26 May 2019).

17 Nosheen Iqbal, 'Birmingham School Row: "This Is Made Out to Be Just Muslims v Gays. It's Not"', *The Guardian* (21 September 2019).

18 'Growing Up LGBT+', *Just Like Us* (June 2021), www.
justlikeus.org.

19 Rafaella Gunz, 'Polish President Considering a Ban
on "Homosexual Propaganda"', *Gay Star News*
(10 November 2018).

20 Michaela Krejcova, 'Ukraine Turns Down the Russian-Style
Anti-Gay Propaganda Bill', GLAAD (29 January 2015),
www.glaad.org.

21 'Hungarian Court Overturns Village's Ban on Islamic
Symbols and "LGBT Propaganda"', *The Independent*
(14 April 2017).

22 'Hungary Passes Law Banning LGBT Content in Schools
or Kids' TV', *The Guardian* (15 June 2021).

23 '2017 County Reports on Human Rights Practices', United
States Department of State (20 April 2018), www.state.gov.

24 'The Countries Where Homosexuality Is Illegal', *The Week*
(3 April 2020).

25 Tom Parfitt and Roland Oliphant, 'Thousands Take Part
in "Anti-Maidan" Protest in Moscow against Uprising in
Ukraine', *Daily Telegraph* (21 February 2015).

26 Todd Starnes, 'School District Forbids Parents from
Opting Kids Out of LGBT Lessons' (25 April 2018),
www.toddstarnes.com.

27 Robert Long, *Relationships and Sex Education in Schools:
What's Changing?*, House of Commons Library
(5 April 2019), https://commonslibrary.parliament.uk.

28 'Success! Humanists UK Celebrates Introduction of
Compulsory Relationships and Sex Education after
More Than 50 Years Campaigning', Humanists UK
(1 September 2020), https://humanism.org.uk.

29 *Teaching Online Safety in School*, Department of Education
(June 2019), www.gov.uk.

Further Reading

Alyson, Sasha, *Young, Gay & Proud!* (New York, 1986)

Blank, Joani, and Marcia Quackenbush, *The Playbook for Kids about Sex* (San Francisco, CA, 1982)

Bösche, Suzanne, *Jenny Lives with Eric and Martin* (London, 1983)

Cashman, Michael, *One of Them* (London, 2020)

Clews, Colin, *Gay in the 80s: From Fighting for Our Rights to Fighting for Our Lives* (Kibworth, 2017)

Lucas, Ian, *OutRage! An Oral History* (London, 1998)

McSmith, Andy, *No Such Thing as Society: A History of Britain in the 1980s* (London, 2010)

O'Connor, Garry, *Ian McKellen: The Biography* (London, 2019)

Otton, Gary, *Religious Fascism: The Repeal of Section 28* (Moray, 2014)

Power, Lisa, *No Bath but Plenty of Bubbles: Stories from the London Gay Liberation Front, 1970–73* (London, 1995)

Rees, David, *The Milkman's on His Way* (London, 1982)

Sanderson, Terry, *Mediawatch* (London, 1995)

Acknowledgements

Thanks to David Watkins at Reaktion Books for his encouragement and diligence, my parents for their love and the many sacrifices they made for me, and Tony McEnery for his support and reading of a draft version.

I would also like to express thanks to Susannah Bowyer, Michael Cashman, Charlie McMillan, Angela Mason, Ian McKellen, Stifyn Parri, Richard Sandells and Chris Smith, who gave me their time and their memories.

I am indebted to Ian Lucas, Colin Clews, Terry Sanderson, Sue Sanders and Gill Spraggs for their scholarship on Section 28, gay social history and media representation.

Thanks to Sunil Gupta for permission to reprint a piece of his artwork, Stefan Dickers and others at the Bishopsgate Institute, Daniel Payne and the London School of Economics archives, and the ProQuest LGBT Magazine archive for providing archive material.

Photo Acknowledgements

The author and publishers wish to express their thanks to the below. Every effort has been made to contact copyright holders; should there be any we have been unable to reach or to whom inaccurate acknowledgement has been given, please contact the publishers, and a full adjustment will be made to subsequent printings.

Mike Forster/*Daily Mail*/Shutterstock: p. 167; Holborn/Mirrorpix/ Getty Images: p. 161; LSE Library: p. 168; Sunil Gupta and Hales Gallery, Stephen Bulger Gallery and Vadehra Art Gallery: p. 211; NLA/reportdigital.co.uk: p. 42; Joanne O'Brien/Bishopsgate Archive: p. 169; Katja Ogrin/EMPICS Entertainment via PA Images: p. 291; PA Images/Alamy Stock Photo: pp. 114, 153, 223, 259; Brenda Prince/ Bishopsgate Archive: p. 91; Reid/Mirrorpix/Getty Images: p. 155; Bryan Wharton: p. 39.

Index

Kellet-Bowman, Elaine
   118–19, 145, 151, 229,
   280
*Kenny Lives with Erica and
   Martina* 278
Kilfedder, James 220–21
Kinnock, Neil 64, 99, 116, 163
Knight, Jill 75, 101–2, 104–5,
   107–8, 125, 127, 131, 137,
   143, 156, 244, 280–81

Last Exit to Brooklyn 35, 40
Lawley, Sue 8–9, 171–5
Learning and Skills Act (2000)
   250, 253, 290
lesbian
   feminism 66, 69, 73–4
   invisibility 67–8
Lesbian Avengers 224–5, 260
Lesbian and Gay Switchboard
   136, 158, 164, 228, 238,
   285
Livingstone, Ken 49–50, 85,
   136
lobbying 142, 144, 178,
   215–17, 233–4
Local Government Act
   (1985) 85
   (1986) 11, 19, 21, 115,
      136
   (1988) 21
   (2003) 273
London Lesbian and Gay
   Centre 85, 135, 218
Longford, Lord 36, 86, 96,
   123, 235, 275, 280
loony left 53, 83, 96, 112, 122,
   209, 252, 284
Lords, House of 20–23, 116,

   146–53, 235–6, 243–5,
   253, 267–73, 275–6
Luce, Richard 82, 99

McClelland, Liam 194–5
McKellen, Ian 128, 131,
   139–44, 151, 157, 160–61,
   188, 203–5, 214–17, 233,
   280, 301–2
McMillan, Charlie 237,
   239–40
Major, John 184, 241
Marriage (Same Sex Couples)
   Act (2013) 285
Mason, Angela 36, 232–3, 241,
   243, 245, 283, 294, 302
Mathias, Sean 203
May, Theresa 253–4, 281
Mendis, Viraj 286
Merck, Mandy 207
Mermaids 288
Milkman's on His Way, The
   105–7, 124
Moffat, Andrew 290–92
Monskwell, Lord 147–8,
   152–4
Monson, Lord 13–14, 124
Morgan, Piers 159, 281–2
Mountford, Kali 263
Murphy, Peter 90–92

National Curriculum 7,
   185–6
Nationwide Festival of Light
   24, 36, 41, 94, 96, 221
Never Going Underground
   154–61, 203
No Outsiders 291–2